THE ASSOCIATION FOR SCOTTISH LITERARY STUDIES
NUMBER THIRTY-ONE

SOMHAIRLE MACGILL-EAIN/
SORLEY MACLEAN

DÀIN DO EIMHIR/
POEMS TO EIMHIR

*

THE ASSOCIATION FOR SCOTTISH LITERARY STUDIES

The Association for Scottish Literary Studies aims to promote the study, teaching and writing of Scottish literature, and to further the study of the languages of Scotland.

To these ends, the ASLS publishes works of Scottish literature (of which this volume is an example); literary criticism and in-depth reviews of Scottish books in *Scottish Studies Review*; short articles, features and news in *ScotLit*; and scholarly studies of language in *Scottish Language*. It also publishes *New Writing Scotland*, an annual anthology of new poetry, drama and short fiction, in Scots, English and Gaelic. ASLS has also prepared a range of teaching materials covering Scottish language and literature for use in schools.

All the above publications are available as a single 'package', in return for an annual subscription. Enquiries should be sent to:

ASLS, c/o Department of Scottish History, 9 University Gardens, University of Glasgow, Glasgow G12 8QH. Telephone/fax +44 (0)141 330 5309 or visit our website at **www.asls.org.uk**

A list of Annual Volumes published by ASLS can be found at the end of this book.

THE ASSOCIATION FOR SCOTTISH LITERARY STUDIES

GENERAL EDITOR – LIAM McILVANNEY

SOMHAIRLE MACGILL-EAIN/ SORLEY MACLEAN

DÀIN DO EIMHIR/ POEMS TO EIMHIR

Edited by

Christopher Whyte

GLASGOW

2002

*

First published in Great Britain, 2002
by The Association for Scottish Literary Studies
c/o Department of Scottish History
University of Glasgow
9 University Gardens
Glasgow G12 8QH

ISBN 0 948877 49 9 (Hardback), 0 948877 50 2 (Paperback)

A catalogue record for this book
is available from the British Library.

The Association for Scottish Literary Studies acknowledges
subsidy from the Scottish Arts Council towards
the publication of this book.

Typeset by AFS Image Setters Ltd, Glasgow
Printed and bound in Great Britain by Bell & Bain Ltd, Glasgow

CONTENTS

FOREWORD

The initial inspiration for this edition of the 'Dàin do Eimhir' came from Ronald Renton, Deputy Headmaster of St Aloysius' College, Glasgow, an enthusiastic proselytizer for Gaelic and, at a stage more distant in the past than either of us now cares to calculate, my own English teacher. It could not and would not have been undertaken without the permission and support of the poet's family and in particular of his daughter Ishbel, to whom I am happy to express a considerable debt. Michael Schmidt of Carcanet Press generously agreed to the reproduction of relevant texts from the 1999 collected volume *O Choille gu Bearradh / From Wood to Ridge*, jointly published with Birlinn of Edinburgh.

The 'Introduction' to this edition sets out the background and charts the complex publishing history of the 'Dàin do Eimhir' ('Poems to Eimhir') sequence. The Gaelic text is then given in its completest possible form, with facing English translations and a list of 'Copytexts and Variant Readings.' A 'List of Titles' charts the appearance of items from the cycle, in a different format, in MacLean's 1977 and 1989 volumes. Significant passages from the poet's correspondence with Douglas Young are presented as a 'Dating Letter' and an 'Autobiographical Sketch'. The 'Commentary' looks briefly at metrical practice, diction, and at the legendary figure who gave her name to the sequence, before examining each single poem in detail. The 'Bibliography' is divided into four sections: unpublished sources, works by Sorley MacLean, works concerning Sorley MacLean, and other works. Finally, an 'Index' of personal and place names, topics and significant Gaelic terms from the 'Introduction', the 'Dating Letter', the 'Autobiographical Sketch' and the 'Commentary' is supplied.

The staff at the National Library of Scotland were consistently welcoming, thoughtful and helpful. An especial thanks goes to Robin Smith, to Kenneth Dunn and to Rachel Craig, who is currently engaged in cataloguing the library's extensive MacLean holdings. I also wish to thank the friends, colleagues and experts who inspected the typescript at various points in its elaboration, offering opinions and corrections: Dr Ann Matheson, formerly of the National Library of Scotland, Ian MacDonald of the Gaelic Books Council, Professor William Gillies and Ronald Black of the University of Edinburgh, Dr John MacInnes, formerly of the School of Scottish Studies, University of Edinburgh and my colleague at Glasgow University, Dr Michel Byrne, whose discovery of unpublished material by MacLean, copied into a notebook by George Campbell Hay, represented a breakthrough in work on the edition.

I am grateful to the Department of Manuscripts at the National Library, and to the Special Collections Department at Edinburgh University Library, for permission to reproduce material. I also wish to thank all those at the Association for Scottish Literary Studies who were involved in the project, notably Dr Christopher MacLachlan, Dr Liam McIlvanney and Duncan Jones. All remaining inaccuracies and oversights are entirely the editor's responsibility.

INTRODUCTION

1.

The present volume offers an edition with commentary of a sequence of love poems which arguably constitutes the major achievement of Scottish Gaelic poetry in the 20th century. Despite this fact, the sequence has never been published in its entirety. Its author clearly took against it in the latter part of his life, going so far as to claim, in the course of a radio interview broadcast in 1989, that 'it's not really a sequence'.[1] A strange fate, then, was reserved for the 'Dàin do Eimhir' or 'Poems to Eimhir', one which is reflected in their chequered publishing history.

In MacLean's 1943 collection *Dàin do Eimhir agus Dàin Eile* (that is, *Poems to Eimhir and Other Poems*), the first item is numbered I and the last LX, followed by a short concluding 'Dimitto'. Yet twelve gaps are constituted by missing poems, so that only 49 out of a notional total of 61 appear.[2] Writing to Douglas Young on February 22nd 1941,[3] MacLean classified most of the deleted items as 'worthless as poetry and capable of misunderstanding'. A notable degree of uncertainty about what to include emerges from the letters. On May 3rd 1941, when LVII to LX were still to be written, he communicates a change of heart about XXII and XXXVI, asks Young to use his discretion regarding XLI, and instructs him to destroy his copies of V, XVI, and XXVI (also XLIX). Luckily Young did not comply, and so was able to supply the first three of these 27 years later, when requested to do so by the poet. On November 9th of the same year, MacLean feels

---

[1] Hendry 1991: 3. MacLean then qualified the statement by adding that 'The only part that could be called a sequence at all is that part called *The Haunted Ebb*'. He is referring to the poems from XXIX to LIX included in the third section of MacLean 1999.

[2] The missing items were V, VI, VII, XII, XV, XVI, XXVI, XXXVI, XL, XLI, XLVI, and XLVII.

[3] MacLean's letters to Douglas Young are in the National Library of Scotland, Acc. 6419 Box 38B.

rather touchy about several of the Eimhir poems, even about some I have not debarred from publication e.g. I, XXII, XXXVI and I think XII ('Ceathrar ann') but they, being pretty worthless, would probably not be included by you at any rate for any other reason than to fill up space. As for the rest I asked you to keep back I still want them kept back.

While VI[4] and XV were moved from the main sequence to the 'Dàin Eile' ('Other Poems'), three more items (XL, XLVI and XLVII) were withheld from publication until 1970, no doubt because of the extraordinarily intimate, even prurient nature of their subject matter.

MacLean reprinted 28 items from the sequence in his 1977 selected volume *Reothairt is Contraigh / Spring tide and Neap tide*, adding a further 8 in the more generous collected volume *O Choille gu Bearradh / From Wood to Ridge*, first issued in 1989.[5] In both cases, poems were given individual titles and allocated to different sections within the book. In the 1989 volume, as if grudgingly, items from the 'Dàin do Eimhir' had their place in the original sequence indicated by an appended Roman numeral, though this was omitted in two cases.

Yet Professor Derick Thomson was not alone in feeling that the poems gain in power and meaning when read in their original context. In an acerbic, if characteristically perceptive, review of the 1986 *Critical Essays* edited by Ross and Hendry, he observes that

> what is most saliently missing is a sustained confrontation with the original "Dàin do Eimhir" sequence of 1943, which is the core of MacLean's work. When that work was published, it passed out of the control of its author. It became a literary fact not subject to distortion or second thoughts. It might be said that the re-arrangement of the poems (and the suppression of some) in *Spring tide and Neap tide* is another fact or artefact, but it is subsidiary to the earlier

---

[4] Possibly VII. See note to this poem in the 'Commentary'.

[5] For details, see the 'List of Titles'. Given the unsatisfactory nature of the Gaelic text in the 1989 volume, the corrected edition of 1999 has been taken as the point of departure for this edition.

one, and has subjected that earlier one to grave distortion. Criticism which does not recognise this, and which does not consider seriously the necessity of analysing the structure of the earlier work, is still a long way from the starting line.[6]

The English versions of 36 items which Iain Crichton Smith published in 1971 under the collective title *Poems to Eimhir* (and which there was a plan to publish alongside the originals for Edinburgh University Press[7]) were an implicit homage to the sequence as an organic whole. Writing in 1994, Aonghas MacNeacail would affirm that 'the sequence "Dàin do Eimhir"... remains central to [MacLean's] oeuvre'.[8]

Drawing on manuscript as well as published sources, the present edition features all but one of the 61 items pertaining to the sequence, making the relevant materials available in their entirety for the first time. VII (which possibly ought to be numbered VI) has not been located. The Gaelic text is translated in full, the poet's own versions being complemented where necessary by literal versions from the editor. This is, however, emphatically an edition with commentary of the Gaelic text, and not of the English versions, even when the latter have been prepared by MacLean.

2.

On March 30th 1942 MacLean gave Young a comprehensive dating of his poetic production till that time, excerpted later in our edition under the title 'Dating Letter'. Of the 'Dàin do Eimhir', I was written in Raasay in August or September 1931, II in Edinburgh the following summer (it was published in 1943 with the indication May 1932), III in Portree in November or December 1936 and IV in Mull in March or April 1938.

---

[6] Thomson 1988: 40.

[7] Young's letters to MacLean can be consulted in National Library of Scotland Acc. 11572/6. This project is mentioned in a letter dated June 6th 1967.

[8] MacNeacail 1994: 34.

After this relatively slow beginning, the remainder of the sequence was completed within two years. V to VIII were written in Edinburgh in September 1939, IX to XVI in Hawick very early in November. At this point in the letter, MacLean turns to 'An Cuilithionn' ('The Cuillin'), and when he goes back to the 'Dàin do Eimhir', it is to say that XXIII was written between December 10th and 13th. No specific mention is made of XVII to XXII. Yet as he had already told Young (on December 7th 1940) that 'It will be enough for you to refer to [items in the sequence] by my own "chronological" numbers' and had given him permission (on May 3rd 1941) to publish it 'without numbers but in the order of the old numbers which is merely chronological', we have every reason to assume that XVII to XXII were written between early November and December 10th 1939.

XXIV to XXVII followed between the 13th and the 18th, while XXVIII to XXXV, and almost certainly XXXVI, were all written on the 20th December. The speed of production at this stage is impressive, nearly a quarter of the sequence having been composed in the space of just 10 days. Such rapidity was facilitated by MacLean's not being a poet who subjected his work to laborious revision. Writing to Hugh MacDiarmid from Hawick on May 25th 1940, he admits that 'Usually a lyric comes to me quite spontaneously as a whole and I don't blot a line'.[9] There is no real contradiction with the statement, in a letter to the same correspondent from Catterick Camp on March 8th, 1941, that 'As for writing verse I just cannot because I can't get the simmering time that is necessary for me'. A period of 'simmering' might regularly have been followed by a brief, rapid spurt of transcription. Concerning XXVIII and XXIX, he told Young that 'I have never changed a word from that first writing down. It seems to me that I composed them simultaneously in a troubled sleep' (letter of March 30th 1942).

There was another burst of activity the following spring, XXXVII to LV being written around March, some possibly in February and some in April. The 'Dimitto' was in existence by this time, as it figures in a list appended to a

---

[9] MacLean's letters to MacDiarmid can be consulted in Edinburgh University Library MS 2954.13.

letter to Young dated May 3rd 1941. LVI was written at Catterick Camp in Yorkshire early in 1941. Though the 'Dating Letter' assigns them to 'the last days of July or first days of August', it is clear from a letter of Sunday 3rd August 1941 that MacLean wrote LVII to LIX in the course of that weekend. LX followed early in September.

Joy Hendry's essay 'The Man and His Work',[10] which heads the *Critical Essays* volume and gives the impression of being written in close consultation with MacLean, differs from this earlier chronology at several points. I is assigned to August or September 1930 (rather than 1931), with the first and last verses being added in December 1939. III is dated November or December 1935 (rather than 1936). Hendry writes that the conflict inspired by the Irishwoman (whose identity is discussed below) 'dominates more than half of "Dàin" IV-XXII, written in 1938 and the first half of 1939. These poems are not ordered chronologically.' The statement is ambiguous. Are all the poems between IV and XXII out of chronological order? Or only those concerning the Irishwoman? Or only those (thirteen out of nineteen) published in 1943? Hendry assigns XXIII to XXXVI, 'which are arranged chronologically, as are all the poems subsequently', to the last three months of 1939. XXXVII to LV were, according to her, completed by March 1940, while LVI to LX date from late June and early July 1941.

Preference is given to MacLean's earlier dating in this edition, not just because more than four decades were to elapse before the publication of Hendry's essay, but because independent evidence shows the later dates to be misleading in specific cases. MacLean's letter of August 3rd 1941 concerning LVII to LIX has already been mentioned. V survives only in a transcript made by Douglas Young not later than February 1941,[11] where it carries the unequivocal indication September 1939 ('an sultuine 1939'). It is hard to tell whether the poet's memory failed him in the later dating, or whether he had more complex reasons for wishing to blur the chronology of the sequence. The relatively high number of omissions between IV and XXII in the 1943 volume (only

---

[10] Ross and Hendry 1986: 9–38.
[11] Letter to MacLean of February 2nd 1941.

matched between XL and XLVII) suggests that they
represent a crucial section of the 'Dàin do Eimhir'. We will
return to this point.

3.

The poems at the start of the 'Dàin do Eimhir' date from
the poet's days as an undergraduate at Edinburgh University,
where he studied from 1929 to 1933, graduating with First
Class Honours in English Language and Literature. Herbert
Grierson was professor, and 'the poetry of most prestige...
was that of the seventeenth-century Metaphysicals',[12] though
MacLean observes that 'the great Grierson himself' was not
'half as pro-Donne as his undergraduate admirers or rather
the undergraduate admirers of Eliot', among whom 'to
suggest that Milton was as great a poet as Donne or Yeats as
great a poet as Eliot' would have been 'blatant heresy'.[13]
Grierson, after all, was 'very very good on nineteenth-century
Romantic poetry too'.[14]

By this time MacLean was writing poetry of his own in
both Gaelic and English, 'the latter in the manner of
Eliot and especially the "Hugh Selwyn Mauberley" manner
of Pound',[15] but upon completing 'A' Chorra-ghridheach'
('The Heron'[16]), he made a conscious decision to abandon
English, because his work in that language was 'over-
sophisticated, over self-conscious'[17] and also 'for patriotic
reasons'.[18] Friendships with James Caird and with the
philosopher George Davie began in the summer term of
1933,[19] and it was they who introduced him to the lyrics in
Hugh MacDiarmid's first two collections and to the long

---

[12] MacLean 1999: xiv.

[13] MacLean 1985: 10–11.

[14] Nicolson 1979: 25.

[15] MacLean 1999: xiv.

[16] Assigned to summer 1934 or 1935 in the 'Dating Letter', but to 1931
or 1932 in MacLean 1999: xiv.

[17] Ross and Hendry 1986: 12.

[18] MacLean 1999: xiv.

[19] Caird's contribution to *Critical Essays* assigns their meeting to the
following year, when MacLean 'was doing teacher training at Moray

poem *A Drunk Man Looks at the Thistle*. According to MacLean,

> The intellectual stimulus of Davie and the literary stimulus of Caird was very great, but the lyrics of Hugh MacDiarmid might very well have destroyed any chances I ever had of writing poetry had my reading of them not been immediately followed by my reading of the *Drunk Man*, *Cencrastus* and *Scots Unbound*.[20]

In the course of a single essay, MacLean rather confusingly remarks both that 'The long poem was always to me a *faute de mieux* compared with the lyric' and that MacDiarmid's *Drunk Man* 'converted me to the belief that the long medley with lyric peaks was the great form for our age'.[21] The latter sounds remarkably like a rationale for 'An Cuilithionn' ('The Cuillin'), the extended and outspokenly political poem which occupied him during the time when many of the 'Dàin do Eimhir' were being written.[22] His ambivalence about the relative merits of 'lyric' and 'medley' offers a tantalising glimpse of what may have been the poet's attitude to these projects. 'An Cuilithionn' is a radical, committed poem with a broad historical sweep which never quite matched up to MacLean's conception of it, while the 'Dàin do Eimhir', which fell so markedly out of favour with their author in the latter years of his life, emerged more spontaneously, rather in the manner of the *canzoniere* which Petrarch defines in his own opening poem as scattered rhymes, *rime sparse*, in contrast to his more serious Latin verse.

After taking a postgraduate diploma at Moray House in Edinburgh, MacLean began his career as a teacher at Portree Secondary School. His letters to MacDiarmid give a vivid picture of living conditions at Elgin Hostel. Writing on December 20th 1936, he complains that

---

House' (Ross and Hendry 1986: 39). In a letter to Douglas Young, however, MacLean writes that he 'met Davie and Caird late in my fourth year' (September 7th 1941).

[20] MacLean 1985: 11.

[21] MacLean 1985: 13, 11.

[22] It now forms the second section of MacLean 1999.

If I am here much longer I shall be extinguished
completely. I can read here but that is about all. I
cannot get the necessary concentration for doing any
real work. I suppose a teacher has sooner or later to
recognise the fact that he cannot use what talents he
has, however modest they are.

Conditions at Tobermory Secondary School on Mull, where
he was appointed teacher of English in January 1938, would
appear to have been easier. In a letter dated February 2nd
1938, MacLean tells MacDiarmid that he now has more time
to work at the English versions of Gaelic verse he had for
some time been supplying to the older poet, and offers a
sober appraisal of the current state of poetry in his chosen
language:

> Of any other modern stuff I do not know anything even
> as worthy apart from Sinclair. You see apart from
> trivial little songs written by people like Old Bannerman
> and Cameron, Paisley there is nothing being published
> in Gaelic verse at present. Of course by delving in
> certain places one has the chance of hitting on talented
> stuff by some local bard.

In the same letter, MacLean confesses to disliking the work
of the Skye poet Neil Macleod, which appealed so much to
Victorian taste. His views of contemporary Gaelic scholar-
ship were similarly disenchanted. Praising MacDiarmid's
version of the 18th century poet Mac Mhaighstir Alasdair's
'Birlinn', he assures him that

> you need not be perturbed by anything that the Gaelic
> scholars may say. Which of them in Scotland has
> produced a piece of criticism worth mentioning? The
> best of them are good grammarians not literary men.
> And which of them has produced a verse-translation of
> a Gaelic poem that is not beneath contempt?[23]

This Modernist sense of dissatisfaction with a decadent and
unambitious tradition is very reminiscent of MacDiarmid's
own stance early in the 1920s. After spending only a matter

---

[23] Letter dated April 1st from Churchton, Raasay. Though no indication
of the year is given, it can with some certainty be assigned to 1935.

of weeks in Mull, MacLean confesses (in a letter dated February 27th) to a degree of homesickness for the island he had left:

> ...we had a good circle in Portree and with it and places like Edinbane I had become a kind of fanatic for Skye or, perhaps at any rate, for a false mystical idea of Skye. There were indeed few places where one felt less cramped than in Skye. The Radical tradition was strong enough to make the teaching of Marxism unnoticed and Portree has no Puritanism about drink. Perhaps your sojourn in Skye will have lessened your belief in Tom MacDonald's[24] estimate of the hold of Secederism[25] on the people of the west; at least it did not trouble us in Portree. A renegade Seceder makes quite a good Marxist and renegades are now very common.

It would be interesting to determine just how far MacLean succeeded in instilling Marxism into his Portree pupils without attracting unwanted attention. Though it had a Skye basis, the poet's radicalism embraced the larger scale situation in Europe. From 1933 onwards he was 'obsessed with what I considered a probable victory of Fascism'. Consequentially, the Scottish nationalist cause had to take second place to 'the immediate thing, the question of immediate importance', that is, 'the fight against Fascism, with Spain, the United Front, and all that'.[26]

The urge to become personally involved in the battle to defend Spain from Franco's 'nationalists' is an important theme in the 'Dàin do Eimhir'. On at least two occasions, in XVIII and XXII, the speaker implies that he has had to choose between pursuing the woman he loved and commit-

---

[24] Thomas Douglas Macdonald (1906–1975), better known by his pen name Fionn MacColla. His novels include *The Albannach* (1932) and *And the Cock Crew* (1945).

[25] A distinctly pejorative term for the Free Presbyterian Church, which seceded from the Free Church of Scotland in 1893. The latter had in its turn seceded from the Church of Scotland in the great Disruption of 1843. MacLean's family worshipped in a church at Holman north of Osgaig. A majority of the Raasay population were adherents of the Free Presbyterian Church at the time the poet grew up.

[26] Nicolson 1979: 29–30.

ment to that struggle. The latter of these two lyrics calls into question the very notion of a choice with its insistence that, had he enlisted, he would surely have died, whereas failing to enlist meant he could never hope to deserve her love. MacLean has, however, warned against the dangers of identifying the man in the lyrics too closely with his own experience:

> the Spanish Civil War, and especially 1937, was a very important year for me because certain circumstances, family circumstances, prevented me from going to fight in the International Brigade. It wasn't a woman fundamentally that kept me from going though there was one.[27]

Though he perhaps overstates his case, the words of the Russian Formalist critic Boris Tomashevsky are relevant in this context:

> The poet considers as a premise to his creations not his actual *curriculum vitae*, but his ideal biographical legend. Therefore, only this biographical legend should be important to the literary historian in his attempt to reconstruct the psychological milieu surrounding a literary work.[28]

The circumstances which led him to hold back, to stay in Scotland and write poetry, are listed in greater detail in the essay 'My relationship with the Muse':

> My mother's long illness in 1936, its recurrence in 1938, the outbreak of the Spanish Civil War in 1936, the progressive decline of my father's business in the Thirties, my meeting with an Irish girl in 1937, my rash leaving of Skye for Mull late in 1937, and Munich in 1938, and always the steady unbearable decline of Gaelic, made those years for me years of difficult choice, and the tensions of those years confirmed self-expression in poetry not in action.[29]

---

[27] Nicolson 1979: 28.
[28] Cited in Bethea 1994: 146.
[29] MacLean 1985: 12.

In January 1939 MacLean moved to Boroughmuir High School in Edinburgh, living in digs in Polwarth, and renewed his acquaintance with Robert Garioch, who in turn introduced him to Sydney Goodsir Smith. Garioch issued from his own hand press in December 1939 a joint collection entitled *17 Poems for 6d.* A corrected second edition appeared early the following year, featuring five poems from the Eimhir sequence: III, IV, XIV, XV and XXIX,[30] along with Garioch's Scots version of III.

Family reasons prevented MacLean from enlisting as a volunteer, and between October 1939 and June 1940 he taught evacuees in Hawick in the Scottish borders.[31] Whichever chronology is preferred, this was the period during which the majority of the poems in the 'Dàin do Eimhir' were written. It is intriguing to reflect that such a milestone in the history of Scottish poetry should have been composed at a considerable distance from the heartland where the Gaelic language was still in everyday use. LVI was written subsequent to MacLean's leaving Edinburgh on September 26th 1940[32] for military training at Catterick Camp, Yorkshire. By September 1941 the sequence had been completed. He left Britain for active service in North Africa as a member of the Signal Corps in December 1941.

4.

From the information contained in Hendry's essay it would appear that the cycle's notional dedication to Eimhir embraces several different women, covered in the fashion of a *senhal* in the work of a Provençal troubadour by this name drawn from Celtic legend.

The first is the girl referred to in the second, third and

---

[30] XV, restored to the sequence in this edition, appears under the title 'Trì Slighean', which it also bore as 'Dàin Eile' XVI in the 1943 volume.

[31] So Hendry (Ross and Hendry 1986: 27). The date 29.7.1940 pencilled in to a letter to Douglas Young, addressed from Langlands Road, Hawick, suggests, however, that MacLean was still in the Borders at the end of July.

[32] See letter of Douglas Young to George Campbell Hay bearing this date (National Library of Scotland Acc. 6419/5).

fourth verses of I. II is an 'abstract' meditation, while III
refers to a girl from Skye who attracted the poet in 1934–35,
without having 'reason to suspect that MacLean had a
strong, if transient feeling for her'.

At a Celtic Congress held in Edinburgh in August 1937,
he met an Irishwoman who is said to be the focus of 'more
than half' of the poems from IV to XXII. According to
Hendry, he saw in her 'a pious Catholic, from a pious family,
and... conservative in politics'. This presumably explains the
Yeatsian epigraph to VIII, and that poem's attribution of
Fascist or pseudo-Fascist leanings to the beloved. Her name
was Nessa Ní Sheaghdha (1916–1993, Nessa O'Shea, later
Mrs Doran) and she had come to Scotland to undertake
research work in the National Library.[33] In December 1939
she married a man who had been training as a Jesuit priest
and who turned into 'something of a socialist'. Hendry tells
us that MacLean's poem about the wedding, XXII, was in
fact written before he got news that the Irishwoman intended
to marry.[34] Her husband is referred to both in XIX ('is ged
bhios tu aig fear-pòsta'[35]) and in XLVI, where she is 'tè nas
rathaile 's nas bòidhche / 's i pòsta thall an Eirinn'.[36]

But the previous spring, most probably in May, MacLean
had met the 'fourth' Eimhir, a Scottish woman he had
already known when she was in her teens:

> In August or September, 1939, he began to feel strongly
> attracted to her, and by December 1939 had committed
> himself by declaring his love for her. Her response gave
> him to understand that because of an operation she had
> been left incapable of enjoying a full relationship with
> a man. This took MacLean by storm. Having declared
> his feeling for her, he could do nothing but have the
> most passionate sympathy for her, being acutely aware
> of what he saw as her tragedy, and, ultimately, his also.
> Her subsequent confessions to him that their friendship

---

[33] Black 1999: xxxiii.
[34] See the note to XIX: 37–38 in the 'Commentary' for an evaluation of
this statement.
[35] 'and, though you will be married to another'.
[36] 'a more fortunate and lovely one / who is married over in Ireland'.

served as a deterrent to suicide only increased his
sympathy and feeling of responsibility towards her.[37]

The implication in XLVII that the woman has been
incapacitated as a result of relationship with another man, a
Lowland Scot ('Carson, a Dhia, nach d' fhuair mi 'n
cothrom, / mun d' shrac an t-òigear Goill do bhlàth'[38]) would
seem to offer a foundation for the hypothesis that she may
well have spoken of an illegal abortion. What MacLean was
subsequently to learn of the man said to have been involved
made it unlikely that he could in fact have assumed the role
assigned to him. He later considered that 'I should have
appreciated [the] truth much earlier than I did', adding that
'Even now I am not altogether sure of it' (letter to Young of
May 27th 1943).

A reference to 'the person, to whom my letters were the
most intimate of all my letters' (writing to Young on
September 11th 1941) hints that MacLean corresponded with
the Scottish woman, and the letter he received on Tuesday
19th December 1939 which, he told Young, 'meant for me
the end of my period of great activity in poetry' (letter of
March 30th 1942), would seem to have contained what
Hendry refers to as this woman's 'confessions'. The account
he gave Young a year later, on December 6th 1940, is
couched in self-deprecating and rather guarded terms:

> I talked to you of feeling my private affairs irreparably
> gone wrong but don't be alarmed about that; that has
> been my normal condition for a few years now. It is
> merely due to an obsession with a woman and regrets I
> cannot overcome. I am afraid that I am one of those
> weaklings who have one love affair that upsets their
> whole lives.

He returned to the question in a letter from Catterick dated
November 9th, 1941:

> I have never given you an explanation of what I hinted
> at in my last letter. The truth is that before I ever met

---

[37] Ross and Hendry 1986: 25.
[38] 'Why, God, did I not get the chance / before the young Lowlander tore
your bloom'.

you, actually just when I finished 'The Cuillin' about
New Year 1940 I had an experience which has nearly
driven me mad and not until July of this year did I
become anything like normal, and even yet I have very
frequent moods that approach the suicidal, though the
real cause of these moods has been removed. That
explains the relative drought of my poetry from the
early months of 1940 until July of this year. Had it not
been that now and again I had moments free from the
terrible fears which I had I could not have written
anything from early 1940 till the end of this July... It is
a matter which concerned primarily not me but someone
else, hence my reticence.

The situation does not develop beyond this within the
confines of the cycle. Indeed, he only saw the woman in
question on one occasion between December 1939 and late
July or early August 1941.[39] The predicament is given more
explicit expression in 'An Cogadh Ceart', set on the eve of
the speaker's departure for active service. He announces his
intention of marrying the woman in question:

> Bha an Gall òg romham
> is rinn e 'n dò-bheairt olc.
>
> Rinn e 'n t-ainneart air do cholainn,
> àmghar do-labhairt ar bròin,
> air chor 's nach eil thu 'n comas laighe
> le fear eile ri do bheò.
>
> Ach pòsaidh sinne, 'ghaoil ghil,
> ann an eaglais fhaoin na brèige
> air eagal 's gum bi 'n saoghal
> glé aognaidh mu do chreuchdan.[40]

---

[39] Nicholson 1986.

[40] 'The Proper War': 'The young Lowlander has been before me / and
he has done the evil deed. // He has done the violence to your body, / the
unspeakable anguish of our grief, / so that you cannot lie / with another
while you live. // But we will marry, fair love, / in the vain false
church, / for fear the world will be / very chill about your wounds.'
MacLean 1999: 198–199.

Late in July 1941 MacLean was given to understand that
the woman had deceived him, and the effect was to induce
'anger at his own quixotic folly'.[41] A bitter quatrain dated
June 1942 and entitled 'Knightsbridge, Libya' defines his
beloved as 'depraved and a liar':

> Ged tha mi 'n diugh ri uchd a' bhatail
> chan ann an seo mo shac 's mo dhiachainn:
> cha ghunnachan 's cha thancan Roimeil,
> ach mo ghaol bhith coirbte briagach.[42]

It is hardly surprising that a feeling of revulsion at the poems
he had dedicated to her should have set in. This helps to
explain the following declaration in a letter to MacDiarmid
dated February 23rd 1942:

> As for my own stuff, I have not done anything since
> September or October and I know now that, if I am ever
> to write any more verse, it will be very different from
> what I have written, that it must be less subjective, more
> thoughtful, less content with its own music, and above
> all that I must transcend the shameful weaknesses of
> petty egoism and doubts and lack of single-mindedness
> that now disquiets [sic] me in much of my own stuff.
> Terrible things happened to me between 1939 and 1941
> and my poetry was a desperate effort to overcome them
> and that left its marks. But now I think I have overcome
> all that and if I survive this fracas, I will certainly cut
> away everything that deters me from a complete
> devotion to Scottish poetry and, if I have no longer
> anything to give that, it will have to be for me complete
> devotion to my political beliefs, which are now more
> uncompromising and far more single-minded than ever.

The presence of different women behind the overarching
figure of Eimhir is explicit in XLVI (quoted above), first
published in 1970. But it can also be detected in the poems
published in 1943. XIX and XX read very like a conclusion,

---

[41] Ross and Hendry 1986: 31.

[42] 'Though I am to-day against the breast of battle, / not here my burden
and extremity: / not Rommel's guns and tanks, / but that my darling is
depraved and a liar.' MacCaig 1959: 64–65. First published in *Poetry
Scotland* 2 in 1945. For a more extended, and equally bitter account, see
MacLean 1946.

with the latter specifying the number of poems so far completed ('chan e naoi deug an àireamh / no a leithid seo de dhàintean / a choisriginn...'[43]). The speaker believes that Eimhir is irremediably lost to him. The two poems signal a caesura to the reader, even though the greater part of the sequence is still to come. The war in Spain, first mentioned in IV and discussed in some detail in XVIII, is not mentioned again after XXII (apart from a passing reference in XXXV), as if with XXIII a new agenda had set in. The phrase 'beothachadh ùr an duain'[44] in XXV may indicate the impulse to write new poems that resulted from MacLean's renewing acquaintance with the Scottish woman.

And yet there are risks in bringing what we know of the poet's life to bear too closely on the text. The stanzas added to the opening poem in December 1939, which address Eimhir as 'A nighean a' chùil ruaidh òir'[45] produce a careful framing effect with the poem which was subsequently to close the cycle, LX, where the sight of her 'cùl ruadh'[46] reawakens old divisions in the soldier's flesh. XXXVI and XXXVIII take up the argument of XIV about selling one's soul, eventually dismissing the notion as foolish blasphemy. Though the lyrics in question may belong to 'different' Eimhirs, we are invited to read them as parts of a single discourse, with a single addressee. The lines quoted above from XX imply that all the preceding poems have been written with one woman in mind. XVII, with its galactic imagery, offers an anticipation of the imagery of stars and constellations which will come to the fore at a later stage, in poems such as L and LII. The 'deich bliadhna'[47] referred to thrice in LII and again in LVI are not linked to any figure from the poet's biography, but rather to a unitary view of the sequence as a single, ongoing experience. Indeed, a significant proportion of the poems lack any reference to an overall plot or to external events, a fact which would facilitate MacLean's subsequent extrapolation of them in his 1977 selected volume.

---

[43] 'nineteen would not be the number / nor these the kind of poems / I would dedicate...' (editor's translation).

[44] 'bringing new life to the poem' (editor's translation).

[45] 'Girl of the red-gold hair' (editor's translation).

[46] 'red hair'.

[47] 'ten years'.

5.

This is a difficult critical problem, and it is possible to conceive of two diametrically opposed responses to it. On the one hand, the sequence can be read as directed towards a single, largely imagined or fantasised addressee, more the expression of a poetic gift than the effect of biographical experience. On the other, a determined effort can be made to assign each individual item from IV to LX to either the Irishwoman or the Scottish woman. The latter approach, however, would be irrelevant to a large number of poems, such as XVII or XLII, which require no background or narrative framing for their understanding. On the other hand, the former approach would lead one wilfully to ignore the evidence of the text itself, what one might call the traces left within the sequence by the circumstances of its composition (its *Entstehungsgeschichte*), such as the mention of two years at XV: 11, as against the ten years mentioned later.

What, for example, is to be made of the range of colour adjectives applied to Eimhir, and specifically to her hair? In IV she is 'A nighean a' chùil bhuidhe, throm-bhuidh, òr-bhuidh',[48] while in V she is repeatedly addressed as 'A nighean ruadh'.[49] Can one woman have hair that is (from natural causes) at the same time yellow and red? And what about the lines added to I in December 1939, where she is 'A nighean a' chùil ruaidh òir'?[50]

The question is worth asking because there is good reason to believe that MacLean's omissions from the cycle were motivated by such inconsistencies and that, in the range of poems from V to XXII, he deliberately withdrew those items too obviously concerned with the 'nighean ruadh', the Scottish girl, so as to leave space for the Irishwoman.[51] VI, for example, must have lived up to MacLean's aesthetic criteria, given that it appeared in 1943 among the 'Dàin

---

[48] 'Girl of the yellow, heavy-yellow, gold-yellow hair.'

[49] 'Red[-haired] girl'.

[50] 'Girl of the red-gold hair' (editor's translation).

[51] In conversation, the poet's daughter Ishbel has offered a different explanation, suggesting that MacLean withheld those items in the sequence which he felt to be too overtly egocentric and personal in nature.

Eile' ('Other Poems'). The suspicion is that he removed it
from the cycle because of its tranquil yet schematic presentation of the way one woman had taken another's place in his
life:

> Am bliadhna roghainn na h-Albann,
> an nighean ruadh, clàr na grèine;
> 's a' bhòn-uiridh an nighean bhàn,
> roghainn àlainn na h-Èireann.[52]

But had she? This item dates from September 1939, and
refers unambiguously to the preparations for combat taking
place on the European mainland ('ùpraid marbhaidh / anns
a' Ghearmailt no san Fhraing'[53]). MacLean had renewed his
acquaintance with the Scottish woman in May or June, and
would declare his love to her in December. At the same time
his imagination continued to be possessed by the Irishwoman. Several of the finest poems linked to her (XVIII,
XIX and XXII) would appear to date at least from early
November and very possibly from December itself.

MacLean's behaviour was honourable in every respect.
The evidence implies, though, that when it came to publication, he did all he could to ensure a smooth transition
between the Irishwoman and the Scottish woman, rather than
having the two, as it were, appear to cohabit in his poetic
imagination. His concerns may have been partly, or even
predominantly, aesthetic. Yet if he did tell Hendry that the
poems from IV to XXII were not chronologically ordered,
the intention may have been to provide himself with a
retrospective alibi against the imputation of a very human,
purely mental infidelity, for which he alone could have
blamed himself. The issue of the different Eimhirs, then,
cannot be ignored, because of its impact not just on the
sequence, but on the fate of specific items in it.

Even when restored to its place, VI does not offer a secure
basis for assigning items to different addressees. While
mentions of 'ruadh' and 'buidhe' in the sequence can be taken
as indications that the Scottish woman or the Irishwoman

---

[52] 'This year the choice of Scotland, / the red-haired girl, sun forehead; /
and the year before last the fair-haired girl, / beautiful choice of
Ireland.'
[53] 'uproar of slaughter / in Germany or in France'.

respectively is intended, 'òr', 'geal' and 'bàn' are more am-
bivalent.[54] The Irishwoman is 'bàn' in the quatrain cited
above, but when the adjective recurs it is in XXIII, the
'concert poem', almost certainly inspired by the Scottish
woman.[55] The addition of the opening and closing stanzas to
I in December 1939 would appear to be a conscious attempt
on the poet's part to blur distinctions where possible, drawing
the various potential Eimhirs into one composite, if shadowy,
addressee. And the wisest critical approach may be to move
between the two opposite positions outlined at the beginning
of this section, combining elements from each in a flexible
manner, according to the demands of individual items or
groups of poems.

6.

Before proceeding further it may be helpful to describe the
landscape of the sequence in terms of its own peaks and
centres of attraction, its own acceleration and slowing down
of rhythm. III and IV set up a tension between love and
political commitment which will reverberate throughout. It is
examined in depth in XVIII 'Ùrnaigh' ('Prayer') (with its
theme of wholeness and splitting, prefigured optimistically in
II) and more pithily in XXII. XIX and XX indicate that his
love can have no happy outcome, but the concert poem,
XXIII, offers a new burst of energy, soon followed by the
haunting, dream-like imagery of XXVIII and XXIX. The
poems from XXX to XXXIX are briefer, more polemical and
comparatively light-hearted in tone, before tragedy sets in
with the unequivocal appearance of the wounded Eimhir in
XL. Poems evoking the speaker's love against a Highland
landscape (XLII, XLIII, XLIX, but also LIV) alternate with
the grimly cerebral knife poem XLV. From L onwards a
new question preoccupies him. How can the matter of the
sequence be safeguarded against the workings of time and
forgetfulness? Galactic imagery figures aptly (the planets
being crucial to human perceptions of time) with Eimhir
becoming a constellation in the best classical style in LII.

---

[54] 'Red-haired', 'yellow-haired', 'golden', 'white', 'fair-haired'. See note
to VI: 5–8 for a detailed account of the application of colour adjectives to
Eimhir throughout the sequence.
[55] See note to XXIII in 'Commentary'.

This question underpins the heavyweight poem LVII, the real point of arrival of the sequence. Increasingly, the poet looks back on what he has achieved (LV, LVI, LIX) and the closing item, LX, recapitulates the theme of splitting and the motif of Eimhir's red hair in an almost musical fashion.

As well as to important aspects of the sequence, too exaggerated an interest in the poet's life risks blinding us to the rich literary heritage from which the work derives so much of its power. In this context, the words of French critic Albert Thibaudet (1874–1936) (even though he had novelists rather than poets in mind) are instructive:

> It's unusual for a writer who reveals himself in a novel to produce a convincing, that is, a living character... The true novelist creates his characters from the infinite directions of his possible life; the false novelist, from the single line of his actual life. The genius of the novel is to bring the possible to life, and not to bring the real back to life.[56]

An admonition of this kind is comforting when dealing with poetry so closely affected by the vicissitudes of one man's fate. It warns us that, rather than a confession, the poetry offers a transmutation, a turning of the material of experience into something different, which cannot be predicated back into crude facts. In so doing, it can hopefully absolve both critics and editors from the accusation of prying unhealthily into the personal history of one individual.

The dichotomy between love and war which runs throughout the 'Dàin do Eimhir' was fundamental to male-authored European love poetry from a very early stage. As much is evident from, for example, the opening of Ovid's *Amores*:

> Arma gravi numero violentaque bella parabam
> edere, materia conveniente modis.
> Par erat inferior versus; risisse Cupido
> dicitur atque unum surripuisse pedem.[57]

---

[56] Editor's translation. Quoted in Gide 1937: 62.

[57] 'Arms, warfare, violence – I was winding up to produce a / Regular epic, with verse-form to match – / Hexameters, naturally. But Cupid (they say) with a snicker / Lopped off one foot from each alternate line.' Ovid 1982: 86.

Ovid has planned to speak of weapons and violent wars in
the appropriate hexameter metre, when the God of Love
intervenes, lopping a foot off his second line to produce an
elegiac distich in which he will be forced to speak of love.
Choosing an amorous subject matter immediately centres
attention on the obligatory, epic topics which are being
avoided. Part of the problem with love poetry was that it
foresaw a predominantly female (and therefore, in Roman
terms, inferior) readership. MacLean's sequence is, of course,
directed throughout to a female recipient, though a modern
audience is less likely to take this as implying it has inferior
value. Ovid's approach is light-hearted and ironic. His immediate predecessor Propertius presents a similar conflict in
more impassioned tones. In Book III, Elegy 3, he relates how
he was preparing to follow in the footsteps of the father of
Latin epic poetry:

> Visus eram molli recubans Heliconis in umbra,
>   Bellerophontei qua fluit umor equi,
> reges, Alba, tuos et regum facta tuorum,
>   tantum operis, nervis hiscere posse meis
> parvaque tam magnis admoram fontibus ora,
>   unde pater sitiens Ennius ante bibit...[58]

The god Apollo intervenes in person, and Calliope, the muse
of epic poetry, warns him off subject-matter which is not
suited to his temperament:

> Contentus niveis semper vectabere cycnis,
>   nec te fortis equi ducet ad arma sonus.
> Nil tibi sit rauco praeconia classica cornu
>   flare nec Aonium tingere Marte nemus,
> aut quibus in campis Mariano proelia signo
>   stent et Teutonicas Roma refringat opes...[59]

---

[58] 'I dreamed that where Bellerophon bestrode / The horse beneath whose
foot a fountain flowed, / On Helicon's soft-shaded slopes I lay, / And felt
within me power to sing and play, / With this momentous subject, Alba's
kings / And those kings' deeds, to task my voice and strings. / Were lips
like mine to touch that mighty stream / Where father Ennius drank...'
Propertius 1968: 127.

[59] 'A team of snow-white swans is yours for life: / No warlike steed shall
neigh you to the strife. / Not yours with trumpet's battle-blare to jar /
The ear, or stain Aonia's groves with war; / Or tell, when Rome beat

MacLean may well have been familiar with both the passages in question, given the quality of the Latin instruction he received in Portree, where the 'Headmaster's teaching of Latin was marvellous, and made me have a great love of Virgil, and a considerable love of Horace'.[60] Sydney Goodsir Smith, a close friend and associate of the poet's, drew inspiration for his own love sequence *Under the Eildon Tree*[61] from the free versions of Propertius done by Ezra Pound.[62] Goodsir Smith's sequence (which can in many respects be read as an ironic reflection on MacLean's) articulates a similar conflict in more flippant terms:

> Forbye, there's ither subjecks for a makar's pen
>   Maist wechtie and profund indeed,
> Maitters o' war and peace and dour debate
> Of foreign levie and domestic malice,
> As the preachers say
>   – But no for me!
> As weill gie me the wale o skillie or drambuie
> As scrieve a leid o' politics or thee![63]

What matters is that an underlying theme of MacLean's sequence was not only relevant to his own predicament but also a characteristic strand in the tradition with which he took care to establish such precise links.[64] Indeed, in deciding which elements of his own experience to foreground, he may well have been guided by his understanding of that tradition.

---

back the Teutons' might, / What plains saw Marius' standards locked in fight...' Propertius 1968: 129.

[60] MacLean 1999: xiii. In conversation with Donald Archie MacDonald, MacLean recalled that, required unexpectedly to take Latin classes in his second last year as Headmaster at Plockton (1970–71), he realised he could still remember nearly all of Book II of the *Aeneid* by heart. 'But oh, we were taught Latin so well in Portree'. See Ross and Hendry 1986: 215.

[61] First published in 1948, and in a revised version in 1955.

[62] Published in 1917 as *Homage to Sextus Propertius*. See Pound 1975: 79–97.

[63] Smith 1975: 150.

[64] See further in this connection the discussion of Platonism, the Petrarchan tradition, and the influence these had on the sequence, in the note to IX in the 'Commentary'.

For the 'Dàin do Eimhir' are much more than a record of
two fruitless emotional involvements. They trace how a
young poet affirms the gift he is conscious of possessing, by
creating a body of work of whose real value he has a very
shrewd notion.[65] The mentions of William Ross, the 18th
century Gaelic love lyricist (in the strictest sense, since his
poems were intended to be sung) occurring in the sequence
are a further index of the dimensions of MacLean's ambitions. XXXI, though uncertain about how Ross will
respond to 'na dàin / a sgaoil mi ealain-shriante, / eachraidh
fhiadhaich bhàrd'[66] when the two meet after death, suggests
that MacLean's lyrics might offer an adequate counterweight
to the earlier poet's 'Òran eile'. XXVI, a poem MacLean
withheld from publication, proudly claims that he can far
outdo his predecessor, provided he is suitably rewarded with
kisses:

> A nighean ruadh, nam faighinn do phòg
> airson gach duanaig luainich òir,
> chuirinn na mìltean dhiubh air dòigh
> thoirt bàrr air Uilleam Ros le stòr.[67]

Tragic love and literary ambition go hand in hand. Their
interrelation can be traced (as so often in the sequence) in the
recurrence of key lexical items; in this case, 'tòir, tòrachd',
meaning pursuit or 'search' (along with the related terms
'ruaig' and 'sireadh', the latter more properly 'seeking'), and
'faodail', which Dwelly (see 'Bibliography') glosses as 'goods
found by chance', 'thing found', 'stray treasure'. The opening
of I informs us that Eimhir is as indifferent to the poet's
'tòir' as she is to his suffering, yet there is a possible underlying ambivalence, an implication that he seeks something
beyond her and distinct from her. XIX, which begins with a
weighing up of accounts between them, makes his debt
explicit:

---

[65] See, for example, the references to the poets of Scotland (among whom
the speaker presumably expects to take his place) in XVI and XXI.

[66] 'the poems / I let loose art-bridled, / a wild cavalry for bards'.

[67] 'Red-haired girl, were I to get your kiss / for every restless golden
lyric, / I should fashion thousands of them / to excel William Ross with
store.'

A nighean bhuidhe àlainn
's ann shrac thu mo threòir-sa
agus dh'fhiaraich mo shlighe
bho shireadh mo thòrachd;
ach ma ruigeas mi m' àite,
coille àrd luchd nan òran,
's tu grìosach an dàin dhomh,
rinn thu bàrd dhiom le dòrainn.[68]

Although Eimhir has diverted his path from what he was seeking, he will, paradoxically, reach his target (affirmation as a poet) thanks to her. In a formulation which must have recalled to MacLean the words of his beloved Mary MacPherson ('Màiri Mhòr nan Òran'), the poet admits that the pain Eimhir has caused him made possible the full exercise of his literary talents. If XXI ('Dè dhòmhsa m' àite / am measg bàird na h-Albann'[69]) takes the trouble to assure the reader that literary fame cannot compensate for her failure to understand or to return his feelings, there is an undeniable implication that, under different circumstances or for a different speaker, such an exchange might just have been acceptable.

LII is a more extended and exhaustive summing up. It concludes that the unexpected treasure or 'faodail' justifies everything that has gone before. In LVI, the 'faodail' is poetry ('riamh cha d' fhuair mi dàn air faodail / cho suaimhneach ri do chuailean craobhach'[70]), while in LVIII it indicates her beauty for which, hopefully, the Muses can offer a secure haven. Again, the function of poetry is crucial to MacLean's discourse. LIX indicates how wrong it would be to read the sequence in uniformly tragic terms. MacLean, who never made a secret of his admiration for the riches of Gaelic oral tradition, does not hesitate to compare his own work with one of its treasures, the 'Hymn of the Graces'

---

[68] 'O yellow-haired, lovely girl, / you tore my strength / and inclined my course / from its aim: / but, if I reach my place, / the high wood of the men of song, / you are the fire of my lyric – / you made a poet of me through sorrow.'

[69] 'What does my place matter to me / among the poets of Scotland' (editor's translation).

[70] 'I never happened upon a treasure poem / as serene as your branching head of hair' (editor's translation).

noted down by Alexander Carmichael for the *Carmina Gadelica*, arguably the most precious 'faodail' that particular collector happened upon:

> agus air latha thàrladh dhòmhsa
> ealaidheachd òir gun luasgan,
> 's i coimhlionta, mar thàinig ortsa,
> gun mheang, an Ortha Bhuadhach.[71]

As a love story, the 'Dàin do Eimhir' end unhappily. As the story of a literary gift finding suitable expression, their conclusion is a triumph.

7.

The 'Dàin do Eimhir' offer a truly dazzling range of literary references and intertextualities, indicative of MacLean's success in turning his bilingual and bicultural situation to advantage. The sections in the 'Commentary' on poems XIII and XIX, for instance, do their best to pay tribute to the rich network of references MacLean sets up, embracing not just the Celtic heritage but also classical Latin poetry and the European tradition since the time of the troubadours. The deployment of the *carpe diem* topos in the last stanza of XIX has a characteristically modern harshness, yet it is not fanciful to detect here reminiscences of Horace, Shakespeare and Marvell, as well as Baudelaire. It is significant that MacLean's access to earlier literary forms, such as the 'composite beauty' notion underlying XIII or the 'Dimitto' with which the sequence closes, is facilitated or at least influenced by a Modernist sensibility, most specifically in the work of Ezra Pound.

Modernist, too, is the challenging, at times jarring, manner in which MacLean pairs Celtic elements with elements from other European traditions. In XXIII, the virgin huntress of the Greek pantheon, Diana, twice appears in adjacent lines

---

[71] 'And one day there came to me / a peaceful golden lyric, / complete, as came to you, / flawless, the Hymn of the Graces.' The word translated by MacLean as 'lyric', 'ealaidheachd', refers to the exercise of his art, and implies that he has more than just one single poem in mind at this point.

with Deirdre, the heroine of Ulster legend, while Beethoven
rubs shoulders with the celebrated piper Patrick Mòr
MacCrimmon (1595–1670). Iain Crichton Smith has said of
MacLean's political stance that

> in no previous Gaelic poetry is there this political
> European commitment, though there is political
> commitment within the Highlands as found, for
> instance, in the work of Iain Lom... However, one of the
> important things that Sorley MacLean did was to open
> Gaelic poetry out to the world beyond purely parochial
> boundaries.[72]

The juxtapositions in XXIII show that the same attitude
informed MacLean's cultural stance. They articulate a claim
for the reintegration of Gaelic culture into a larger frame of
reference than it had enjoyed since the late Middle Ages, just
as the political agenda of the sequence looks beyond the
immediate concerns of those who speak the Gaelic language
or even of Scotland as a whole.

The trinity of poets envisaged in XX is made up of William
Ross and two contemporary poets, one Anglo-Irish, the other
Russian. As with the protagonist of the Eimhir cycle, it is
crucial that these figures should not merely be luckless lovers
but at the same time poets, and therefore able to express
and even immortalise their experience in metrically patterned
language. The three have in common a passion for a named
woman and an associated body of verse, in Ross's case
Marion Ross of Stornoway.[73] The Russian poet's situation
was rather different. He had the good luck, or more likely the
misfortune, to marry the woman he had idealised so in-
tensely, and would appear to have been prodigiously
unfaithful to her later on in life. How familiar MacLean was
with such details is uncertain. It is more than likely that Blok
was brought to his attention because MacDiarmid
incorporated versions of two poems into *A Drunk Man Looks
at the Thistle*.[74]

---

[72] See 'Introduction' to MacLean 1971.
[73] See the note on X: 12 in the 'Commentary' for more detailed
information.
[74] See note on XX: 18–19 in the 'Commentary'.

Of the three poets involved, MacLean has the most
sustained and troubled confrontation with Yeats. It is
interesting to note that he figured alongside William Ross in
an early draft of XXXIII. Few readers familiar with the Irish
poet's work will read poems III or IV in the 'Dàin do Eimhir'
sequence without recalling 'Politics':

> How can I, that girl standing there,
> My attention fix
> On Roman or on Russian
> Or on Spanish politics?
> Yet here's a travelled man that knows
> What he talks about,
> And there's a politician
> That has read and thought,
> And maybe what they say is true
> Of war and war's alarms,
> But O that I were young again
> And held her in my arms![75]

There are obvious parallels between Yeats's protracted obsession with Maud Gonne and MacLean's own experiences.
Yet the protagonist of the 'Dàin do Eimhir' only arrives at
the indifference towards political matters, when set against
amorous or sensual passion, which is so unhesitatingly avowed
by the Irish poet, after the self-torment and laceration
narrated in the sequence. Yeats is not just a presence, but an
influence throughout it.[76] It gave MacLean pleasure when
Young found LI to be 'in the later style of Yeats' and he
freely admitted that a core inspiration for LVII was 'Where
had her sweetness gone' from *The Winding Stair and Other
Poems*. He told Young that 'I did not read Yeats at the
university at all and only read him in bulk about 1936, and it
is only in the last two years that his poetry has become one
of my obsessions. I now read and re-read him'.[77]
    Writing on January 10th 1940 he assured MacDiarmid
that 'all the people whose opinions I value are now certain

---

[75] Yeats 1983: 348.
[76] Notwithstanding the following disclaimer from MacLean, listing
influences on him, in a letter to Douglas Young dated September 11th
1941: 'Of course Yeats, but I don't think stylistically...'
[77] Letter of September 11th 1941.

that this century has seen two major poets in the British
Islands, yourself and Yeats'. Fully three years earlier, however, he was already characterising Yeats as 'a man full of all
sorts of misgivings and indecisions, making half-hearted
attempts to make the best of a few worlds' (letter to
MacDiarmid of December 20th 1936). In the continuation of
a letter to Young already quoted above, dated December
6th 1940, MacLean says of his own unhappiness that

> No doubt many a bourgeois Philistine is in the same
> predicament but so were Yeats and William Ross. At
> least Ross was. I now am come very much to doubt the
> depth of Yeats's feelings. That's not what I mean. What
> I really mean is that most of his finest poetry is just a
> specious camouflage for his feelings. He had to erect the
> Anglo-Irish aristocratic myth to cover his self-contempt.
> I even doubt the depth of his feelings to Maud Gonne.
> After all he did not become a revolutionary for her sake.
> He just remained a crossed troubled aesthete.

He found the Irish poet's 'aristocratic yearnings... very
bourgeois and vulgar' (letter to Young of September 11th
1941) and, on reading George Moore's *Confessions*, wrote
that he found the book 'a great commentary on Yeats's
pretensions, being so much more honest than Yeats. I think it
gives the whole show away for good' (December 18th 1941).
The problematics of the 'Dàin do Eimhir' peep through in
the private correspondence of the writer. For Yeats's passion
to be believable, it would have had to translate itself into
direct action, preferably at the risk of the poet's own life.
There is an element of self-projection here, evident in this
passage from a letter to MacDiarmid of May 25th 1940:

> I sometimes imagine that I could be a humble follower
> of the School of Yeats, who essentially is a very mun-
> dane poet compared with you. I am especially interested
> in Yeats because I am certain a sense of inferiority is
> one of the main dynamics of his poetry, though this
> sense of inferiority frequently, as in his Anglo-Irish
> ascendancy aristocratic sense, is an inferiority complex.
> I don't think I have the complex but I have the
> inferiority feeling quite clearly.

One cannot help wondering if those words about the 'crossed

troubled aesthete' were a reproach MacLean directed, in private, against himself. Perhaps the final word on his relationship to the work of the Irish poet can be taken from an essay entitled 'Some Gaelic and non-Gaelic Influences on Myself' first published in 1981:

> I have always believed that the highest poetry is either that which is a passionate comment on life of 'high seriousness' or that which gets near to saying the unsayable. MacDiarmid's lyrics said the unsayable. Some years later, I came to believe that much of Yeats's middle and later poetry was, of the modern poetry I knew, the most consistently and convincingly passionate comment on life, much as I disliked Yeats's élitism and some of his other attitudes.[78]

8.

Given the active presence of such a wide range of references to European culture in the 'Dàin do Eimhir', it becomes hard to define MacLean as a purely Gaelic poet in any simplistic sense. Young told MacLean, in a letter of April 2nd 1943, that

> my comment about your sprung rhythm... arose from your brother John's horror, expressed about last April, in being confronted with your productions. He roundly *denied* they were Gaelic poetry at all, and proceeded to propound a series of utterly idiotic academic would-be emendations.[79]

Dr John MacInnes insists that

> when *Dàin do Eimhir* appeared, it was not any traditional quality, as that is more usually defined, which

---

[78] MacLean 1981: 501. See also the note on X: 12 in the 'Commentary'.
[79] Letter of April 4th 1943. On this occasion George Campbell Hay (1915–1984) leapt to MacLean's defence, observing, when Young told him about the remarks made by the poet's elder brother, that 'General Rommel was quite enough of an assailant for one bard to contend with at a time...'

seized the imagination of his Gaelic readers. There were
some who criticised the poetry for its strangeness; others
for its difficulty.[80]

Since many of those who have written and continue to write
about his work cannot read his Gaelic texts, or Gaelic texts
of any kind, a degree of projection must be hard to avoid.
The English translations the poet himself increasingly
supplied mould perceptions of a Gaelic culture, of which he is
then cast as the expression, but to which readers in this group
have no direct access. A closed circle of this kind risks being
dangerously solipsistic.

It goes, of course, without saying that MacLean was
steeped in Gaelic lore, poetic, musical and lexicographical,
thanks to his upbringing on Raasay. He was born at
Osgaig on the island on October 26th 1911, to Malcolm and
Christina MacLean, the second son of five sons and two
daughters. His father's forebears, who most likely came from
North Uist, had been on the island for at least seven
generations, his father's grandfather John being the sole
member of the family not to have emigrated in the 1830s or
the 1850s. His father's mother, Mary Matheson from Braes
in Skye, had a 'vast store of song... not only from Skye and
Raasay but also from Lochalsh and Kintail'. She lived with
the family, dying in 1923 at the age of 84 or 86, when the
poet was not quite 12. From her he heard 'Cumha Iain
Ghairbh', 'Luinneag MhicLeòid' and a host of other songs.[81]
His mother's brother Alexander Nicolson would make special
trips to the island for the purpose of taking these down from
his grandmother, along with herbal and other lore. His
father's sister Peigi, the eldest of that family, was a colourful
figure who would visit for a month each year:

> ...we had to go out fishing with her. I used to go
> out, and I was terribly keen on boats, and Peigi, she'd
> get up about eleven o'clock and away out to fish. We'd
> come back home for dinner and out again after that,
> and again in the evening... I used to go out alone with
> her, and it was all songs. She was full of old songs. I

---

[80] MacInnes 1981: 15.
[81] MacLean 1977b: 378.

used to threaten to go on strike unless she sang songs!
...What fights and arguments would be going on
about politics... she had become a Tory about that
time because of the First World War, though she had
been a Socialist and a Nationalist and a Suffragette
before...[82]

Something of the atmosphere surrounding her visits may be
gleaned from MacLean's recalling how 'One forenoon in
1936 my Aunt Peggie announced that she had remembered
three songs that she had forgotten for many years'.[83] He
believed her to be 'almost as good, perhaps quite as good, as
my grandmother in the number of songs she had'.[84] Both
Peigi's younger sister Flora and the poet's father were also
gifted singers. Of his father (also a fine piper) MacLean wrote
that 'in some songs his timing and weight was such that I
now find it difficult to listen to those songs from anyone else'.
He had a keen interest in the work of the great 18th century
poets, the object of engrossing discussions with MacLean's
Nicolson uncle, though sadly 'in anti-Catholic Free Presbyterian Raasay not even my father knew much about
Alexander MacDonald'.
     Of his mother's immediate family 'two brothers were
pipers, two others were singers, one a bard, and one sister a
very good singer'. The network of MacLean's sources for
traditional Gaelic song included his elder brother John, who
had a prodigious memory, as well as their great friend from
Portree School, John Matheson of Kilmuir, an aunt and
uncle in Braes, and another brother of his mother's, Angus
Nicolson, whose 'great store of songs' derived from his
mother, Isabel MacLeod, from neighbours in Braes, and
from other sources on Skye and the mainland.
     The poet's mother, however, was not a singer and neither
was he. Even though he 'could not forget the words of any
Gaelic song I liked even if I heard it only once', from about

---

[82] Ross and Hendry 1986: 213. The interview with Donald Archie
MacDonald featured in *Critical Essays* is an invaluable source of
information about MacLean's Raasay background.
[83] MacLean 1977b: 391.
[84] Nicolson 1979: 24.

1924 MacLean looked upon himself as 'a traditional Gaelic singer manqué'.[85] He would later comment that:

I was fond of poetry of all kinds from the age of 14 onwards, but I think I was even fonder of old Gaelic song, and I consider the fusion of poetry and music in those Gaelic songs as it were the very last word in what the Gaels have done. And there was a kind of impotence about me in the sense that I couldn't sing. I was one of the few of our family who couldn't sing or play the pipes or something like that, but I was passionately fond of it.[86]

Though a significant tradition bearer, his maternal grandmother was a devout Free Presbyterian, a member of a sect which considered 'the secular arts dangerous vanities'.[87] Yet MacLean would come to feel that he had overestimated the destructive influence of religious radicalism on Gaelic lore which, rather than vanishing, went underground.

Wherever the truth may lie, the church played a vital role in supplying him with a more exalted and intellectual register of the language. On the Friday of a communion ceremony, preaching could go on for four and a half hours, with as many as twenty elders, exhibiting distinctive varieties of the language, 'speaking to the question'. This encouraged an acute awareness of linguistic variation, reflected in discussions of a philological slant between the poet's father and his Nicolson uncle, who was himself the author of a Gaelic grammar. Among the preachers MacLean was privileged to hear he singled out Ewen MacQueen, who had

a wonderful register, a marvellous Gaelic... with the kind of ability to change the registers and to use the local colour, to use everything... if his sermons could have been recorded in toto you would have a Gaelic prose amazing in its richness, variety and raciness.[88]

---

[85] MacLean 1985: 5–7.

[86] Hendry 1991: 1.

[87] MacLean 1985: 10.

[88] Ross and Hendry 1986: 218. For the influence of Gaelic sermons and related intellectual debate on MacLean's work, see MacInnes 1981 and the notes to poem XVIII in the 'Commentary'.

Writing to Douglas Young on September 7th, 1941, MacLean
would insist that

> constant sermonising made me very familiar with
> Seceder metaphysics and imagery and vocabulary. I
> have retained this knowledge (in fact, at present I think
> I could make a very fine Seceder sermon if my tongue
> were loosened with a little strong drink).

Though he spoke no English when he first went to school
aged 6, it would be a mistake to conceive of the Raasay
environment he grew up in as a uniformly Gaelic one. The
workforce brought from the Scottish Lowlands at the end of
the previous century to operate the local mine meant that the
language of the school playground (and not just of the
classroom) was English (or Scots) rather than Gaelic. And
there are indications that, in the course of time, both
languages were used by the poet's immediate family.[89]

9.

MacLean was wounded three times in all while fighting in
North Africa. As a consequence of the serious injuries he
received when a mine exploded close to him during the battle
of El Alamein on November 2nd 1942, he spent nine months
in a series of military hospitals, a period which coincided with
the final preparations for seeing the 'Dàin do Eimhir' through
the press. His letters to Young allow us to trace his changing
feelings about the sequence. Indeed, to use Joy Hendry's
words, 'so completely did he turn against his own poetry that
it spilled over to affect his appreciation of other poets'.[90]

It was mooted that at least extracts from 'An Cuilithionn'
might be included in the volume, and on November 9th 1941
MacLean recommended using the closing section (beginning
'Có seo, có seo oidhche dhona'[91]) which Hay had 'thought
the very best thing in it'. He spoke of his 'very precise

---

[89] According to Dr John MacInnes, MacLean's younger sister Mary had
a largely passive knowledge of Gaelic.
[90] Ross and Hendry 1986: 31.
[91] 'Who is this, who is this on a bad night' MacLean 1999: 128–129.

reasons' for already deleting 12 items from the sequence, involving 'the other business' (presumably the 'wounded Eimhir') and proposed 'extra exclusions of poems' if these would not 'spoil your scheme'. His painful uncertainty about what and what not to print (no doubt provoked in part by his imminent departure on active service) is unmistakable when he comes to the untraced poem 'Do A. M.' ('To A. M.'):

> ...I think you had better leave it out. I think I have advertised the unsuccess of my love sufficiently without giving it 'local habitation and a name'. This is a point on which I change my mind almost as often as I think about it but, unless you hear from me to the contrary, just leave it out. But I may change my mind before I go. If I do I'll tell you. I suppose it is something which can be decided almost at the last minute at any rate.

In the same letter he asks for the 'Dimitto' to be omitted, but ten days later is content to leave the decision up to Young. He must have explained the circumstances surrounding the 'wounded Eimhir' to both Young and his brother John in person before leaving Britain, for on December 18th we read that he is

> very grateful for our last meeting as I felt that you, as well as John, should know the real reasons for my apparent weakness. I may have been a bloody fool but, at any rate, I wasn't a weakling in the business, but, for God's sake, never think that I feel any resentment against the other person chiefly concerned and any vague doubts I may have expressed to you are very probably my own fault and an injustice to a person of a very open and unsuspicious nature, towards whom I have the same feelings as ever...

This attitude was to change within six months, with 'Knightsbridge, Libya' as eloquent testimony. In a letter from North Africa dated March 15th 1942, MacLean expresses a growing antipathy towards the cycle:

> ...nowadays I am always finding my own stuff false, shallow and meretricious... I am very much ashamed of my preoccupation with my own private troubles and think of many of the other enthusiasms of my

poetry as silly idolatries. I could now write a pretty crushing review of all my own poetry, especially of my 'high falutins of love' but they are probably fairly harmless.

Writing two weeks later with nothing but a thin canvas to protect him from a sandstorm, MacLean inveighs against Yeats, whose 'great lyrics' are merely 'the splendid expressions of a weakling's moments of self-realisation, hopelessly tangled with his posturings, often just arrant nonsense...' If, as seems probable, the MacLean who produced the 'Dàin do Eimhir' had an unusually symbiotic and tormented relationship with the Irish poet, it is understandable that the revulsion the sequence had begun to inspire in him should colour his attitude to Yeats. On October 6th, he tells Young that many of his own poems 'which formerly pleased me well enough, now fill me with shame and disgust...' If he is to write more in the future, it will not be after the manner of the 'Dàin do Eimhir' but in the style of 'Ban-Ghàidheal' ('A Highland Woman'), 'Calbharaigh' ('Calvary') or parts of 'An Cuilithionn'. In other words, a politically committed poetry of social responsibility.

MacLean corrected the proofs of the 1943 volume, where he found that MacKechnie had 'corrected a great many errors in the original Gaelic texts which he would never have noticed himself'.[92] But he was now preoccupied with bringing out a separate edition of 'An Cuilithionn', if necessary in Gaelic only, at a price the average crofter could afford. Writing from Raasay on May 2nd 1943, four days before he was due to return to Raigmore Hospital in Inverness, he tells Young that 'For the "Dàin do Eimhir", I simply don't care, but I expect they will be out fairly soon... surely [the sequence] shows how tainted I am with bourgeois-dom'. The same degree of antipathy transpires in a letter dated June 15th, where he is 'in no hurry' for the 'Dàin' 'but would like to see them off my hands as soon as possible, and for good'.

Young, on his side, was alarmed when 'your brother John threw a spanner in the works by forbidding the atheistic stuff

---

[92] Letter from Young to MacKechnie dated March 31st 1943 (National Library of Scotland Acc. 6419/6).

like Dan XVIII' at a stage when 'I had everything set... to start printing' (airgraph, June 1942). The following January, in a further airgraph, he warned MacLean that Glasgow publisher William Maclellan was advertising the projected volume at 10/6

> with illustrations by William Crosbie, the ablest younger painter in Scotland. It should be out any day now, but I have had *nothing* to do with its final form.

Young's term in prison, because of his repeated public opposition to conscription by the London governement, effectively removed him from the scene, though he devoted part of his confinement to making an English 'projection' of 'An Cuilithionn'.[93] The illustrations were a source of further headaches, as transpires from Young's letter of April 21st 1943:

> With regard to illustrations, my own thought was for two photographs, the ones you gave me, 1933 and 1940. John thought of a third, in uniform with cap. It was at this stage MacColl[94] introduced me to William Crosbie, with whom he was staying. So far as my recollection goes... there was no question of Crosbie illustrating the 'Dàin'; but I had mentioned the notion of a handsome edition of 'The Cuillin' with your parallel translation or another, illustrated by Crosbie... At any rate I certainly had no conception that Maclellan was launching into a big-page edition with a good half-dozen pieces by Crosbie. You in the firing-line could not authorize that, nor could I. Nor did either of us expressly authorize it.

---

[93] See National Library of Scotland MS 14978 (Papers of James B. and Janet Caird) and, for another copy, Acc. 10090/208 (Robert McIntyre Papers). National Library of Scotland Acc. 6419 Box 101 contains a further, incomplete copy of the English version of 'An Cuilithionn' carried out by Young while incarcerated, between January 8th and February 12th 1943. He proposed including a sample of his translation in *Auntran Blads*, but MacLean had 'the Gaelic readers first in mind' and did not wish 'any version to precede the original by what would now be most likely a great length of time...' (letter dated May 2nd 1943 from Churchton, Raasay).

[94] Dugald MacColl: see section on Hugh MacDiarmid in note to poem XV in the 'Commentary'.

Two days later Young had a meeting to discuss the legal aspects of the question, and concluded that Maclellan had the right to include the art work of his choice, while privately commenting that 'Crosbie's illustrations resemble heavily blitzed telephone-exchanges, but will doubtless rank five centuries hence with the Book of Kells'.[95]

In the last but one of the letters to Young preserved in the National Library of Scotland, dated June 6th 1950, the treatment to be given the sequence in the 1977 and 1989 volumes is clearly prefigured. While calculating the total number of lines of his work which are to appear in an anthology Young is editing, MacLean instructs him: 'Do not use the name "Dàin do Eimhir" or the numbers thereof; just give the poems first lines if there is no title...'

10.

The Gaelic text of the 'Dàin do Eimhir' is presented here in the currently accepted form of Gaelic spelling[96] but with absolute respect for the phonetic and phonological particularities of MacLean's originals. Exhaustive use is made of the poet's letters, our primary source of information as to his work and his views, and in particular of his correspondence with Douglas Young between 1940 and 1943. In quoting letters, spelling and punctuation have been silently normalised where this appeared desirable. The English translations opposite the Gaelic text have been reproduced from the 1999 collected volume, supplemented where necessary from the 1943 volume, from manuscript sources, and by the editor's own translations (clearly marked with an asterisk).

The translations to be appended to the 1943 Gaelic text were a source of some disquiet for MacLean. On July 25th 1942, he tells Young that he is

---

[95] Letter to George Campbell Hay, March 31st 1943 (National Library of Scotland Acc. 6419/6).

[96] For further details of the solutions adopted, see the introductory note to the 'Copytexts and Variant Readings' section of this edition. Quotations of MacLean's work not from the sequence reproduce the spelling of the source being cited.

a bit perturbed at the idea of the appearance of my
versions of the things. I should much have preferred
yours in, leaving those not done by you as untranslated,
as some of them are terribly poor in the original and in
my bald English will look awful scarecrows.

Five days later, the situation has changed. MacLean is
'terribly pleased that your translations and not mine will
appear', since 'the idea of the appearance of my bald
translations left me sick', and he thanks Young 'for your
stand in that matter'. On March 22nd, 1943, however,
matters have changed again, and the publisher William
Maclellan wishes to use 'either my own literal versions or
MacKechnie's'. The proofs which arrived five days later
included versions by the latter which, on examining them,
MacLean found he objected to no less than he had to earlier
versions by MacColl. He was also unhappy with the choice
of poems translated. On March 30th we find him 'plodding
through' versions of his own which are 'hellish at best, especially when I see yours of the rant' (that is, 'An Cuilithionn').
He is 'keeping quite a lot of MacKechnie's and MacColl's
ideas' and asks Young to 'touch up what I do myself'. He
has no alternative, as Maclellan refuses to print Young's
Scots versions, while Young himself was convinced that
'there must be English versions' and that 'they must be in
straightforward prose', as he wrote to MacLean on March
31st. It would appear, then, that the English versions featured
in the 1943 volume were a collaborative effort, even if the
principal contribution was MacLean's.

He had the enviable good fortune to see items from the
sequence translated into Scots by poets (and friends) of
considerable stature in their own right.[97] The fact that the
1977 and 1989 volumes were accompanied solely by the
poet's own English versions indicates how much the cultural
climate had changed in the intervening years. Discussing

[97] For Scots versions of LIV, 'Calbharaigh', XLIII, LI, 'Dàin Eile' XVII,
XXVIII, XXXIII, XXXIV, LIII, LV, 'Gealach ùr', 'Ban-ghàidheal' and
XLII see Young 1943: 11–19; of 'Reothairt' and LVII, Young 1947:
33–37; of III, Garioch 1983: 120; and of 'An Trom-laighe', Goodsir Smith
1946: 19. A fine, unpublished Scots version of LVII by Sydney Goodsir
Smith is in National Library of Scotland Acc. 10397/3.

three recent bilingual publications in a polemical essay
published in *Chapman* magazine, Wilson McLeod highlighted
the perils of a situation where Gaelic poets are required, as
a matter of course, to provide parallel English texts if they
desire to see their work in print:

> All the poems in all three volumes are given in Gaelic
> and in English, with the English on the eye-catching
> right, with both languages printed in the same typeface.
> The English texts are not described as translations of
> the Gaelic – their presence is not explained at all – and
> no translator is identified: one may assume that the
> poets themselves provided the English texts as well as
> the Gaelic.
>
>   Presenting this poetry in such a fashion has serious
> consequences. The two texts can be understood as two
> functionally equivalent versions of the same thing, the
> same ideal 'original' – the difference being essentially
> one of format... Or the two texts can be seen as two
> distinct and different compositions, two 'originals' of
> essentially identical legitimacy and importance, each the
> fruit of the author's labour, and not necessarily de-
> pendent on each other. What no longer seems a realistic
> interpretation is the most obvious one – that the Gaelic
> texts are the originals, and their English translations
> are ancillary and mediated compositions in whose pro-
> duction 'something has been lost'.[98]

The temptation to regard the English versions as an
acceptable substitute for, even an equivalent of the originals,
in much greater when the poet has himself provided them.
Who better than he could extract and convey in another
language the quintessence of his own productions?
   The damage brought about by such a practice is at least
twofold. First of all, studies of the poetry are prone to a kind
of slippage by which it becomes unclear which texts are
the focus of discussion, the Gaelic originals or the author's
versions. Vagueness of this kind is a serious defect of the
1986 *Critical Essays*, which fail to make a hard and fast
distinction between contributors who deal with MacLean's

---

[98] McLeod 1998: 149.

originals, and those whose knowledge is limited to translations. Secondly, it brings about a distortion in the corpus of
the poet's work, a distortion from which the 'Dàin do Eimhir'
sequence of love poems has suffered notably. MacLean's
poetic output is identified, to all intents and purposes, with
his own translations into English. Those parts of the 1943
collection which were not available in English could, it seems,
be ignored.

Poetic translation of any kind involves selection among a
range of possible resonances and at least a degree of interpretation. When it is the poet himself who does this, the
danger is that he may be held to have produced the definitive
interpretation of his text, whereas in fact the choice of a
word or shade of meaning may well have been a question of
elegance and naturalness of expression in the target language,
and therefore irrelevant to the original poem. In an engaging
essay, where he describes the effect of hearing his own work
lectured on by a professor at the Sorbonne, no less a figure
than Paul Valéry implies that the one person who should
never translate a poem is the poet himself, given that his
experience of the process of writing blinds him to the nature
of the end product:

> If I am questioned, then; if someone is perturbed (as
> people can be, and sometimes quite deeply) about what
> I 'wanted to say' in such and such a poem, I reply that I
> did not *want to say*, but *wanted to do*, and that it was
> the intention of *doing* which *wanted* what I *said*... As to
> his interpretations of the *letter*, I have already explained
> my views on this elsewhere; but one can never insist
> too much upon this point. *There is no such thing as 'the
> real meaning' of a text.* The author has no special
> authority. Whatever he may have *wanted to say*, he has
> written what he has written. Once published, a text is,
> so to speak, a mechanism which everyone can use in his
> own way and as best he can: it is not certain that its
> constructor uses it better than the next man. Besides, if
> he really knows what he *wanted* to do, this knowledge
> always interferes with his perception of what he has
> *done*.[99]

---

[99] Valéry 1971: 87, 93.

One could argue that it is a condition of creative work of any kind that one should never be fully conscious of the implications of one's choices, or of the nature of the artefact one is producing. And the idea that the poet can offer an authoritative rendering, a sanctioned and therefore exclusive interpretation of the original, is inimical to the very notion of translation, which rests on multifariousness and the possibility, indeed the necessity of constant repetition, re-translation.

The audience for MacLean's poetry goes far beyond the restricted body of readers who have access to it in the original language. In view of this fact, Gaelic citations are in this edition provided with an English translation in a footnote. The resulting transparency is, though, a double-edged sword. It is likely to exacerbate the slippages and inaccuracies discussed in the preceding paragraph. Yet there is another possibility. At the close of an interview with the poet published in 1979, Aonghas MacNeacail referred to those 'who have learned Gaelic so that they could read the poems of Sorley MacLean'.[100] The editor was inspired to do just that, not by the poet's own translations, but by infinitely freer versions from the hand of Iain Crichton Smith. If the deeper understanding of MacLean's love poetry which this edition aims to facilitate can spur on even a handful of readers to take him at his word (*den Dichter beim Wort zu nehmen*), encountering him in the language of his choice, then the effort that went into it will have been richly rewarded.

---

[100] Nicolson 1979: 36.

DÀIN DO EIMHIR
Poems to Eimhir

I*

Girl of the red-gold hair,
far from you, o love, my aim;
girl of the red-gold hair,
far from you my sorrow.

Tonight on the Sound of Raasay
my hand is on the helm,
listlessly the wind shakes the sail,
my heart is dumb, aching for your music,
today and tomorrow indifferent to my expectation.

Grey is the mist that creeps over Dun Caan,
fretful the coarse moor grass and bog cotton,
the west wind touches the surface of the sea,
my hopes are gone, gloom overshadows me.

A white cleft to the bottom of the wave,
the wind skirls round the tip of the mast,
but let it blow, I am indifferent
to a battle awakening on a bare sea.

Girl of the red-gold hair,
far from you, o love, my aim,
girl of the red-gold hair,
very far from you my sorrow.

II
Reason and Love

If our language has said that reason
is identical with love,
it is not speaking the truth.

When my eye lighted on your face
it did not show the reason in love,
I did not ask about that third part.

I

A nighean a' chùil ruaidh òir,
fada bhuat, a luaidh, mo thòir;
a nighean a' chùil ruaidh òir,
gur fada bhuatsa mo bhròn.

Mi nochd air linne Ratharsair
's mo làmh air an stiùir,
a' ghaoth gu neo-airstealach a' crathadh an t-siùil,
mo chridhe gu balbh, cràiteach an dèidh do chiùil,
an là an-diugh 's a-màireach coingeis ri mo dhùil.

Ciar an ceò èalaidh air Dùn Cana,
frionasach garbh-shliabh is canach,
a' ghaoth an iar air aghaidh mara,
dh'fhalbh mo dhùil is dùiseal tharam.

Am bristeadh geal gu làr an tuinn,
a' ghaoth 'na sgal mu bhàrr a' chroinn,
ach sèideadh sgal, chan eil mo shuim
ri cath a dhùisgeas air muir luim.

A nighean a' chùil ruaidh òir,
fada bhuat, a luaidh, mo thòir;
a nighean a' chùil ruaidh òir,
gur glè fhada bhuat mo bhròn.

II
A Chiall 's a Ghràidh

Ma thubhairt ar cainnt gu bheil a' chiall
co-ionann ris a' ghaol,
chan fhìor dhi.

Nuair dhearc mo shùil air t' aodann
cha do nochd e ciall a' ghràidh,
cha do dh'fheòraich mi mun trian ud.

When I heard your voice it did not make
this division in my flesh;
it did not the first time.

But that came to me without my knowing
and it tore the root of my being,
sweeping me with it in its drift.

With all I had of apprehension
I put up a shadow of fight;
my reason struggled.

From the depths of this old wisdom
I spoke to my love:
You are not worthy of me, nor from me.

　On the inside my love,
　my intellect on the elegant side,
　and the foolish door was broken.

And my intellect said to my love:
Duality is not for us;
we mingle in love.

May 1932

III

Never has such turmoil
nor vehement trouble been put in my flesh
by Christ's suffering on the earth
or by the millions of the skies.

And I took no such heed of a vapid dream –
green wood of the land of story –
as when my stubborn heart leaped to the glint
of her smile and golden head.

And her beauty cast a cloud
over poverty and a bitter wound
and over the world of Lenin's intellect,
over his patience and his anger.

Nuair chuala mi do ghuth cha d' rinn
e 'n roinneadh seo 'nam chrè;
cha d' rinn a' chiad uair.

Ach dhiùchd siud dhomh gun aithne dhomh   10
is reub e friamh mo chrè,
gam sguabadh leis 'na shiaban.

Leis na bha dhomh de bhreannachadh
gun d' rinn mi faileas strì;
gun d' rinneadh gleac lem chèill.   15

Bho dhoimhne an t-seann ghliocais seo
's ann labhair mi rim ghaol:
Cha diù liom thu, cha diù bhuam.

   Air an taobh a-staigh mo ghaol,
   mo thuigse air an taobh ghrinn,   20
   is bhristeadh a' chòmhla bhaoth.

Is thubhairt mo thuigse ri mo ghaol:
Cha dhuinn an dùbailteachd:
tha 'n coimeasgadh sa ghaol.

                                      an cèitean 1932

III

Cha do chuir de bhuaireadh riamh   1
no thrioblaid dhìom 'nam chrè
allaban Chrìosda air an talamh
no milleanan nan speur.

'S cha d' ghabh mi suim de aisling bhaoith –   5
coille uaine ùr an sgeòil –
mar leum mo chridhe rag ri tuar
a gàire 's cuailein òir.

Agus chuir a h-àilleachd sgleò
air bochdainn 's air creuchd sheirbh   10
agus air saoghal tuigse Lenin,
air fhoighidinn 's air fheirg.

IV

Girl of the yellow, heavy-yellow, gold-yellow hair,
the song of your mouth and Europe's shivering cry,
fair, heavy-haired, spirited, beautiful girl,
the disgrace of our day would not be bitter in your kiss.

Would your song and splendid beauty take
from me the dead loathsomeness of these ways,
the brute and the brigand at the head of Europe
and your mouth red and proud with the old song?

Would white body and forehead's sun take
from me the foul black treachery,
spite of the bourgeois and poison of their creed
and the feebleness of our dismal Scotland?

Would beauty and serene music put
from me the sore frailty of this lasting cause,
the Spanish miner leaping in the face of horror
and his great spirit going down untroubled?

What would the kiss of your proud mouth be
compared with each drop of the precious blood
that fell on the cold frozen uplands
of Spanish mountains from a column of steel?

What every lock of your gold-yellow head
to all the poverty, anguish and grief
that will come and have come on Europe's people
from the Slave Ship to the slavery of the whole people?

IV

A nighean a' chùil bhuidhe, throm-bhuidh, òr-bhuidh,
fonn do bheòil-sa 's gaoir na h-Eòrpa,
a nighean gheal chasarlach aighearach bhòidheach,
cha bhiodh masladh ar latha-ne searbh 'nad phòig-sa.

An tugadh t' fhonn no t' àilleachd ghlòrmhor   5
bhuamsa gràinealachd mharbh nan dòigh seo,
a' bhrùid 's am meàirleach air ceann na h-Eòrpa
's do bhial-sa uaill-dhearg san t-seann òran?

An tugadh corp geal is clàr grèine
bhuamsa cealgaireachd dhubh na brèine,   10
nimh bhùirdeasach is puinnsean crèide
is dìblidheachd ar n-Albann èitigh?

An cuireadh bòidhchead is ceòl suaimhneach
bhuamsa breòiteachd an adhbhair bhuain seo,
am mèinear Spàinnteach a' leum ri cruadal   15
is 'anam mòrail dol sìos gun bhruaillean?

Dè bhiodh pòg do bheòil uaibhrich
mar ris gach braon den fhuil luachmhoir
a thuit air raointean reòta fuara
nam beann Spàinnteach bho fhòirne cruadhach?   20

Dè gach cuach ded chual òr-bhuidh
ris gach bochdainn, àmhghar 's dòrainn
a thig 's a thàinig air sluagh na h-Eòrpa
bho Long nan Daoine gu daors' a' mhòr-shluaigh?

V*

Red-haired girl, heavy the burden
that depleted my vigour
and, white love, harsh the affliction
that cleft my heart;
I plan no feats of valour
since your bright features rose,
my spirit has lost its winning way,
thrown in turmoil with your essence.

Many long anxious nights
my eagerness was darting
and [many] evenings of torment
iron entered my hopes,
my rigid, steeled heart
set tottering by your gaze
and my swift, strong blood
agonising for your love.

O, beautiful, red-haired girl,
you mutilated a strength
that was haughty and proud
before your tranquil splendour:
your beauty wounds me
with a numbing grief
and your white, kindly face
has chased me from my aim.

And, red-haired girl, my burden is not
that I am a ransom for Europe,
and my abundant weeping is so bitter
not because I no longer know myself,
but because I failed to get your love
through the foolishness of conventions,
through the vanity of the world,
through the obliqueness of my approach.

September 1939

V

A nighean ruadh, 's trom an èire
rinn an lèireadh 'nam chlì,
's, a ghaoil ghil, cruaidh an t-àmhghar
rinn an sgàineadh 'nam chrìdh:
cha bhi m' aigne ri treuntas   5
bhon dh'èirich do lì
no mo spiorad ri suairceas,
air a bhuaireadh led bhrìgh.

'S iomadh oidhche fhada iomagain
bha iomaluas 'nam shùrd   10
agus feasgar na h-iargain
bha an t-iarann 'nam dhùil,
mo rag chridhe cruadhach
ann an luasgan led shùil
agus m' fhuil shiùbhlach, làidir   15
ann an cràdhlot led mhùirn.

O, a nighean ruadh àlainn
rinn thu màbadh air treòir
a bha àrdanach, uallach
ro shuaimhneas do ghlòir: 20
tha do bhòidhchead gam chiùrradh
ann an dùiseal is bròn
agus t' aghaidh gheal, shuairce
air mo ruagadh bhom thòir.

'S, a nighean ruadh, chan e m' èire   25
mi bhith an èirig na h-Eòrp',
's chan e goirteas mo shàth-ghal
mi bhith fàgte gun m' eòl,
ach nach d' fhuair mi do ghaol-sa
tre bhaothaireachd dhòigh   30
agus faoineachd an t-saoghail
agus claoine mo sheòil.

                                          an sultuine 1939

VI

In spite of the uproar of slaughter
in Germany or in France
I shall remember a table in this house
two nights and I there:

this year the choice of Scotland,
the red-haired girl, sun forehead;
and the year before last the fair-haired girl,
beautiful choice of Ireland.

VIII

> *The innocent and the beautiful*
> *Have no enemy but time.*
>   W. B. Yeats

I thought that I believed from you
the shapely words of that little poem,
and it seems to me that I did not think
that I would see the declension of their deceit.

But I understood that your thought was idle
when I saw on that Monday,
with my own eyes, the steel helmet
on my darling's very beautiful head.

IX

I spoke of the beauty of your face
yesterday and today, not often but always;
and I will speak of the beauty of your spirit
and death will not say it is idle talk.

VI

A dh'aindeoin ùpraid marbhaidh
anns a' Ghearmailt no san Fhraing
bidh mo chuimhne air bòrd san taigh seo
dà oidhche 's mi ann.

Am bliadhna roghainn na h-Albann,   5
an nighean ruadh, clàr na grèine;
's a' bhòn-uiridh an nighean bhàn,
roghainn àlainn na h-Èireann.

VIII

> *The innocent and the beautiful*
> *Have no enemy but time.*
>   W. B. Yeats

Bha dùil leam gun do chreid mi bhuatsa
briathran cuimir an duain ud;
agus ar leam nach do shaoil mi
gum faicinn aomadh an cluaine.

Ach thuig mi gum b' fhaoin do smuain-sa   5
nuair chunnaic mi an Diluain sin
lem shùilean fhìn an clogad stàilinn
air ceann àlainn mo luaidhe.

IX

Rinn mi luaidh air àilleachd t' aodainn
an-dè 's an-diugh, cha thric ach daonnan;
's nì mi luaidh air àilleachd t' anama
's cha chan am bàs gur h-e an arraghloir.

X*

Maybe the variously swift lyric art
is not part of my predicament,
eloquent as the clamour of bagpipe drones,
with sounding strings, or mild and restful,
though there came to me as much love,
as many restless thoughts,
as much anxiety, as much pain
as would suffice a band of poets,
as would suffice the band lacking stillness,
lacking succour, patience or rest,
who are assigned a place here
together with Yeats and William Ross.

XI

Often when I called Edinburgh
a grey town without darting sun,
it would light up with your beauty,
a refulgent, white-starred town.

XII*

There were four to whom I gave love,
four allegiances triumphing in turn:
the great cause and poetry,
the beautiful island and the red-haired girl.

X

Theagamh nach eil i 'nam chàs
ealain iomaluath an dàin,
labhar mar ghleadhraich nan dos,
teud-mhodhanach, no caoin le fois,
ged a thàrr dhomh uiread gràidh,   5
uimhir smuaintean gun tàmh,
uiread iomagain, uiread cràidh,
's a dh'fhòghnadh do chòmhlan bhàrd,
's a dh'fhòghnadh don chòmhlan gun tost,
gun fhurtachd, gun fhoighidinn, gun fhois,   10
dha bheil an t-àite seo a-bhos
cuide ri Yeats is Uilleam Ros.

XI

Tric 's mi gabhail air Dùn Èideann
baile glas gun ghathadh grèine,
's ann a lasadh e led bhòidhche,
baile lòghmhor geal-reultach.

XII

Ceathrar ann dan d' thug mi luaidh,
do cheathrar seirbheis caochladh buaidh, –
an t-adhbhar mòr agus a' bhàrdachd,
an t-Eilean àlainn 's an nighean ruadh,

XIII

To my eyes you were Deirdre
beautiful in the sunny cattle-fold;
you were MacBride's wife
in her shining beauty.
You were the yellow-haired girl of Cornaig
and the Handsome Fool's Margaret,
Strong Thomas's Una,
Cuchulainn's Eimhir and Grainne.
You were the one of the thousand ships,
desire of poets and death of heroes,
you were she who took the rest
and the peace from the heart of William Ross,
the Audiart who plagued De Born
and Maeve of the drinking horns.

And if it is true that any one
of them reached your beauty,
it must have been with a gracious spirit
shaped in a beautiful face.
And therefore I ought
to fashion for you the Dàn Dìreach
that would catch every beauty
that has kindled the imagination of Europe.
There ought to appear in its course
the vehemence of Spain complete,
the acuteness of France and Greece,
the music of Scotland and of Ireland.

I ought to put every effect
that Norway and Ireland
and old Scotland gave to my people
together in mellowness
and to offer them to the wonder
that is fair and shapely in your face.

XIII

Dom shùilean-sa bu tu Deirdre
's i bòidheach sa bhuaile ghrèine;
bu tu bean Mhic Ghille Bhrìghde
ann an àilleachd a lithe.
Bu tu nighean bhuidhe Chòrnaig   5
is Mairearad an Amadain Bhòidhich,
an Una aig Tómas Làidir,
Eimhir Chù-chulainn agus Gràinne,
bu tu tè nam mìle long,
ùidh nam bàrd is bàs nan sonn,   10
's bu tu an tè a thug an fhois
's an t-sìth bho chridhe Uilleim Rois,
an Audiart a bhuair De Born
agus Maebhe nan còrn.

Agus ma 's eadh is fìor gun d' ràinig   15
aon tè dhiubhsan t' àilleachd,
tha fhios gum b' ann le spiorad gràsmhor
air a dhealbh an aghaidh àlainn.
Agus uime sin bu chòir dhomh
'n Dàn Dìreach a chur air dòigh dhut   20
a ghlacadh gach uile bhòidhchead
a las mac-meanmna na h-Eòrpa.
Bu chòir nochdadh 'na iomchar
dianas na Spàinne gu h-iomlan,
geur-aigne na Frainge is na Grèige,   25
ceòl na h-Albann 's na h-Èireann.

Bha còir agam gach uile èifeachd
a thug Lochlann is Èire
is Alba àrsaidh do mo dhaoine
a chur cuideachd an caoine   30
agus an ìobairt don ioghnadh
tha geal dealbhte an clàr t' aodainn.

And since I am not one of them –
MacBride or Naoise,
Thomas Costello or MacDonald,
Bertrans or the Handsome Fool,
Cuchulainn or great Fionn or Diarmad –
it is my dilemma to seize
in tormented verses the longing
that takes the spirit of sad poets,
to raise and keep as I would like,
direct and well-formed in the poem for you,
old and new and full,
the form and spirit of every beauty:
together in the image of joy,
paean-like, deep, jewel-like,
the acuteness of France and Greece,
the music of Scotland and of Ireland.

XIV
The Selling of a Soul

A poet struggling with the world's condition,
prostitution of talents and the bondage
with which the bulk of men have been deceived,
I am not, I think, one who would say
that the selling of the soul would give respite.

But I did say to myself, and not once,
that I would sell my soul for your love
if lie and surrender were needed.
I spoke this in haste without thinking
that it was black blasphemy and perversion.

Your forgiveness to me for the thought
that you were one who would take a poor creature
of a little weak base spirit
who could be sold, even for the graces
of your beautiful face and proud spirit.

Agus a chionn nach mise aon diubh –
Mac Ghille Bhrìghde no Naoise,
Tómas Ua Custuil no MacDhòmhnaill,   35
Bertrans no 'n t-Amadan Bòidheach,
Cù-chulainn no Fionn mòr no Diarmad –
's e mo chàs-sa an iargain
a ghabhas spiorad nam bàrd cianail
a ghlacadh anns na ranna pianta,   40
a thogail 's a chumail mar a b' àill leam
dìreach, cuimir anns an dàn dhut,
sean agus ùr is lànmhor,
cumadh is meanmna gach àilleachd;
còmhla an ìomhaigh an èibhneis,   45
luathghaireach, domhainn, leugach,
geur-aigne na Frainge 's na Grèige,
ceòl na h-Albann is na h-Èireann.

XIV
Reic Anama

Bàrd a' strì ri càs an t-saoghail,
siùrsachd bhuadhan is an daorsa
leis na mhealladh mòr-roinn dhaoine,
cha mhise fear a chanadh, shaoil leam,
gun tugadh reic an anama faochadh.   5

Ach thubhairt mi rium fhìn, 's cha b' aon-uair,
gun reicinn m' anam air do ghaol-sa
nam biodh leum air breug in uorradh
Thubhairt mi an deifir sin gun smaointinn
gum b' e an toibheum dubh 's an claonadh.   10

Do mhaitheanas dhomh airson na smuaine
gum b' thusa tè a ghabhadh truaghan
de spiorad beag lag suarach
a ghabhadh reic, eadhon air buadhan
t' aodainn àlainn 's do spioraid uallaich.   15

Therefore, I will say again, now,
that I would sell my soul for your sake
twice, once for your beauty
and again for that grace
that you would not take a sold and slavish spirit.

XV
Three Paths
To Hugh MacDiarmid

I could not keep within sight
of the narrow high-mountain road
that was indicated across the core of your poetry:
and, therefore, MacDiarmid,
farewell: but, if I liked,
I could comfortably follow that petty,
dry, low road
that Eliot, Pound, Auden,
MacNeice and Herbert Read and their clique have:
I could were it not for the twist,
put in my heart for two years
by my own land, the fate of Spain,
an angry heart and a beautiful girl.

XVI*

How could I deserve
such choice conversation?
How on earth did I encounter
a gift of this sort?
How on earth did I find
in the shifting unsteadiness of the world
good fortune of this sort
opened at my side?

Uime sin, their mi rithist, an-dràsta,
gun reicinn m' anam air do sgàth-sa
dà uair, aon uair airson t' àilleachd
agus uair eile airson a' ghràis ud,
nach gabhadh tu spiorad reicte tràilleil.   20

XV
Trì Slighean
Do Ùisdean MacDhiarmaid

Cha b' urrainn domhsa cumail fàire
air slighe chumhang nan àrd-bheann
a nochdadh thar cridhe do bhàrdachd:
agus, uime sin, MhicDhiarmaid,
soraidh leat: ach nam bu mhiann leam   5
b' urrainn domh an t-slighe chrìon ud,
thioram, ìseal, leantainn tìorail
th' aig Eliot, Pound agus Auden
MacNeice, is Herbert Read 's an còmhlan:
b' urrainn, mur b' e am fiaradh   10
a chuireadh 'nam aigne dà bhliadhna
lem dhùthaich fhìn is càs na Spàinnte,
cridhe feargach is nighinn àlainn.

XVI

Carson a bhithinn-sa dligheach   1
air an roghainn de chòmhraidh?
Ciamar idir a thachair
leithid de thabhartas dhòmhsa?
Ciamar idir a fhuair mi   5
an crath luasgain an t-saoghail
a leithid de fhortan
air fhosgladh rim thaobh-sa?

What thrust of the wheel
brought my degree the highest?
Even for one night
what did I deserve of its triumph?
How on earth did it come about
amidst the ill fortune of my circuit
that my wish and my intellect
reached high-spirited exultation?

O girl, o girl,
what misfortune was in the laughter
that mocked your bright,
shapely, comely visage?
What set you at my side
where I thought of you being?
What gave me one night
the joyous glory of your laughter?

O girl, o girl,
the fever of the turning,
the movement of the wheel
has set me reeling with longing:
how on earth was I borne
to alight on its summit,
though all I did was fall
speedily and completely?

I desired the dream
though that was all it was:
I desired the glimmer
of joy in the troubled mist:
but what on earth set your shadow,
bright, red-haired girl, there?
You had not an inkling
of the poets of Scotland.

Dè an spàirn air a' chuibhle
thug m' uidhe air uachdar? 10
Eadhon aon oidhche
dè thoill mi de 'buaidh-se?
Ciamar idir a thàinig
am measg ànradh mo chuairt-sa
gun deach mo mhiann agus m' eanchainn 15
gu meanmnach ri luathghair?

A nighean, a nighean,
dè tubaist a' ghàire
rinn fanaid air t' aghaidh
ghil fhoinnidh àlainn? 20
Dè chuir thu rim thaobh-sa
far an do shaoil mi a bha thu?
Dè thug dhomhsa aon oidhche
glòir aoibhneach do ghàire?

A nighean, a nighean, 25
tha breisleach an tionndaidh,
tha iomairt na cuibhle
air mo ruidhleadh le ionndrainn:
ciamar idir a thàrr mi
air a bàrr-se le iomchar, 30
ged nach d' rinn mi ach tuiteam
gu clis is gu h-iomlan?

Bu mhiann leam an aisling
ge b' e aisling a bh' ann dith:
bu mhiann an t-aiteal 35
de aiteas an allacheo:
ach dè idir chuir t' fhaileas,
a nighean ruadh gheal, ann?
Cha robh agad fiù 's fathann
air filidhean Albann. 40

XVII

Multitude of the skies,
golden riddle of millions of stars,
cold, distant, lustrous, beautiful,
silent, unfeeling, unwelcoming.

Fullness of knowledge in their course,
emptiness of chartless ignorance,
a universe moving in silence,
a mind alone in its bounds.

Not they moved my thoughts,
not the marvel of their chill course;
to us there is no miracle but in love,
lighting of a universe in the kindling of your face.

XVIII
Prayer

Since there is no God
and since Christ
is only the vain reflection of a story,
there is only: Let me strengthen
my own spirit against agony.

For I have seen Spain lost,
a sight that has made my eyes salt,
and a tingling cry that has slowed
the movement of my heart of pride
with the nothingness and the death of the great.

We see again, now,
the oppression of the heart and the death of pride
and the miserable nothingness
of every brave generous hope
by which we are separated from chill death.

XVII

Lìonmhoireachd anns na speuran,
òr-chriathar milleanan de reultan,
fuar, fad às, lòghmhor, àlainn,
tostach, neo-fhaireachdail, neo-fhàilteach.

Lànachd an eòlais man cùrsa,   5
failmhe an aineolais gun iùl-chairt,
cruinne-cè a' gluasad sàmhach,
aigne leatha fhèin san àrainn.

Chan iadsan a ghluais mo smaointean,
chan e mìorbhail an iomchair aognaidh,   10
chan eil a' mhìorbhail ach an gaol dhuinn,
soillse cruinne an lasadh t' aodainn.

XVIII
Ùrnaigh

A chionn nach eil Dia ann
agus a chionn nach eil Crìosda
ach 'na fhaileas faoin sgialachd,
chan eil ann ach: Dèanam làidir
m' aigne fhìn an aghaidh àmhghair.   5

Oir chunnaic mi an Spàinn caillte,
sealladh a rinn mo shùilean saillte,
agus gaoir a chùil maille
air iomchar mo chridhe àrdain
le neoinitheachd is bàs nan sàr-fhear.   10

Chì sinn a-rithist an-dràsta
claoidh cridhe 's bàs an àrdain
agus neoinitheachd neo-àghmhor
anns gach dòchas treun faoilidh
len sgarar sinn bhon bhàs aognaidh.   15

Young Cornford had this in his heroism,
the fear of the thought of his love being near him
when Spain was a fast-day for him:
fear of his loss in the man,
fear of the fear in the hero.

What fear will I have
before the chill floods of the surge
now since I have heard their murmur?
It is said that a nightmare will be seen,
death and famine choking gladness,

that famine will be seen in the fields,
the mighty feebleness in her leanness
that will take life and love from us,
that will lay low to the grave
with hunger and spiritless despair.

But do you think I will pray
to my own spirit against my own desire,
stoppage of my heart, blinding of eyes?
Will I beg that love of you be torn
from the roots of my choked heart?

Will I ask that my heart be purified
from the weakness of my pure white love,
will I ask for a flayed spirit
even in order that I be found in the madness
as brave as Dimitrov or as Connolly?

Just now I understand
that a fragmentation has come in this case,
the struggle of deathless humankind:
the being before the hardest choice,
death in immortal life or a death-like life.

My life the death-like life
because I have not flayed the heart of my fullness of love,
because I have given a particular love,
because I would not cut away the love of you,
and that I preferred a woman to crescent History.

Bha seo aig Cornford òg 'na ghaisge,
eagal smuain a ghaoil bhith faisg air
nuair bha an Spàinn 'na latha-traisg dha,
eagal a challa air an duine,
eagal an eagail air a' churaidh.   20

Dè an t-eagal a bhios ormsa
ro thuiltean aognaidh an onfhaidh
a-nis on chuala mi am monmhar?
Theirear gum faicear trom-laighe,
am bàs 's a' ghort a' tachdadh aighir;   25

gum faicear a' ghort air na raointean,
an eislig chumhachdach 'na caoile,
a bheir a' bheatha is an gaol bhuainn,
a leagas sìos a dh'ionnsaigh uaghach
le acras is eu-dòchas neo-uallach.   30

Ach saoil sibh an dèan mi ùrnaigh
rim spiorad fhìn an aghaidh m' ùidhe,
stad mo chridhe, dalladh shùilean?
An guidh mi do ghaol bhith air a shracadh
à friamhaichean mo chridhe thachdte?   35

An iarr mi mo chridhe bhith glainte
bho anfhannachd mo ghaoil ghlain ghil,
an iarr mi spiorad 's e air fhaileadh
eadhon gum faighear anns a' bhoile mi
cho treun ri Dimitrov no ri O Conghaile?   40

Tha mi a' tuigsinn an-dràsta
gun tàinig lìonsgaradh sa chàs seo,
gleac a' chinne-daonna neo-bhàsmhoir:
an neach mu choinneamh roghainn sàr-chruaidh,
bàs sa bheatha bhiothbhuain no beatha bhàsail.   45

Mo bheatha-sa a' bheatha bhàsail
a chionn nach d' fhail mi cridhe mo shàth-ghaoil,
a chionn gun tug mi gaol àraidh,
a chionn nach sgarainn do ghràdh-sa
's gum b' fheàrr leam boireannach na 'n Eachdraidh   50
  fhàsmhor.

I saw the branching blood rising,
the bonfire of the spirit on the mountains,
the poor world losing its wounds:
I sensed and understood the meaning of the cry
though my heart had not been flayed.

He whose heart has been washed
will go through fire without turning;
he will ascend the great mountain without homesickness;
I did not get such a spirit
since my heart is only half flayed.

This prayer is the hard and sorry prayer,
the blasphemous imperfect prayer,
the crooked perverted prayer that turns back,
the prayer that I may pray
without praying to reach the substance.

I have heard of unhappy death
and about the hunger of loathsome famine
coming in pursuit of treachery.
How will I stand up against their cavalry
since my heart is but half flayed?

When the spirit has been flayed,
it will lose every shadow,
it will lose every faintness.
But who will call my white love
surrender, faintness or shadow?

No catechist or examiner is needed
to see that there is not in my prayer
Effectual Calling or Sincerity,
and though I am clear-sighted in scripture
that my spirit is not one-fold.

Since the blame will not be put on gods,
who are only the shadow of desire,
and to avoid the man Christ,
I do not feel kindly towards Nature,
which has given me the clear whole understanding,
the single brain and the split heart.

Chunnaic mi 'n fhuil chraobhach ag èirigh,
tein-aighir an spioraid air na slèibhtean,
an saoghal truagh a' call a chreuchdan:
thuig is thùr mi fàth an langain
ged nach robh mo chridhe air fhaileadh.   55

Esan dha bheil an cridhe air ionnlaid,
thèid e tro theine gun tionndadh,
dìridh e bheinn mhòr gun ionndrainn;
cha d' fhuair mise leithid de dh'anam
's mo chridhe ach air leth-fhaileadh.   60

'S e 'n ùrnaigh seo guidhe na duilghe,
an guidhe toibheumach neo-iomlan,
guidhe cam coirbte an tionndaidh,
an guidhe gun dèan mi guidhe,
gun guidhe 'n t-susbaint a ruigheachd.   65

Chuala mi mu bhàs neo-aoibhneach
agus mu acras gorta oillteil
a' tighinn an tòrachd na foille.
Ciamar a sheasas mi rim marc-shluagh
's gun mo chridhe ach leth-fhailte?   70

An uair tha 'n spiorad air fhaileadh,
caillidh e gach uile fhaileas,
caillidh e gach uile fhannachd.
Ach cò a ghabhas air mo gheal ghaol
nomadh, fannachd no faileas?   75

Cha ruigear a leas ceistear no sgrùdair
a dh'fhaicinn nach eil 'nam ùrnaigh
a' Ghairm Èifeachdach no 'n Dùrachd,
's ged tha mi soilleir anns an fhìrinn
nach eil mo spiorad aon-fhillte.   80

A chionn nach cuirear coire air diathan,
nach eil ach 'nam faileas iarraidh,
agus a sheachnadh an duine Crìosda,
chan eil mo chaomhachd ris an Nàdar
a thug an tuigse shoilleir shlàn dhomh,   85
an eanchainn shingilte 's an cridhe sgàinte.

XIX

I gave you immortality
and what did you give me?
Only the sharp
arrows of your beauty,
a harsh onset
and piercing sorrow,
bitterness of spirit
and a sore gleam of glory.

If I gave you immortality
you gave it to me;
you put an edge on my spirit
and radiance in my song.
And though you spoiled
my understanding of the conflict,
yet, were I to see you again,
I should accept more and the whole of it.

Were I, after oblivion of my trouble,
to see before me
on the plain of the land of youth
the gracious form of your beauty,
I should prefer it there,
although my weakness would return,
and to peace of spirit
again to be wounded.

O yellow-haired, lovely girl,
you tore my strength
and inclined my course
from its aim:
but, if I reach my place,
the high wood of the men of song,
you are the fire of my lyric –
you made a poet of me through sorrow.

XIX

Thug mise dhut biothbhuantachd
is dè thug thu dhòmhsa?
Cha tug ach saighdean
geura do bhòidhchid.
Thug thu cruaidh shitheadh   5
is treaghaidh na dòrainn,
domblas an spioraid,
goirt dhrithleann na glòire.

Ma thug mise dhut biothbhuantachd
'stusa thug dhòmhs' i;   10
'stu gheuraich mo spiorad
's chuir an drithleann 'nam òran;
's ged rinn thu mo mhilleadh
an tuigse na còmhraig,
nam faicinn thu rithist   15
ghabhainn tuilleadh 's an còrr dheth.

Nam faicinn mum choinneamh
air magh Tìr na h-Òige
an dèidh dìochuimhn' mo dhragha
clàr foinnidh do bhòidhichid,   20
b' fheàrr leam an siud e
ged thilleadh mo bhreòiteachd,
'sna suaimhneas an spioraid
mi rithist bhith leòinte.

A nighean bhuidhe àlainn   25
's ann shrac thu mo threòir-sa
agus dh'fhiaraich mo shlighe
bho shireadh mo thòrachd;
ach ma ruigeas mi m' àite,
coille àrd luchd nan òran,   30
's tu grìosach an dàin dhomh,
rinn thu bàrd dhiom le dòrainn.

I raised this pillar
on the shifting mountain of time,
but it is a memorial-stone
that will be heeded till the Deluge,
and, though you will be married to another
and ignorant of my struggle,
your glory is my poetry
after the slow rotting of your beauty.

XX*

If I had the capacity I would wish,
with art entwined in my abundant love,
nineteen would not be the number
nor these the kind of poems
I would dedicate to your beautiful face
and to your proud, gracious spirit.
They would only be poems intertwining
music and mildness and thoughts
and a marvellous imagination
with sun's vehemence and sky's swiftness,
gentle as the falling of night
and mild as the breaking of brilliant day
and new as the onset of joy,
exultant poems without seeking,
deep, elegant and playful,
poems where would be united
the plaited qualities of that threesome,
poems where one would see the cross
borne by Yeats and Blok and William Ross.

Thog mi an calbh seo
air beinn fhalbhaich na tìme
ach 's esan clach-chuimhne   35
a bhios suim dheth gu dìlinn,
is ged bhios tusa aig fear-pòsta
is tu gun eòl air mo strì-sa,
's e do ghlòir-sa mo bhàrdachd
an dèidh cnàmhachd do lithe.   40

XX

Nan robh an comas mar a b' àill leam,
le ealain fuaighte ri mo shàth-ghaol,
chan e naoi deug an àireamh
no a leithid seo de dhàintean
a choisriginn do t' aodann àlainn   5
agus dod spiorad uallach gràsmhor.
Chan e ach dàintean sam fuaigheadh
ceòl is caoine is smuaintean
is mac-meanmna 'na mhìorbhail
le dianas grèine 's iomaluas iarmailt,   10
ciùin mar chamhanaich na h-oidhche
's caoin mar bhristeadh latha boillsgeadh
agus ùr mar thoiseach aoibhneis,
dàintean luathghaireach gun shireadh,
doimhne, finealta, le mire,   15
dàintean sam faighte singilt'
buadhan an triùir 's iad fillte,
dàintean sam faicte chrois
bh' air Yeats is Blok is Uilleam Ros.

XXI*

What does my place matter to me
among the poets of Scotland
even if I put into Gaelic
a transient elegance and beauty?
You will not understand my love
or my lofty vain prattling,
beautiful yellow girl,
though you are my transient beauty.

XXII

I walked with my reason
out beside the sea.
We were together but it was
keeping a little distance from me.

Then it turned saying:
Is it true you heard
that your beautiful white love
is getting married early on Monday?

I checked the heart that was rising
in my torn swift breast
and I said: Most likely;
why should I lie about it?

How should I think that I would grab
the radiant golden star,
that I would catch it and put it
prudently in my pocket?

I did not take a cross's death
in the hard extremity of Spain
and how then should I expect
the one new prize of fate?

XXI

Dè dhòmhsa m' àite
am measg bàird na h-Albann
ged chuireas mi an Gàidhlig
loinn is àilleachd fhalbhach?
Cha tuig thusa mo ghràdh bhuam   5
no m' àrdan arraghloir,
a nighean bhuidhe àlainn,
ge tu m' àilleachd fhalbhach.

XXII

Choisich mi cuide ri mo thuigse
a-muigh ri taobh a' chuain;
bha sinn còmhla ach bha ise
a' fuireach tiotan bhuam.

An sin thionndaidh i ag ràdha: 5
A bheil e fìor gun cual
thu gu bheil do ghaol geal àlainn
a' pòsadh tràth Diluain?

Bhac mi 'n cridhe bha 'g èirigh
'nam bhroilleach reubte luath   10
is thubhairt mi: Tha mi cinnteach;
carson bu bhriag e bhuam?

Ciamar a smaoinichinn gun ghluaim
an rionnag leugach òir,
gum beirinn oirre 's gun cuirinn i   15
gu ciallach 'na mo phòc?

Cha d' ghabh mise bàs croinn-ccusaidh
an èiginn chruaidh na Spàinn
is ciamar sin bhiodh dùil agam
ri aon duais ùir an dàin?   20

I followed only a way
that was small, mean, low, dry, lukewarm,
and how then should I meet
the thunderbolt of love?

But if I had the choice again
and stood on that headland,
I would leap from heaven or hell
with a whole spirit and heart.

XXIII

Deaf, agitated, angry,
anguish in the great heart,
the sweetness of the dawn music of birds,
the young morning of the music of Beethoven.

Dear, in the close packed hall,
dumb under the new art of the great one,
there rose together before my desire
the piercing music and your beauty.

Girl, fair-haired girl,
the great music was folded in your beauty,
the great choir was wound in your grace,
the big house surged with my love.

My eyes shut before the music
that was in pursuit of joy,
Diana appeared in smooth stone,
Deirdre by the side of Loch Etive.

It was your image and the music
that gathered the company of the lustrous ones,
that sent Deirdre to Glen Da Ruadh,
Diana to the rout of the Greeks.

Girl, girl of my love,
the joy of the big music was your face,
Beethoven and Maol Donn
extended on the bare plain of a heart.

Cha do lean mi ach an t-slighe chrìon
bheag ìosal thioram thlàth,
is ciamar sin a choinnichinn
ri beithir-theine ghràidh?

Ach nan robh 'n roghainn rithist dhomh   25
's mi 'm sheasamh air an àird,
leumainn à nèamh no iutharna
le spiorad 's cridhe slàn.

XXIII

Bodhar, neo-shuaimhneach, am feirg,
àmhghar an cridhe na mòrachd,
binneas ceòl camhanaich nan eun,
òg-mhadainn ceòl Bheethoven.

A luaidh, anns an talla dhlùth,   5
balbh fo ealain ùir an t-sàr-fhir,
dhiùchd còmhla fa chomhair mo rùin
gathadh a' chiùil is t' àilleachd.

A nighean, a nighean bhàn,
dh'fhilleadh an ceòl mòr 'nad àilleachd,   10
shuaineadh a' chòisir 'nad loinn,
bhàrc an taigh mòr lem ghràdh-sa.

Dhùin mo shùilean ris a' cheòl
a bha air tòrachd an èibhnuic,
dhiùchd Diana an cloich chaoimh   15
agus Deirdre taobh Loch Èite.

B' e t' ìomhaigh-sa agus an ceòl
a chruinnich còmhlan nan leugach,
chuir Deirdre do Ghleann Da Ruadh,
Diana an ruaig nan Greugach.   20

Nighean, a nighean mo luaidh,
b' e aoibhneas a' chiùil mhòir t' aodann,
Beethoven agus Maol Donn
air magh lom cridhe sgaoilte.

Deaf, agitated, angry,
the anguishing and suffering of the Muse:
fair, very beautiful, with mild pride,
the girl fresh in her beauty.

Will one neatly set up
in the synthesis the world's deceit,
the distress of the great and of the wretched,
and the mild paean of your face?

Will a synthesis be made of Fate,
of the misery and glory of the universe,
the frail bruised loathsome wretched filth,
your beauty and the nobleness of lyrics?

Fever has choked many a poor one
and has left many a father bruised, sore and frail,
but the music of Patrick's Lament
left the distress of his children glorious.

There have died in misery with no illusion
child and old man together,
but there came no music or poem
to put beauty on sorrow.

High-headed Deirdre in the grave,
in the unsought eternity,
and my love in the great choir
graced above poet's paean.

No synthesis will be made of fortune,
the glory and the distress of the universe,
the feverish wasting and Patrick Mor,
slavery, Beethoven and you.

Deaf, agitated, in anger;
sweet, stormy, gentle, glorious music,
fair, beautiful, calm, with no flaw,
unexcelled the aspect of your beauty.

Bodhar, neo-shuaimhneach, am feirg,   25
àmhghar, allaban a' Cheòlraidh:
geal, àlainn, le uaill chiùin
an nighean ùr 'na bòidhche.

An cuirear gu cuimir suas
anns a' chochur cluaineas saoghail,   30
ànradh an duine mhòir 's an truaigh
agus ciùin luathghair t' aodainn?

An dèanar an cochur dhen dàn,
de thruaighe 's de ghlòir na cruinne,
a' bhrèine bhreòite oillteil thruagh,   35
t' àilleachd is uaisle luinneag?

Thachd an fhiabhras ioma truagh
is dh'fhàg i ioma athair breòite,
ach dh'fhàg ceòl cumha Phàdraig Mhòir
àmhghar a chloinne glòrmhor.   40

Bhàsaich an truaighe gun sgleò
leanabh is seann duine còmhla,
ach cha dàinig ceòl no dàn
a chur àilleachd air dòrainn.

Deirdre ghuanach anns an uaigh,   45
anns an t-sìorraidheachd gun shireadh,
agus mo ghaol sa chòisir mhòir
buadhmhor thar luathghair filidh.

Cha dèanar an cochur dhen chàs,
glòir agus ànradh na cruinne,   50
an èitig fhiabhrais 's Pàdraig Mòr,
daorsa, Beethoven is thusa.

Bodhar, neo-shuaimhneach, am feirg,
ceòl binn, gailleanach, ciùin, glòrmhor,
geal, àlainn, socair, gun aon ghiamh,   55
gun bharrachd fiamh do bhòidhche.

XXIV

When you said that beauty
was only relative and with a defect
what I thought was:
Think, lovely fool,
would that be said to Naoise
when he approached Argyll?

XXV*

I would rather than the theft of fire
from heaven for people's sake
the theft that did not make a spoiling
in the seeking of what it found,
the theft of beguilement from your eyes,
bringing new life to the poem.

XXVI

Red-haired girl, were I to get your kiss
for every restless golden lyric,
I should fashion thousands of them
to excel William Ross with store.

XXVII*

The critic said that my art
was getting overblown, its clusters
radiant, gracious, flashing.
But, o love, from your face
it got its beguiling brilliance,
its joy of musical laughter,
its serenity of aspect.

XXIV

Nuair thuirt thu nach robh bhòidhche
ach cosamhlach is le fàiling
's ann bha mise smaointinn:
Saoil, òinseach àlainn,
an cainte sin ri Naoise   5
nuair thaobh e Earra-Ghàidheal?

XXV

B' fheàrr leam na goid an teine
à nèamh air sgàth an t-sluaigh
a' ghad nach d' rinn am milleadh,
aig sireadh na fhuair,
gad meallaidh bho do shùilean,   5
beothachadh ùr an duain.

XXVI

A nighean ruadh, nam faighinn do phòg
airson gach duanaig luainich òir,
chuirinn na mìltean dhiubh air dòigh
thoirt bàrr air Uilleam Ros le stòr.

XXVII

Thubhairt an sgrùdair gu robh m' ealain
a' dol gu laomadh le meallan
drithleannach, foinnidh, caoireach.
Ach, a ghaoil, 's ann bho t' aodann
a fhuair i mealladh a leugachd,   5
a fhuair i ceòl-gàire h-èibhneis,
a fhuair i suaimhneas a h-aogais.

XXVIII
The Ghosts

If I had won your love,
perhaps my poems would have
no empty waste of eternity,
the sort of immortality which fate accords them.
From far-off, forlorn shores
my love, their cry will come,
yearning, shouting for your love.
They will take the way of the high mountain-tops
of generations, ever wailing,
ever mourning for your love,
ever making mention of your beauty.
They will go naked on the streets
of History and Poetry:
they will be seen on the highways
of the heart, ever marching:
they will meet in the night
poets in their white shrouds of art:
they will keep the candlelight wake;
the horizon, breaking for day, will not smother their gleam.
They will stand about the coffin
where the clay is lying,
the grey clay of the love of joyless poets.
They will stand beyond the grave,
without the ruddiness of life, their cheeks grey.

They will go, a rose, on mountains
where the sun of the poets is rising.

XXVIII
Na Samhlaidhean

Nan robh mi air do ghaol fhaotainn
theagamh nach biodh aig mo dhàintean
an t-sìorraidheachd fhalamh fhàsail,
a' bhiothbhuantachd a tha an dàn dhaibh.
'S ann, a ghaoil, bho na taobhan   5
fad às, cianail a bhios an glaodhaich,
ag iargain, ag èigheach air do ghaol-sa.
Gabhaidh iad mullaichean nan àrd-bheann
ghinealach, a' sìor rànaich,
a' sìor iargain do ghràidh-sa,   10
a' sìor dhèanamh luaidh air t' àilleachd:
falbhaidh iad nochdta air sràidean
na h-Eachdraidh agus na Bàrdachd:
chithear iad air rathaidean àrda
nan cridheachan a' sìor mhàrsail: 15
tachraidh iad anns an oidhche
ris na bàird 'nan suaineadh loinn-gheal:
ni iad caithris solas choinnleir;
cha mhùch bristeadh fàire 'm boillsgeadh.
Seasaidh iad mun chiste-laighe   20
far a bheil a' chrè 'na laighe,
crè ghlas gaol nam bàrd gun aighear:
seasaidh iad thar na h-uaghach,
gun rudhadh, glaisneulach an gruaidhean.

Falbhaidh iad 'nan ròs air slèibhtean   25
far bheil grian nam bàrd ag èirigh,

XXIX
Dogs and Wolves

Across eternity, across its snows,
I see my unwritten poems,
I see the spoor of their paws dappling
the untroubled whiteness of the snow:
bristles raging, bloody-tongued,
lean greyhounds and wolves
leaping over the tops of the dykes,
running under the shade of the trees of the wilderness,
taking the defile of narrow glens,
making for the steepness of windy mountains;
their baying yell shrieking
across the hard barenesses of the terrible times,
their everlasting barking in my ears,
their onrush seizing my mind:
career of wolves and eerie dogs
swift in pursuit of the quarry,
through the forests without veering,
over the mountain-tops without sheering;
the mild mad dogs of poetry,
wolves in chase of beauty,
beauty of soul and face,
a white deer over hills and plains,
the deer of your gentle beloved beauty,
a hunt without halt, without respite.

XXIX
Coin is Madaidhean-allaidh

Thar na sìorraidheachd, thar a sneachda,
chì mi mo dhàin neo-dheachdte,
chì mi lorgan an spòg a' breacadh
gile shuaimhneach an t-sneachda:
calg air bhoile, teanga fala,   5
gadhair chaola 's madaidhean-allaidh
a' leum thar mullaichean nan gàrradh,
a' ruith fo sgàil nan craobhan fàsail,
a' gabhail cumhang nan caol-ghleann,
a' sireadh caisead nan gaoth-bheann;   10
an langan gallanach a' sianail
thar loman cruaidhe nan àm cianail,
an comhartaich bhiothbhuan 'na mo chluasan,
an deann-ruith a' gabhail mo bhuadhan:
rèis nam madadh 's nan con iargalt   15
luath air tòrachd an fhiadhaich
tro na coilltean gun fhiaradh,
thar mullaichean nam beann gun shiaradh;
coin chiùine caothaich na bàrdachd,
madaidhean air tòir na h-àilleachd,   20
àilleachd an anama 's an aodainn,
fiadh geal thar bheann is raointean,
fiadh do bhòidhche ciùine gaolaich,
fiadhach gun sgur gun fhaochadh.

XXX

A Bolshevik who never gave heed
to queen or to king,
if we had Scotland free,
Scotland equal to our love,
a white spirited generous Scotland,
a beautiful happy heroic Scotland,
without petty paltry foolish bourgeoisie,
without the loathsomeness of capitalists,
without hateful crass graft;
the mettlesome Scotland of the free,
the Scotland of our blood, the Scotland of our love,
I would break the legitimate law of kings,
I would break the sure law of the wise,
I would proclaim you queen of Scotland
in spite of the new republic.

XXXI

William Ross, what should we say
meeting beyond death?
I should mention your 'Òran Eile'.
What would you say about the poems
I let loose art-bridled,
a wild cavalry for bards?

XXXII

Let me lop off with sharp blade every grace
that your beauty put in my verse,
and make poems as bare and chill
as Liebknecht's death or slavery,
let me burn every tree branch
that grew joyous above grief,
and put the people's anguish
in the steel of my lyric.

XXX

'S mi 'm Bhoilseabhach nach tug suim
riamh do bhànrainn no do rìgh,
nan robh againn Alba shaor,
Alba co-shìnte ri ar gaol,
Alba gheal bheadarrach fhaoil,   5
Alba àlainn shona laoch;
gun bhùirdeasachd bhig chrìon bhaoith,
gun sgreamhalachd luchd na maoin',
's gun chealgaireachd oillteil chlaoin,
Alba aigeannach nan saor,   10
Alba 'r fala, Alba 'r gaoil,
bhristinn lagh dligheach nan rìgh,
bhristinn lagh cinnteach shaoi,
dh'èighinn 'nad bhànrainn Albann thu
neo-ar-thaing na Poblachd ùir.   15

XXXI

Uilleim Rois, dè chanamaid
a' coinneachadh taobh thall a' bhàis?
Dhèanainn luaidh air t' Òran Eile;
dè theireadh tusa mu na dàin
a sgaoil mi ealain-shrianta,   5
eachraidh fhiadhaich bhàrd?

XXXII

Sgatham le faobhar-roinn gach àilleachd
a chuir do bhòidhche 'nam bhàrdachd,
's dèanam dàin cho lom aognaidh
ri bàs Liebknecht no daorsa;
loisgeam gach meanglan craoibhe   5
a dh'fhàs aoibhneach thar duilghe
's cuiream diachainn an t-sluaigh
an iarann-cruadhach mo dhuain.

XXXIII

The lot of poets is not
divorced from others' dispensation:
fortune was with Duncan Ban
and William Ross got his fill
of anguish, of consumption and death.

XXXIV

When I speak of the face
and of the white spirit of my fair love
one might well say that my blind eyes
had not lighted on the moss,
on the loathsome ugly morass
in which the bourgeoisie is drowning;
but I have seen from the height of the Cuillin
darts of glory and bruised frail sorrow:
I have seen the gilding light of the sun
and the black morass of filth;
I know the sharp bitterness of the spirit
better than the swift joy of the heart.

XXXV

Come before me, gentle night,
starred blue sky and dew,
though there is not purged from any airt
the world's poverty and Spain's shivering cry,
a night when Maol Donn sings
a *ceòl mòr* of gentleness on the mountain,
a night with my love in her beauty,
a night whose completeness hides
from my own eyes the shadow
I cast on the horizon;
come to me blue and round,
and I will thoughtlessly comprehend
the piercing music of Maol Donn's theme.

XXXIII

Chan eil freastal nam bàrd
dealaichte bho fhreastal chàich:
bha 'm fortan le Donnchadh Bàn
is fhuair Uilleam Ros a shàth
den àmhghar, den chaitheamh 's den bhàs.   5

XXXIV

An uair a labhras mi mu aodann
agus mu spiorad geal mo ghaoil ghil
's ann a theireadh neach nach d' ràinig
mo shùilean dalla air a' chàthar,
air a' bhoglaich oillteil ghrànda   5
sa bheil a' bhùirdeasachd a' bàthadh:
ach chunnaic mi bho àird a' Chuilithinn
gathadh glòir is breòiteachd duilghe:
chunnaic mi òradh lainnir grèine
agus boglach dhubh na brèine: 10
's eòl dhomh seirbheachd gheur an spioraid
nas fheàrr na aoibhneas luath a' chridhe.

XXXV

Thig am chomhair, oidhche chiùin,
gorm reultachd adhair agus driùchd,
ged nach glanar bho aon àird
bochdainn saoghail, gaoir na Spàinn,
oidhche is Maol Donn a' seinn   5
ceòl mòr ciùine air a' bheinn,
oidhche is mo ghaol 'na lì,
oidhche air nach fhaicear mì
lem shùilean fhìn, a chionn lànachd,
a' cur dubhair air an fhàire: 10
thig am chomhair gorm, cruinn,
is cuiridh mi air dòigh gun shuim
gathadh ùrlair ciùil Maoil Duinn.

XXXVI

I should have sold my soul
without pricking of conscience for your sake:
because of your refusal I shall make of it steel
to split the rock of vicissitudes.

XXXVII

It is not the beauty of your body,
the beauty shaped in your face,
the beauty blinding my eyes
though it has gone beyond thought;
but the beauty of the spirit
that took form in your face,
the beauty of the spirit,
the heart-marrow of my love.

XXXVIII*

I spoke about selling a soul
for your sake, o love:
blasphemy, blasphemy, ugly blasphemy,
a blasphemy of foolish rigmarole:
the soul sold for your sake
would not become free,
the soul sold for your sake
would become enslaved.

XXXIX

As the slow embers of the fire
become a pure sparkling flame,
so my love for you
becomes a white adoration.

XXXVI

Bhithinn air m' anam a reic
gun bhioradh cuimhseis air do sgàth:
a chionn do dhiùltaidh nì mi dheth
cruas sgoiltidh creag nan càs.

XXXVII

Chan e àilleachd do dhealbha,
àilleachd cruth t' aodainn,
àilleachd mo dhallabhrat
ged a dh'fhalbh i thar smaointean;
ach àilleachd an anama   5
bha dealbhach 'nad aodann,
àilleachd an spioraid,
smior cridhe mo ghaoil-sa.

XXXVIII

Labhair mi mu reic anama
air do sgàth, a ghaoil:
toibheum, toibheum, toibheum grànda,
toibheum ràbhain bhaoith:
an t-anam a reicteadh air do sgàth-sa,   5
chan e a dh'fhàsadh saor,
an t-anam a reicteadh air do sgàth-sa,
's ann dh'fhàsadh e daor.

XXXIX

Mar thèid grìosach mhall an teine
'na caoir-lasair ghlain,
's ann tha 'n gaol a th' agam ortsa
a' dol 'na adhradh geal.

XL

I am not striving with the tree that will not bend for me,
and the apples will not grow on any branch;
it is not farewell to you; you have not left me.
It is the ebb of death with no floodtide after it.

Dead stream of neap in your tortured body,
which will not flow at new moon or at full,
in which the great springtide of love will not come –
but a double subsidence to lowest ebb.

XLI

My love for you has gone beyond poetry.
beyond imagination, beyond pride,
beyond love-talk, beyond hummed song,
beyond art, beyond laughter-music,
beyond joy, beyond loveliness,
beyond grief, beyond agony,
beyond reason, beyond nature,
beyond the great surging world.

XLII
Shores

If we were in Talisker on the shore
where the great white mouth
opens between two hard jaws,
Rubha nan Clach and the Bioda Ruadh,
I would stand beside the sea
renewing love in my spirit
while the ocean was filling
Talisker bay forever:
I would stand there on the bareness of the shore
until Prishal bowed his stallion head.

XL

Chan eil mi strì ris a' chraoibh nach lùb rium
's cha chinn na h-ùbhlan air gèig seach geug:
cha shoraidh slàn leat, cha d' rinn thu m' fhàgail:
's e tràigh a' bhàis i gun mhuir-làn 'na dèidh.

Marbh-shruth na conntraigh 'nad chom ciùrrte   5
nach lìon ri gealaich ùir no làin,
anns nach tig reothairt mhòr an t-sùgraidh –
ach sìoladh dùbailt gu muir-tràigh.

XLI

Chaidh mo ghaol ort thar bàrdachd,
thar mac-meanmna, thar àrdain,
thar sùgraidh, thar mànrain,
thar ealain, thar ceòl-gàire,
thar èibhneis, thar àilleachd,   5
thar dòlais, thar àmhghair,
thar cèille, thar nàdair,
thar an t-saoghail mhòir bhàrcaich.

XLII
Tràighean

Nan robh sinn an Talasgar air an tràigh
far a bheil am bial mòr bàn
a' fosgladh eadar dà ghiall chruaidh,
Rubha nan Clach 's am Bioda Ruadh,
sheasainn-sa ri taobh na mara   5
ag ùrachadh gaoil 'nam anam
fhad 's a bhiodh an cuan a' lìonadh
camas Thalasgair gu sìorraidh:
sheasainn an siud air lom na tràghad
gu 'n cromadh Priseal a cheann àigich.   10

And if we were together
on Calgary shore in Mull,
between Scotland and Tiree,
between the world and eternity,
I would stay there till doom
measuring sand, grain by grain,
and in Uist, on the shore of Homhsta
in presence of that wide solitude,
I would wait there forever
for the sea draining drop by drop.

And if I were on the shore of Moidart
with you, for whom my care is new,
I would put up in a synthesis of love for you
the ocean and the sand, drop and grain.
And if we were on Mol Stenscholl Staffin
when the unhappy surging sea dragged
the boulders and threw them over us,
I would build the rampart wall
against an alien eternity grinding (its teeth).

XLIII

But for you the Cuillin would be
an exact and serrated blue rampart
girdling with its march-wall
all that is in my fierce heart.

But for you the sand
that is in Talisker compact and white
would be a measureless plain to my expectations
and on it the spear desire would not turn back.

But for you the oceans
in their unrest and their repose
would raise the wave-crests of my mind
and settle them on a high serenity.

Agus nan robh sinn cuideachd
air tràigh Chalgaraidh am Muile,
eadar Alba is Tiriodh,
eadar an saoghal 's a' bhiothbhuan,
dh'fhuirichinn an siud gu luan   15
a' tomhas gainmhich bruan air bhruan.
Agus an Uibhist air tràigh Hòmhstaidh
fa chomhair farsaingeachd na h-ònrachd,
dh'fheithinn-sa an siud gu sìorraidh
braon air bhraon an cuan a' sìoladh.   20

Agus nan robh mi air tràigh Mhùideart
còmhla riut, a nodhachd ùidhe,
chuirinn suas an cochur gaoil dhut
an cuan 's a' ghaineamh, bruan air bhraon dhiubh.
'S nan robh sinn air Mol Steinnseil Stamhain   25
's an fhairge neo-aoibhneach a' tarraing
nan ulbhag is gan tilgeil tharainn,
thogainn-sa am balla daingeann
ro shìorraidheachd choimhich 's i framhach.

XLIII

Mur b' e thusa bhiodh an Cuilithionn
'na mhùr eagarra gorm
a' crioslachadh le bhalla-crìche
na tha 'nam chridhe borb.

Mur b' e thusa bhiodh a' ghaineamh   5
tha 'n Talasgar dùmhail geal
'na clàr biothbhuan do mo dhùilean,
air nach tilleadh an rùn-ghath.

'S mur b' e thusa bhiodh na cuantan
'nan luasgan is 'nan tàmh   10
a' togail càir mo bhuadhan,
ga cur air suaimhneas àrd.

And the brown brindled moorland
and my reason would co-extend –
but you imposed on them an edict
above my own pain.

And on a distant luxuriant summit
there blossomed the Tree of Strings,
among its leafy branches your face,
my reason and the likeness of a star.

XLIV*

Though I put from myself the garment
of deceitful feeling
and set off bare and trim
as a firebrand of triumphant reason,
there I would reach the love-core
of my ardent devotion
and would deliver to your joy
the firebrand of triumphant reason.

XLV

The knife of my brain made incision,
my dear, on the stone of my love,
and its blade examined every segment
and my eye took its colour.

I turned every jewel fragment
under a sharp cold glass
and under the flame of my reason,
which tried them hundreds of times.

After knife, glass, fire,
and the sharp-pointed blades,
lopping, cutting, burning, scrutiny,
there was no change on its aspect.

'S bhiodh am monadh donn riabhach
agus mo chiall co-shìnt' –
ach chuir thusa orra riaghladh 15
os cionn mo phianaidh fhìn.

Agus air creachainn chèin fhàsmhoir
chinn blàthmhor Craobh nan Teud,
'na meangach duillich t' aodann,
mo chiall is aogas rèil. 20

XLIV

Ged chuirinn dhiom èideadh
faireachaidh na cluaineis
's nam falbhainn lom gleusta
'nam chaoir cèille buadhmhoir,
ruiginn an sin crè-ghaol 5
mo chèille luaidhe
's liùbhrainn do t' èibhneas
caoir na cèille buadhmhoir.

XLV

Rinn sgian m' eanchainn gearradh
air cloich mo ghaoil, a luaidh,
is sgrùd a faobhar gach aon bhearradh
is ghabh mo shùil a thuar.

Thionndaidh mi gach mìrean lèige 5
fo ghloine gheur fhuair
is fo mo lasair chèille,
a dh'fhiach iad ceudan uair.

An dèis sgeine, gloine, teine
is gath nam faobhar giar, 10
beumadh, gearradh, losgadh, sgrùdadh,
cha robh caochladh air a fiamh.

The charm-stone cut in a thousand fragments
as whole as it ever was,
ground into a powder
but dense, jewelled, sharp.

As it increased in the number
of cut and brittle fragments,
so it took unity,
alone hard and taut.

It swelled to the size of a thousand oceans
and every fragment became a drop,
but it was a water that went to hardness
with the tightening swelling of love.

The stone that was cut
out of my own narrow spirit
was clipped to the greatness
that would contain the land of the world.

Pick-axed out of my body, its great size
was above my farthest measurement,
and like a fragment, its mother-rock crouched
in the star Betelgeuse.

The love-stone that came from my brain
took on the strong mettle
that it was a mother-spirit
to its own mother brain.

The love begotten by the heart
is the love that is in free chains
when it takes, in its spirit,
a brain love of its love.

And the stone that is broken
is the clear whole jewel
when it is pounded by a brain
to a greater hardness of its love.

An t-sian-chlach geàrrt' am mìle mìrean
cho slàn 's a bha i riamh,
air a prannadh ann am fùdar   15
ach dùmhail leugach giar.

Mar a rachadh i an àireamh
nam bruan geàrrte prann
's ann a ghabhadh i aonachd
'na h-aonar cruaidh teann.   20

Dh'at i gu meud mìle chuantan
is chaidh gach bruan 'na bhraon,
ach b' i uisge chaidh an cruadal
le teannachadh at gaoil.

Bha a' chlach a fhuair a gearradh   25
à m' aigne chumhang fhìn
air a bearradh gus a' mhòrachd
a thoilleadh domhain-thìr.

Pioct' às mo chom, bha a miadachd
os cionn mo thomhais chèin   30
's mar bhruan chrùb a creag-màthar
am Betelgeuse nan reul.

A' chlach ghaoil a thàinig à m' eanchainn,
's i ghabh am meanmna treun
gu robh i 'na màthair-meanmna   35
da màthair-eanchainn fhèin.

'S e 'n gaol ginte leis a' chrìdhe
an gaol tha 'n geimhlich shaoir
an uair a ghabhas e 'na spiorad
gaol eanchainn air a ghaol.   40

Agus 's e a' chlach tha briste
an leug shoilleir shlàn
nuair phrannar i le eanchainn
gu barrachd cruais a gràidh.

Dear, if my heart love
of you were not like the hardness of the jewel,
surely it could be cut
by a hard sharp brain.

XLVI

We are together, dear,
alone in Edinburgh,
and your serene kind face
hides the hurt of your wounds.
I have as my share of you
a beautiful head and a torn body.

My misery is small tonight
beside the evil of your wounded body,
but with your misery my love
turns to white leaping flame,
burning in the turmoil of my head
my memory of the other,
of a more fortunate and more lovely one
who is married over in Ireland.

XLVII

Remorse after the kisses
wounding me all the night:
that the pride of my love
is mocking your unhappy fate;
that the young strength of my body
was mocking the cause of your sorrow,
and your sad beauty going away, a ghost
on the grey broken road of your agony.

Why, God, did I not get the chance
before the young Lowlander tore your bloom,
before your beauty was made a thing of pity,
and before a golden banner was laid to the ground?

A luaidh, mur biodh gaol mo chridhe   45
ort mar chruas na lèig,
tha fhios gun gabhadh e gearradh
le eanchainn chruaidh gheur.

XLVI

Tha sinn còmhla, a ghaoil,
leinn fhìn ann an Dùn Èideann,
is t' aodann suaimhneach còir
a' falach leòn do chreuchdan.
Tha agamsa mar chuibhreann dhiot   5
ceann grinn is colainn reubte.

Is beag mo thruaighe-sa a-nochd
seach olc do cholainn creuchdaich,
ach le do thruaighe-sa tha m' ghaol
air dhol 'na chaoir ghil leumraich,   10
a' losgadh am bruaillean mo chinn
mo chuimhne air an tèile,
air tè nas rathaile 's nas bòidhche
's i pòsta thall an Eirinn.

XLVII

Aithreachas an deaghaidh nam pòg
ga mo leòn fad na h-oidhche:
gu bheil uabhar mo ghaoil
a' magadh air do chòr mi-aoibhneach;
gu robh neart òg mo cholainn   5
a' fanaid air adhbhar do thùrsa,
is t' àilleachd bhròin a' falbh 'na manadh
air rathad briste glas do chiùrraidh.

Carson, a Dhia, nach d' fhuair mi 'n cothrom,
mun d' shrac an t-òigear Goill do bhlàth,   10
mun d' rinneadh culaidh-thruais dhed bhòidhche
's mun d' leagadh suaithneas òir ri làr?

O God, the beauty of the garden,
though the grey canker is under the sheen of its blossoms,
which will not stay for the yellow gratitude of autumn
since time and root and top are plucked.

XLVIII

With you my humility
is equal to my pride
and my submission and pride
are a permanent laughter-music.

Prostrate at your feet
my spirit is on high tip-toe
and my mind's pain and unrest
are an impetuous serene repose.

And with you the meeting
that I have with myself
is as near me as my heart's marrow
when it goes on a far-off peak.

I have burst from the husk
which my life's condition imposed,
and my spirit's blossom has come
out of distress an adamant.

XLIX

My boat was under sail and the Clarach
laughing against its prow,
my left hand on the tiller
and the other in the winding of the sheet-rope.

On the second thwart to windward,
darling, you sat near me,
and your lit rope of hair
about my heart, a winding of gold.

A Dhia, 's e bòidhche a' ghàrraidh
ged tha 'n giamh glas fo lì nam blàth,
nach fhan ri buidheachas an fhoghair   15
on bhuaineadh tìm is bun is bàrr.

XLVIII

Mar riutsa tha m' irisleachd
co-ionann ri m' uaill
agus tha m' ùmhlachd is m' àrdan
'nan ceòl-gàire buan.

Sleuchdt' aig do chasan tha mo spiorad   5
air chorra-bhioda àrd
agus tha pian is luasgan m' aigne
'nam bras shuaimhneas tàimh.

'S 'nad fhaisge tha a' chòmhail
a th' agam rium fhèin   10
cho dlùth rium ri smior mo chridhe
's e falbh air binnean cèin.

Fhuair mi faoisgneadh às a' chochall
a rinn cor mo rèis
is dhiùchd bàrr-gùc m' anama   15
bho arraban 'na lèig.

XLIX

Bha 'm bàt' agam fo sheòl 's a' Chlàrach
a' gàireachdaich fo sròin,
mo làmh cheàrr air falmadair
's an tèile 'n suaineadh sgòid.

Air dara tobhta 'n fhuaraidh   5
shuidh thu, luaidh, 'nam chòir
agus do ròp laist' cuailein
mum chrìdh 'na shuaineadh òir.

God, if that course had been
to the destination of my desire,
the Butt of Lewis would not
have sufficed for my boat under sail.

L

Grief is only a nothing
and love is only a crumb
in the face of the stars extending
and the Earth going round.

And the many millions of years
since the Earth has gone as a flame
and the many million times
its course has encircled love.

What do I care for its circuits,
for its distant ancient course
since it will not give with its sunlight
any kind of permanence to my love.

Let it romp for the race of its permanence
through the grey fields of the skies
since it cannot be triumphantly fashioned
as a form of love to my reason.

Since there is no heed of our desires
in the perverse eternal circlings,
I do not heed its hundreds
or millions of tales of love.

If the face of my love could be
beautiful and lasting forever
I would defy Time with its powers
with its novelty and paean of growth.

A Dhia, nan robh an cùrsa ud
gu mo cheann-uidhe deòin, 10
cha bhiodh am Bùta Leòdhasach
air fòghnadh do mo sheòl.

L

Chan eil anns a' bhròn ach neoini
's chan eil anns a' ghaol ach bruan
fa chomhair nan reul a' sgaoileadh
's an saoghal a' dol 'na chuairt.

Agus liuthad millean bliadhna 5
on thriall an Talamh 'na chaoir
agus liuthad millean iadhadh
a thug e le thriall air gaol.

Dè dhomhsa a mhillean iadhadh,
dè dhomhsa a chian chùrs' aost 10
a chionn nach toir e le ghrian-leus
gnè shìorraidheachd do mo ghaol!

Seatadh e fad rèis a bhuantachd
tro chluaintean glasa nan speur
a chionn nach dealbhar le buaidh e 15
'na chumadh luaidhe dom chèill!

A chionn nach eil suim dar miannan
anns an iadhadh bhiothbhuan chlaon,
chan eil mo shuim-sa ra chiadan
no mhilleanan sgialachd gaoil. 20

Nam b' urrainn aodann mo luaidhe
bhith àlainn is buan gu bràth
bheirinn dùbhlan do Thìm le bhuadhan
le nodhachd 's luathghair fàis.

LI

My prudence said to my heart
when the very stars were being spoilt:
you are adding to a beauty
that will be your own wound;
it's on you that the wearying oppression will come
when the skies burst and stream with terror.

My spirit, bruised and decrepit, lay
in the loneliness of its pain,
shuddering before the monster
of the sharp cold floods,
and the chill cry of death choked
the brave green blossoming.

I myself would understand the torment
that is in the mere drowning
and the power of mutilation
that is in the roaring of the waves,
if you did not raise your face
to put the change of death on reason.

LII

To my steady gaze you were a star
alone in the skies;
and you were given the two rays
by my fertile spirit and my grief.

And then you shone with a three-
in-one direct trinity of rays;
but my own vehement rays were
only the children of your beauty in grief.

I was waiting for the blow
that would spoil your sway with its blight;
but I gave you the three for yourself
at the end of the course of ten years.

LI

Thuirt mo chrìonnachd ri mo chridhe
'n àm milleadh nan reul:
Tha thu cur ri bòidhchid
a bhios gud leònadh fhèin,
's ann ortsa thig an claoidheadh   5
le maoim-shruth nan speur.

Laigh mo spiorad breòite
ann an ònrachd a phèin,
a' plosgartaich ro uilebheist
nan tuiltean fuaraidh geur',   10
is thachd a' ghaoir aognaidh
an gorm-fhaoisgneadh treun.

Gun tuiginn fhìn an cràdhlot
a th' anns a' bhàthadh lom
agus brìgh a' mhàbaidh   15
th' an gàirich nan tonn,
mur togadh tusa t' aodann
chur caochlaidh air conn.

LII

Dom dhùr-amharc bha thu 'nad reul
's tu leat fhèin san iarmailt:
is thugadh dhut an dà leus
le m' aigne dhoirrach 'o m' iargain

'S an uair sin bhoillsg thu le trì-   5
an-aon leus dìreach trianaid;
ach cha robh 'nam leòis dhian fhìn
ach clann do lìthe 'n iargain.

Bha mi feitheamh ris a' bheum
a mhilleadh do rèim le chrìonadh;   10
ach thug mi dhut na trì dhut fhèin
an ceann rèis deich bliadhna.

For if it were only my own begotten rays
that created beauty in your ray,
it was certain that they would lose their power
with the greying of ten years' time.

O frankness and o generous heart
luminous in a face;
O charm of heart and of eye,
your loved image her face!

The pursuit was not long
that took more than ten years
when the treasure-trove was more
than would suffice for an eternal hope.

LIII

I lightly hold the great revolution
that will suffice the lot of man
since I have seen the image of all that is generous
fashioned in the beauty of a face.

LIV

You were dawn on the Cuillin
and benign day on the Clarach,
the sun on his elbow in the golden stream
and the white rose that breaks the horizon.

Glitter of sails on a sunlit firth,
blue of the sea and aureate sky,
the young morning in your head of hair
and in your clear lovely cheeks.

My jewel of dawn and night
your face and your dear kindness,
though the grey stake of misfortune is
thrust through the breast of my young morning.

Oir nam b' iad mo leòis gin fhìn
a bheothaich lì 'nad lias-sa,
bu chinnt gun cailleadh iad am brìgh   15
le glasadh tìm deich bliadhna.

A shuilbhireachd 's a chridhe chòir
's sibh lòghmhor ann an aodann;
a mheallaidh cridhe 's a mheallaidh sùla,
ur n-ìomhaigh rùin a h-aogas!   20

Cha b' ann fada bha an tòir
a thug còrr 's deich bliadhna
an uair a bha an fhaodail còrr
's na dh'fhòghnadh dòchas sìorraidh.

LIII

Gur suarach leam an t-ar-a-mach mòr
a dh'fhòghnas do chor nan daoine,
on chunnaic mi ìomhaigh na tha còir
's i dealbhte 'm bòidhichid aodainn.

LIV

Bu tu camhanaich air a' Chuilithionn
's latha suilbhir air a' Chlàraich,
grian air a h-uilinn anns an òr-shruth
agus ròs geal bristeadh fàire.

Lainnir sheòl air linne ghrianaich,   5
gorm a' chuain is iarmailt àr-bhuidh,
an òg-mhadainn 'na do chuailean
's 'na do ghruaidhean soilleir àlainn.

Mo leug camhanaich is oidhche
t' aodann is do choibhneas gràdhach,   10
ged tha bior glas an dòlais
tro chliabh m' òg-mhaidne sàthte.

LV

I do not see the sense of my toil
putting thoughts in a dying tongue
now when the whoredom of Europe
is murder erect and agony;
but we have been given the million years,
a fragment of a sad growing portion,
the heroism and patience of hundreds
and the miracle of a beautiful face.

LVI*

In my ten years of labour
I never happened upon a treasure poem
as serene as your branching head of hair,
as beautiful and open as your face.

LVII

A face haunts me,
following me day and night,
the triumphant face of a girl
is pleading all the time.

It is saying to my heart
that a division may not be sought
between desire and the substance
of its unattainable object;

that mischance will not come on beauty
in spite of the growth of failings
because a day that has declined
is as free as the day tomorrow;

and that this period of time is
above every change and denial
that will shout insurrection
against its rule tomorrow;

LV

Chan fhaic mi fàth mo shaothrach
bhith cur smaointean an cainnt bhàsmhoir,
a-nis is siùrsachd na Roinn-Eòrpa
'na murt stòite 's 'na cràdhlot;
ach thugadh dhuinn am millean bliadhna   5
'na mhìr an roinn chianail fhàsmhoir,
gaisge 's foighidinn nan ciadan
agus mìorbhail aodainn àlainn.

LVI

'Na mo dheich bliadhna saothrach
riamh cha d' fhuair mi dàn air faodail
cho suaimhneach ri do chuailean craobhach,
cho àlainn fosgailte ri t' aodann.

LVII

Tha aodann ga mo thathaich,
ga mo leantainn dh'oidhche 's latha:
tha aodann buadhmhor nìghne
's e sìor agairt.

Tha e labhairt ri mo chridhe   5
nach fhaodar sgaradh a shireadh
uudaı ırıann ngıın ougbaint
a' chuspair dho-ruighinn,

nach tig tubaist air àilleachd
a dh'aindeoin cinntinn nam fàiling   10
a chionn gu bheil là aomte
cho saor ri là màireach,

agus gu bheil an tràth seo
os cionn gach caochlaidh 's àichidh
a nì ceannairc èigheach   15
ra rèim a-màireach,

because it now is
that its form and being will always be,
and that change cannot
maim its unity;

that the choice of the eye's desire
is as eternal as the secret thoughts
that have taken their lasting shape
in new words;

that it is quite as full of grace
as the art of the two Patricks
though it may not be expressed
by melody or cut stone,

and though the pictured board may not
offer its shape and colour
to the new generations
without the smooring that perverts.

O face, face, face,
will you lose, will you lose the wonder
with which your beauty has seized
a generous joy?

If stone or board will not take your likeness,
what will the art of music or verse do
if there is no way of putting this time
in a circumscribed predicament;

if there is no way of checking
this hour and holding it
in the sand of change
with the fluke of an anchor,

before it raises the new sails
on a course to oblivion
and before its sails are lost
to the sight of eye.

a chionn gu bheil i 'n-dràsta
gum bi 'cruth 's a bith gu bràth ann
agus nach urrainn caochladh
a h-aonachd a mhàbadh,   20

gu bheil roghainn miann na sùla
cho biothbhuan ris na rùintean
a ghabh an cumadh sìorraidh
am briathran ùra,

gu bheil i cheart cho àghmhor   25
ri ealain an dà Phàdraig
ged nach cuir an cèill i
ceòl rèidh no clach gheàrrte,

's ged nach fhaod clàr dealbha
a cruth 's a dreach a thairgsinn   30
do na gineil ùra
gun smùradh coirbte.

O aodainn, aodainn, aodainn,
an caill, an caill thu 'n t-ioghnadh
leis na ghlac do bhòidhche   35
sòlas faoilidh?

Mur gabh clach no clàr do shamhladh
dè nì ealaidh chiùil no ranntachd
mur eil seòl an tràth seo
chur an càs staimhte,   40

mur eil seòl air bacadh
na h-uarach seo 's a glacadh
an gainmhich a' chaochlaidh
le faobhar acrach,

mun tog i na siùil ùra   45
gu dìochuimhne air chùrsa
's mun caillear a brèidean
bho lèirsinn sùla?

O face that is haunting me,
beautiful face that is speaking,
will you go away with this time
in spite of your pleading?

When the hoard of every memory decays
that will give you love or thought or care,
will you lose the delight of your unity,
vain and forgotten?

For you I would never seek
any lastingness for your beauty
but what would render it complete
exactly as it is.

I would not seek the action of music
that speaks many things to one's care:
I would not ask for one new thing
that I myself did not see in your face.

And painted board would give
memory only one gleam
though a third of your graces were kept
stored in its colours.

Thus, o time and face,
you must be always together
so that at the end of the hour
graces are not surrendered.

O tract of time, when your reign
departs like the troubled mist,
to what newly lit consciousness
will your agitated motion be manifest?

O tract of time, and what ceases
of us with your steps,
where is the course
that will care for us or tell of us?

O aodainn a tha gam thathaich,
aodainn àlainn a tha labhairt,   50
an triall thu leis an àm seo
neo-ar-thaing t' agairt?

Nuair chrìonas tasgadh gach cuimhne
a bheir gaol no smuain no suim dhut,
an caill thu mealladh t' aonachd   55
's tu faoin gun chuimhn' ort?

Chan iarrainn-sa gu bràth dhut
aon bhiothbhuantachd do t' àilleachd
ach na liùbhradh slàn i
dìreach mar a thà i.   60

Chan iarrainn gnìomhachd a' chiùil
's e ioma-bhriathrach ri ùidh:
chan iarrainn aon ni ùr
nach fhaca mi fhìn 'nad ghnùis.

Agus cha tugadh clàr dathte   65
do chuimhne ach aon aiteal
ged chuimteadh trian ded bhuadhan
'na thuar an tasgadh.

Mar sin, a thràth is aodainn,
feumar ur cuideachd daonnan   70
los nach bi 'n ceann na h-uarach
buadhan aomte.

A thràth de thìm, nuair dh'fhalbhas
do rèim mar an allacheo,
dè am breannachadh ùr-laist   75
don diùchd t' fhalbhan?

O thràth de thìm, 's na thrèigeas
dhinne le do cheuman,
càit a bheil an cùrsa
bheir ùidh dhuinn no sgeul oirnn?   80

What was and what is now of us,
though they would last forever,
how would a tale of them come
from distant shores?

What eye will see them
or what ear will hear them
on their exposed forlorn journey
beyond a mind's thoughts?

What is the fourth dimension
that will bring this beauty to the ken
of eye, reason or any sense-perception
over the wastes of the abyss?

And what sense beyond senses
will perceive their beauty
when neither eye nor ear will show it,
nor taste nor touch nor smell,

and when it is not folded
in a living memory or near
the swift-journeying thoughts
that renew their treasure?

If there is not found, for perception,
one other sense or dimension,
will your beauty have form or being
in the bounds of time and the eternal deep?

O face that is haunting me,
o eloquent marvel,
is there any port in time for you
or march-wall but earth?

O shapely human paean,
is there a dimension in the universe
that will give you a greater wholeness
than music, board or lyric?

Na bha, 's na tha an-dràsta,
ged mhaireadh iad gu bràth dhinn,
ciamar thigeadh sgeul orr'
bho chèin-thràighean?

Dè 'n t-sùil a nì am faicinn   85
no chluas a nì an claisteachd
's iad air turas faondraidh
bharr smaointean aigne?

Ciod e an ceathramh seòl-tomhais
a bheir an àilleachd seo fa chomhair   90
sùla, reusain no aon chàileachd
thar fàsaichean glomhair?

Is dè a' chàil thar chàiltean
a mhothaicheas an àilleachd,
nuair nach nochd sùil no cluas i,   95
blas, suathadh no fàileadh,

's nuair nach bi i paisgte
an cuimhne bheò no 'm faisge
ris na smuainteannan siùbhlach
a dh'ùraicheas an tasgadh?   100

Mur faighear, air chor 's gum mothaich,
aon chàil eile no seòl-tomhais,
am bi cruth no bith aig t' àilleachd
an àrainn tìme 's domhainn?

O aodainn a tha gam thathaich,   105
a mhìorbhail a tha labhar,
a bheil aon phort an tìm dhut
no balla-crìch ach talamh?

O luathghair dhaonda chuimir,
a bheil seòl-tomhais sa chruinne   110
a bheir dhut barrachd slànachd
na ceòl no clàr no luinneag?

Though the Red Army of humanity is
in the death-struggle beside the Dnieper,
it is not the deed of its heroism
that is nearest my heart,

but a face that is haunting me,
following me day and night,
the triumphant face of a girl
that is always speaking.

LVIII*

O girl who enriches
a fleeting moment,
how are we to detain
the swift running of its flowing step?
How are we to seize
the showering blossom of its May?
How are we to store it away
in baskets of jewels?

O girl and your pale forehead
inflamed with beauty
together with the half-light
inflamed with its youth,
it is you who set all of
my faculties rushing
and kindle in a rush
the cavalry of the Muses.

O calm, open gaze,
inspiring right feelings,
how am I to check
the flowering thicket of your roses
when you reveal to me
the poverty of my skill
as I seek to suck out
the steadiness of its beauty?

Ma tha Arm Dearg a' chinne
an gleac bàis ri taobh an Dniepeir,
chan e euchd a ghaisge 115
as fhaisg' air mo chridhe,

ach aodann a tha gam thathaich,
ga mo leantainn dh'oidhche 's latha,
aodann buadhmhor nìghne
's e sìor labhairt. 120

LVIII

A nighean 's tu beairteachadh
tacan tha trèigsinn,
ciamar a bhacar leinn
cas-ruith a cheum-shruth?
Ciamar a ghlacar leinn 5
fras-bhlàth a chèitein?
Ciamar a thasgar leinn
'm basgaidean leug e?

O nighean 's do mhala gheal
laiste le bòidhichid 10
mar ris a' chamhanaich
laiste le h-òige,
's tu chuireas brasadh air
m' aignidhean còmhla
's a ghrìosas gu cabhagach 15
marc-shluagh a' cheòlraidh.

O sheallaidh chiùin fhosgailte,
mosgladh na còireid,
ciamar a chosgar leam
dos-bhlàth do ròsan, 20
agus tu nochdadh dhomh
bochdainn mo sheòltachd
's mi fiachainn ri deocadh às
socrachd à bhòidhichid?

Abundantly chiselled face
under your white joyous gladness,
how are we to seize
the fashion of its enchantment;
how are we to store away
its showers of jewels
before it is hidden
across in a far land?

O pure face, face,
could your beauty not be freed
from the power of every foolishness,
decline and iniquity!
Could it not be kept as a chance treasure
mildly stowed away
in the shelter of every free
mildness the Muses possess!

LIX

Carmichael, I often think
of every treasure you chanced on;
and of your wealth every day
without bitter wrestling and delirium:
that you got the grace and happiness of the Muse
without struggle against loneliness and terror,
and that it will be very different for us
against the venomous blast to windward.

But, Alexander Carmichael,
there came to me without striving
a paean in the fair beauty of a girl's face
in spite of its troubling;
and one day there came to me
a peaceful golden lyric,
complete, as came to you,
flawless, the Hymn of the Graces.

O aodainn shàr-shnaidhte   25
fo t' aighear geal èibhneach,
ciamar a ghlacar leinn
fasan a sheuntachd;
ciamar a thasgar leinn
frasan a leugachd   30
mum bi e falaichte
thairis an cèin-thir?

O aodainn ghlain, aodainn,
nach saoirteadh do bhòidhichead
bho chumhachd gach baothalachd   35
aomadh is dò-bheairt!
Nach cuimteadh mar fhaodail e
caoin air a stòradh
am fasgadh gach caomhalachd
saoir th' aig a' cheòlraidh!   40

LIX

Mhic Gille-Mhìcheil, 's tric mi smaointinn
air gach faodail a fhuair thu;
agus do shaoibhreas gach aon latha
gun charachd gheur, gun bhruaillean:
gun d' fhuair thu àgh is sonas ceòlraidh   5
gun ghleac ri ònrachd 's fuathas,
's nach ann mar sin a bhitheas dhuinne
ri sgal guineach an fhuaraidh.

Ach, Alasdair Mhic Gille-Mhìcheil,
thàinig gun strì dhomh luathghair   10
ann an geal mhaise aodann nìghne
a dh'aindeoin brìgh a bhuairidh:
agus air latha thàrladh dhòmhsa
ealaidheachd òir gun luasgan,
's i coimhlionta, mar thàinig ortsa,   15
gun mheang, an Ortha Bhuadhach.

LX*

When I saw the red hair last night
and the joyous, beautiful forehead,

beneath the king's wretched coat
the foolish heart leapt.

As far as human company went,
no-one else, my love, was like you:

as far as sharp perception went,
you alone were my company:

as far as greatness of intellect went,
you alone could satisfy me:

as far as great sincerity went,
it was not that which pained my flesh:

I saw the red hair last night
and the opulent, beautiful forehead.

I saw the red hair and an old
new division awakened in my flesh.

Dimitto

Go, little ineffective book,
look into her shining eyes:
though lame, you are no liar:
in the time of wing spreading you will be over mountains.

LX

Nuair chunna mi 'n cùl ruadh a-raoir
's a' bhathais aoibhinn bhòidheach,

's ann fo chòta truagh an rìgh
a leum an cridhe gòrach.

Air na bh' ann a chòmhlan sluaigh   5
cha robh, a luaidh, do sheòrs' ann:

air na bh' ann a dh'aigne gheur
b' e thus' thu fhèin mo chòmhlan:

air na bh' ann a dh'inntinn mhòir
's tu fhèin a dh'fhòghnadh dhòmhsa: 10

air na bh' ann a dhùrachd mhòir
cha b' i siud dòrainn m' fheòla:

chunna mi 'n cùl ruadh a-raoir
's a' bhathais shaoibhir bhòidheach.

Chunna mi 'n cùl ruadh is dhùisg   15
seann roinneadh ùr 'nam fheòil-sa.

Dimitto

Thalla, a leabhair bhig uallaich nochdnich;
amhairc a-steach 'na sùilean leugach:
ge bacach thu, chan eil thu breugach:
'n àm sgaoileadh sgiath bidh tu thar shlèibhtean.

Note on the Gaelic text

This text represents what might be called a 'conservative modernising' of MacLean's practice, in general lines with current principles of Gaelic spelling. Acute and grave accents over long vowels have been unified as grave. The neutral 'schwa' vowel is written 'a' rather than 'u'. Personal forms of the preposition have initial apostrophe in the case of 'ann' ('nam', ''nad' etc.) but not of 'aig' ('gam', 'gad' etc.) The careful distinction made in MacLean's later versions of his texts between diphthong ('bial') and monophthong ('beul') pronunciations of the same word has been preserved. Direct speech is represented by a colon followed by a capital. Capital letters bear accents as appropriate. Separate forms ''s e' and ''s ann' are used (rather than 'se' or 'sann'). The cluster -sd(-) has generally been standardised to -st(-).

It is hoped that in due course all the poet's surviving poems can be submitted to the same process of standardisation and modernisation, always maintaining absolute respect for the phonetical and phonological integrity of the text.

Obvious errors and insignificant spelling variants (such as the presence or absence of a hyphen) are not noted in the list that follows. On the other hand, variants in punctuation have been listed scrupulously, since they offer an insight not just into the syntax but also into the breath and rhythm of lines as perceived by the poet (sometimes differently at different stages in his lifetime).

The Gaelic text of 1999 has been used as a point of departure, given the frequency of misprints in the Gaelic text in the first, 1989 edition of the collected poems.

Copytexts and Variant Readings

A   Somhairle Mac Ghill Eathain *Dàin do Eimhir agus Dàin Eile* (Glasgow, William MacLellan 1943) 103pp

B   Sorley MacLean / Somhairle MacGill-Eain *Reothairt is Contraigh* [sic]: *Taghadh de Dhàin 1932–72 / Spring tide and Neap tide: Selected Poems 1932–72* (Edinburgh, Canongate 1977) ix + 181pp

C   Somhairle MacGill-Eain / Sorley MacLean *O Choille gu Bearradh: Dàin Chruinnichte / From Wood to Ridge:*

Collected Poems (Manchester, Carcanet and Edinburgh, Birlinn 1999) (a reprint of the 1989 and 1990
editions, with corrected Gaelic text) xvi + 317pp

a   Somhairle Mac Ghill-Eathain and Robert Garioch
17 Poems for 6d (Edinburgh, The Chalmers Press
1940) (Second edition with alterations and corrections)

b   *The New Alliance* Vol.1 No.5 New Series (Aug-Sept
1940) p. 6

c   *Lines Review* 34 (1970) 'A special issue devoted to
Sorley MacLean' pp. 32–34

m   Letters from Sorley MacLean to Douglas Young
(National Library of Scotland Acc.6419 Box 38b)

n   Manuscript notebook of poems compiled by George
Campbell Hay in the late 1930s (National Library of
Scotland MS 26722)

o   Transcripts of eight items from the cycle accom-
panying a letter of April 3rd 1968 from Douglas
Young to Sorley MacLean (National Library of
Scotland Acc 11572/6)

I
copy text **A** 10
16   sgal,] **A** sgal
20   òir,] **A** òir

II
copy text **C** 4
1   a' chiall] **A** an ciall
2   ghaol,] **B** ghaol
6   do dh'fheòraich] **A** d' fheòraich
8   'n] **A** an
11   friamh] **A** freumh
      chrè,] **B** chrè
16   dhoimhne] **A** dhoimhneachd
18   Cha] **A** 'Cha **BC** cha
      bhuam] **A** bhuam'
23   Cha] **A** 'Cha **BC** cha
24   'n] **A** an
      ghaol] **A** ghaol'

III
copytext **C** 6
8   's] **a** is
11   Lenin] **aAB** Leninn

IV
copytext **C** 8
1   throm-bhuidh,] **B** throm-bhuidh
           òr-bhuidh,] **a** òr-bhuidh
3   gheal chasarlach aighearach] **a** gheal, chasurlach,
           aighearach,
           bhòidheach,] **aAB** bhòidheach
7   meàirleach] **A** mèirleach
8   bhial-sa] **aA** bheul-sa,
           uaill-dhearg] **aA** uaill-dhearg,
19   reòta] **A** reòta,
21   òr-bhuidh] **a** or laist (sic)

V
copytext **o**
1   ruadh,] **o** ruadh
7   suairceas,] **o** suairceas
17   O,] **o** O
25   'S,] **o** 'S
           ruadh,] **o** ruadh

VI
copytext **A** 83
3   chuimhne] **o** chuimhn'
6   grèine;] **o** gréine,

VIII
copytext **C** 10

IX
copytext **C** 10
4   arraghloir] **A** arraghlòir

X
copytext **A** 13
11   dha] **A** d' am

XI
copytext **C** 10
3   bhòidhche] **A** bhòidhichid
4   lòghmhor] **A** lòghmhor,

XII
copytext **o**
2   sheirbheis] **o**

XIII
copytext **C** 12
2   ghrèine;] **AB** ghrèine:
5   nighean bhuidhe Chòrnaig] **m** May 25th 1941 Morag
         Mhic Dhomhnaill (deleted)
7–8   **m** May 25th 1941 shows that these lines were initially
         placed after 12, with 11 beginning 'agus' rather than
         'bu tu'
10   bàs] **m** May 25th 1941 gràdh
14   Maebhe] **B** Maoibhe
21   bhòidhchead] **A** bhòidhichead
37   Diarmad -] **A** Diarmad,-
43–44   **m** May 25th 1941 shows that the order of these two
         lines was initially reversed

XIV
copytext **C** 14
3   na] **a** an
13   beag lag suarach] **aA** beag, lag, suarach,
20   reicte] **aA** reicte,

XV
copytext **A** 82
3   nochdadh] **a** nochd
         bhàrdachd:] **a** bhàrdachd
4   Mhic Dhiarmaid,] **a** Mhic Dhiarmaid
5   ach] **a** ach,
         leam] **a** leam,
7   tìorail] **a** tiorail,
8   Eliot,] **a** Eliot
         Auden,] **a** Auden
9   MacNeice,] **a** Macneice **A** Macneice,
         còmhlan:] **a** còmhlan.
10   b'] **a** B'

XVI
copytext **n** 58v–59r
4   dhòmhsa] **no** dhomh-sa
10   air] **o** an
19   rinn] **o** a rinn
20   ghil fhoinnidh] **o** ghil, fhoinnidh,
22   so **o**; **n** bha
30   iomchar,] **o** iomchar
34   dith] **o** dhith
36   allacheo:] alla-cheò
38   ruadh] **o** ruadh,
         gheal,] **n** gheal

amendments made to **o** after April 3rd 1968 as follows:
18   a' ghàire] ànraidh
21   rim] gu m'
22   far an do shaoil mi bhà thu] le d' fhaoilteachd chòir
         àghmhor
23   dhomhsa aon] dhomh ?coma [illegible]
24   glòir aoibhneach do ghàire] ròs aoibhinn do ghràidh
         dhomh [cancelled and corrected to] ghràidh-sa
32   gu clis is] 's tu bris [cancelled] 's thusa briste

XVII
copytext **C** 16
5   man] **n** 59r 'nan
8   leatha fhèin san] **A** leis fhèin anns an

XVIII
copytext **C** 16
1   Dia] so **m** May 2nd 1943; **ABC** dìon
2   Crìosda] so **m** May 2nd 1943 **ABC** m' iarrtas
4   Dèanam] so **A**; **BC** dèanam
25   aighir;] **A** aighir,
28   is] **A** 's
32   ùidhe,] **A** ùidhe?
33   stad] **A** Stad
         shùilean?] **A** shùilean.
35   friamhaichean] **A** freumhaichean
37   ghil,] **A** ghil?
38   an] **A** An
40   O Conghaile] **A** Connolly

43   neo-bhàsmhoir:] **A** neo-bhàsmhor, **B B** neo-bhàsmhor:
45   's a'] **B** 'sa'
       bhiothbhuain] **A** bhiothbhuan
52   tein-aighir] **A** teine-aighir
56   dha] **A** d' am, **BC** dh' am
       ionnlaid,] **AB** ionnlaid
57   tionndadh,] **A** tionndadh;
58   ionndrainn;] **A** ionndrainn:
59   dh'anam] **A** anam
65   guidhe] **AB** ghuidhe
71   faileadh,] **A** fhaladh **B** fhaileadh
81   diathan,] **A** diathan
82   iarraidh,] **A** iarraidh
85   a thug] **A** thug

XIX
copytext **A** 20
26   ann] **A** an

XX
copytext **A** 21

XXI
copytext **A** 21
6   arraghloir] **A** arraghlòir

XXII
copytext **C** 22
5   ràdha] **A** ràdh
6   A] so **A**; **BC** a
11   Tha] so **A**; **BC** tha
18   an] **B** ann an
15   gun cuirinn] **B** cuirinn
21   chrìon] **A** chrìon,
22   bheag ìosal thioram thlàth,] **A** bheag, ìosal, thioram,
       thlàth:
24   beithir-theine] **A** bheithir-theine
27   neamh] **A** nèamh

XXIII
copytext **C** 24
6   sàr] **A** sàir
11   chòisir] **A** chòisir mhór
27   le] **A** socair le
28   bòidhche] **A** bòidhichead
33   an cochur] **A** a' cho-chur
35   bhreòite oillteil] **A** bhreòite, oillteil,
43   dàinig] **A** tàinig
45   uaigh,] **A** uaigh
49   an cochur dhen] **A** a' cho-chur de 'n
52   is] **A** 's
56   bhòidhche] **A** bhòidhichid

XXIV
copytext **C** 38
1   thuirt] **A** thubhairt
         bhòidhche] **A** bhòidhichead
4   Saoil] **BC** saoil
         òinseach] **A** òinsich
5   cainte] **A** abradh

XXV
copytext **A** 26

XXVI
copytext **m** April 15th 1942
1   ruadh,] **m** ruadh
2   òir] so **o**; **m** òir

XXVII
copytext **A** 27

XXVIII
copytext **A** 29

XXIX
copytext **C** 134
1   sneachda,] **a** sneachda
2   neo-dheachdte,] **a** neo-dheachdte; **A** neo-dheachdte:
4   t-sneachda:] **aAB** t-sneachda;
5   fala,] **a** fala

6   madaidhean-allaidh] **A** madaidhean-allaidh,
7   gàrradh,] **a** gàrradh **AB** gàradh
8   fàsail,] **B** fàsail
9   caol-ghleann,] **B** caol-ghleann
13   na mo] **a** 'nam
      chluasan,] **B** chluasan
14   bhuadhan:] **A** bhuadhan;
16   an fhiadhaich] **a** na fiadhach **A** na fiadhaich,
18   shiaradh;] **a** shiaradh,
19   caothaich na bàrdachd] **aA** cuthaich mo bhàrdachd
23   bhòidhche ciùine gaolaich] **a** bhòidhichid chiùin ghaolaich **A** bhòidhichid chiùin, ghaolaich
24   sgur] **A** sgur,

XXX
copytext **C** 134
2   bhànrainn] **A** bhàn-righinn
6   àlainn] so **AB**; **C** gheal
      laoch;] **A** laoch,
7   bhaoith] **n** 60r mhaoith (influenced by 'mhaoin' in following line?)
8   na maoin'] **A** a' mhaoin
9   's gun] **A** gun
11   'r fala] **A** ar fala
      'r gaoil] **A** ar gaoil
15   bhànrainn] **A** bhàn-righinn
      thù] **ABC** thu

XXXI
copytext **A** 31
3   dè] **A** Dé

XXXII
copytext **C** 136
2   bhòidhche] **A** bhòidhichead
      bhàrdachd,] **A** bhàrdachd;
4   daorsa;] **A** daorsa:
5   craoibhe] **A** craoibhe,
6   duilghe] **A** duilghe,
8   iarann-cruadhach] **A** iarunn cruadhach

XXIII
copytext **C** 136

XXXIV
copytext **C** 136
7   Chuilithinn] **A** Chuilthinn

XXXV
copytext **C** 138
4   Spàinn;] **A** Spàinn:
12   cuiridh] **A** cuireadh

XXXVI
copytext **o**

XXXVII
copytext **C** 138
4   smaointean;] **A** smaointean,

XXXVIII
copytext **A** 34

XXXIX
copytext **C** 140
2   ghlain,] **A** ghlain
3   agam] **A** 'gam

XL
copytext **C** 140
5   ciùrrte] **c** ciùrrte,

XLI
copytext **m** April 15th 1942

XLII
copytext **C** 140
6   ag ùrachadh gaoil 'nam] **n** 60r a' dòrtadh mo ghaoil
         'nad
10   Priseal] **n** 60r Preasail **A** Preiseal
13   Alba] **A** Albainn
16   bhruan] **A** bhruain
17   Hòmhstaidh] **n** 60v Hòstaidh

20   bhraon] **A** bhraon,
25   Mol] **A** Moll

XLIII
copytext **C** 142
1   Cuilithionn] **A** Cuilthionn
14   co-shìnt' -] **A** co-shìnt'
17   fhàsmhoir] **A** fhàsmhor

XLIV
copytext **A** 37

XLV
copytext **C** 144
6   fo] **A** fo 'n
7   is fo mo] **A** a tha 'nam
      chèille,] **A** céille
9   sgeine] **A** sgine
13   geàrrt'] **A** geàirrt
18   geàrrte] **A** geàirrte
26   à] **A** as
33   a thàinig] **A** thàinig
      eanchainn,] **AB** eanchainn
46   lèig,] **AB** léig

XLVI
copytext **C** 146

XLVII
copytext **C** 148
4   mì-aoibhneach] **cB** mi-aoibhneach
10   bhlàth,] **cB** bhlàth
15   fhoghair] **cB** fhaghair

XLVIII
copytext **C** 148
15   bàrr-gùc] **A** barr-guc **B** barr-gùc

XLIX
copytext **C** 150
6   luaidh] **n** 60v ghaoil
8   chrìdh] so **AB**; **C** chrìdh'

9   Dhia,] **A** Dhia
         'n] **A** an
10   mo cheann-uidhe deòin] **A** ceann ùidh mo dheòin

L
copytext **C** 152
4   saoghal] **A** t-saoghail
7   dhomhsa] **A** dhòmhsa
8   dhomhsa] **A** dhòmhsa
12   ghaol!] **A** ghaol?
18   chlaon,] **A** chlaon

LI
copytext **C** 512
2   reul:] **A** reul.
3   Tha] so **A**; **BC** tha
         bòidhchid] **A** bòidhichid
4   fhèin,] **A** fhéin:
7   ann an] **A** an
10   geur',] **A** geur

LII
copytext **C** 154
6   trianaid;] **A** trianaid:
14   bheothaich] **A** bheòthaich
         lias-sa,] **A** lias-sa
18   aodann;] **A** aodann:
19   sùla,] **A** sùla

LIII
copytext **A** 43

LIV
copytext **C** 156
1   Chuilithionn] **A** Chuilthionn
6   àr-bhuidh,] **b** òr-bhuidh'
7   chuailean] **b** chuailein
10   is] **A** 's
12   òg-mhaidne] **b** ògalachd

LV
copytext **C** 156
7   foidhidinn] **b** faighidinn

LVI
copytext **A** 43

LVII
copytext **C** 158
28   gheàrrte] **AB** gheàirrte
30   dreach] **AB** a dreach
40   staimhte] **B** staimhnte
46   dìochuimhne] **B** diochuimhne
35   bhòidhche] **A** bhòidhichead
60   thà] **AB** tha
73   thìm,] **B** thìm
74   allacheo] **AB** allacheò
88   bharr] **A** bhàrr
95   i,] **AB** i
106   a] **A** o

LVIII
copytext **A** 48

LIX
copytext **C** 164
1   Gille] **A** Ghille
2   thu;] **A** thu:
4   gheur,] **A** gheur
9   Ath,] **A** Ath
           Gille] **A** Ghille
13   dhòmhsa] **AC** dhomhsa
15   ortsa,] **A** ortsa
16   mheang,] **A** mheang

LX
copytext **A** 50

Dimitto
copytext **A** 50

LIST OF TITLES

Items from the 'Dàin do Eimhir' appearing in MacLean's 1977 selected volume were printed with titles as follows (an asterisk indicates a title already appearing in the 1943 volume):

II	A Chiall 's a Ghràidh*	Reason and Love
III	Am Buaireadh	The Turmoil
IV	Gaoir na h-Eòrpa	The Cry of Europe
VIII	An Clogad Stàilinn	The Steel Helmet
XIII	A' Bhuaile Ghréine	The Sunny Fold
XIV	Reic Anama*	The Selling of a Soul
XVII	Lìonmhoireachd	Multitude
XVIII	Urnuigh*	Prayer
XXII	An Roghainn	The Choice
XXIV	An Oinseach	The Fool
XXIX	Coin is Madaidhean-allaidh*	Dogs and Wolves
XXX	Am Boilseabhach	The Bolshevik
XXXII	Sgatham...	Let Me Lop...
XXXIII	Mac an t-Saoir is Ros	Macintyre and Ross
XXXV	Oidhche Chiùin	Gentle Night
XL	Muir-tràigh	Ebb
XLII	Tràighean*	Shores
XLIII	Am Mùr Gorm	The Blue Rampart
XLV	An Sgian	The Knife
XLVI	An Dithis	The Two
XLVII	Aithreachas	Remorse
XLVIII	Irisleachd	Humility
XLIX	Fo Sheòl	Under Sail
LI	Crìonnachd	Prudence
LIV	Camhanaich	Dawn
LV	Chan fhaic mi...	I Do Not See...
LVII	An Tathaich	The Haunting

In this volume, II and III (along with 'A' Chorra-ghridheach' ('The Heron') formed an untitled first section; the second section, 'Roghainn' ('A Choice') contained IV, XI, XIII, XIV, XVIII and XXII; the third, 'Aiteal' ('A Gleam'), contained VIII, XVII and XXIV; and the remaining items from the cycle were grouped in the fourth of the volume's nine sections, under the title 'An Tràigh Thathaich' ('The Haunted Ebb').

In the 1989 collected volume, MacLean printed 9 additional items from the cycle, as follows:

IX	Rinn mi luaidh...	I spoke of...
X	Dùn-éideann	Edinburgh
XXIII	Cochur	A Synthesis
XXXIV	An uair a labhras mi...	When I speak...
XXXVII	Chan e àilleachd...	It is not the beauty...
XXXIX	Grìosach	Embers
L	Chan eil anns a' bhròn...	Grief is only...
LII	Trì Leòis	Three Rays
LIX	Mhic Gille-Mhìcheil...	Carmichael...

The grouping into sections was more straightforward on this occasion. II to XXIII formed part of the first section '1932–1940', while the remaining items from XXIX to LIX formed the third section, 'An Tràigh Thathaich / The Haunted Ebb December 1939-July 1941'.[1]

---

[1] This should in fact be 'August 1941'. See note to LVII in 'Commentary'.

DATING LETTER

Extract from a letter to Douglas Young dated March 30th 1942

You ask about dates or parts of '[The] Cuillin' and 'Dàin [do Eimhir]' and about 'Coin' etc. I hope this is only for your own information, that you are not going to include notes of any kind with anything you publish of my stuff, especially the Eimhir poems. You will appreciate my worries about them in particular.

Dàn I was written in Raasay in September[1] or August 1931, Dàn II in Edinburgh in summer 1932, Dàn III in Portree in November or December 1936, Dàn IV in Mull in March or April 1938. Of 'The Cuillin' the first thing was the 'Ann an talla' lyric[2] written in Mull in the spring of 1938. I cannot remember whether 'Ban-ghàidheal' was written in Portree in 1937 or in Mull early in 1938. 'Dàin do Eimhir' V, VI and VII and VIII were all written in Edinburgh in September 1939. The Cuillin was started in Edinburgh in April or May 1939, was being rapidly written and had reached the line before 'Seo la eile'[3] when a chance meeting with E[imhir] brought back the old passion and it was completely interrupted,[4] until it was restarted in Hawick in November 1939.

'Dàin do Eimhir' IX-XVI were written in Hawick very early in November 1939. I don't actually know when in November 'The Cuillin' was restarted, but there was a short break between the end of Part II and the beginning of Part III and then again after the end of Part IV and again after [the] end of Part VI, but it was being written in November

---

[1] Names of months are silently expanded throughout.
[2] From Part I (MacLean 1999: 68–69).
[3] II, 110 (MacLean 1999: 80).
[4] Cp. the later statement that 'The Cuillin' 'stopped abruptly with the conclusion of the second part in late May or June 1939...' (MacLean 1999: 63).

and early December 1939. By the 13th December I know 'Eimhir' XXIII was written, sometime between the 10th and the 13th. 'Eimhir' XXIV to XXVII were written between 13th and 18th of December. On the 20th December 'Eimhir' XXVIII to XXXVI were all written. Meanwhile 'The Cuillin' was certainly all finished except 'Có seo'[5] before the 23rd December. 'Có seo' to the end was composed in bed in Raasay in the early hours of January 1st 1940. I had a bad throat and went to bed, I think, immediately the New Year was in. I think 'The Cuillin' was finished apart from that before December 20th 1939.

'Eimhir' XXXVII to LV were written in Hawick about March 1940, possibly some in February and some in April, I am not sure. 'Eimhir' LVI in Catterick sometime in early 1941, LVII-LIX in London in the last days of July [August scored out] or first days of August 1941[6] and LX in early Sept 1941.

Of[7] the other poems, 'An Soitheach' was written in Edinburgh in May or June 1934, 'Conchobar', 'Am Bàta Dubh', 'This is fair'[8] were written in 1933 or '34, I don't exactly remember. 'Chan eil mo shùil'[9] and 'An Crann Dubh' and 'Cornford' were all written in November or December 1939 but 'Gealach ùr' was a bit later, probably in February, March or April 1940 (in Hawick too). I forget whether 'Craobh nan Teud' was in November or December 1939 or in the early months of 1940, but 'Coilltean Ratharsair' was in spring or early summer 1940. The two things on John Maclean[10] were in November or December 1939, also 'Ceann Loch Aoineart' and 'An t-Eilean', 'An t-Eilean' must have been pretty early in November 1939 to go into *17 Poems [for 6d]*. 'Ceann Loch' was later. 'A' Chorra-ghridheach' is an old thing written in Raasay in the summer of 1934 or 1935. 'Fuaran' too is old but I can't tell when.

---

[5] The opening words, incessantly repeated, of the incantatory closing section of the poem: VII, 156ff. (MacLean 1999: 128).

[6] See note to LVII in 'Commentary' for an exact dating.

[7] Paragraph division in original. All other paragraphs are editorial.

[8] Untraced.

[9] Opening words of the poem titled 'Calbharaigh'.

[10] Presumably 'Clann Ghill-Eain' (MacLean 1999: 46–47) and 'Do 'n bhreitheamh a thubhairt ri Iain Mac Ghill-Eathain gum b' e gealtair a bh' ann' (MacLean 1943: 94).

Then there was the batch written in London in September 1941 and sent you early in October 1941: 'An té'[11] etc. 'Théid mi thun nan Eileanan'[12] was written in Portree, I think in 1936. The rest of 'Eisgeachd' was November or December 1939 or early 1940. I hope this screed will serve and I am sorry I can't be more precise as to [the] dates of many.

As to 'Samhlaidhean' and 'Coin'[13] this is all I can say. On Tuesday 19th December 1939 (I remember the date because I travelled home to Raasay on Christmas Day 1939, which was Monday) I got a letter that meant for me the end of my period of great activity in poetry. All Tuesday I was depressed and wrote nothing but about 2 or 3 a.m. on Wednesday 20th I got up out of bed and very quickly wrote down 'Samhlaidhean' and 'Coin', of which, as far as I remember, I have never changed one word from that first writing down. It seems to me that I composed them simultaneously in a troubled sleep. When I got up on Wednesday I felt more serene and that day I wrote 'Eimhir' XXX-XXXV and perhaps XXXVI as well.

---

[11] 'An té dh' an tug mi...' (MacLean 1999: 186). Young responded on October 11th 1941: 'Many thanks for the latest batch of Immortality, all of which I liked immensely, especially "An té d' an d' thug mi uile ghaol". If your new style is that I entirely approve.' NLS Acc. 11572/6.

[12] MacLean 1943: 95, where it is entitled 'Road to the Isles' and appears as VII in the section called 'Eisgeachd' ('Satire'), which in all contains five poems.

[13] 'Dàin do Eimhir' XXVIIII and XXIX.

AUTOBIOGRAPHICAL SKETCH

MacLean supplied the information that follows in two letters to Douglas Young, dated 7th and 11th September 1941 from the Old Town Hall in Hammersmith, London, with a view to the critical piece Young was planning to write. They offer an invaluable account of the poet's background and tastes, written down around the time when the 'Dàin do Eimhir' cycle was completed. Anomalies of spelling and punctuation have been silently normalised. Unless otherwise indicated, division into paragraphs is editorial.

To begin with Secederism.[1] At the age of twelve I began to get over my Secederism. I was never properly reconciled to it even as a child. As a young child, as far as I can remember, my general feelings were I could probably make shift to be 'saved' myself, but since only about 2 or 3 per cent, even of Seceders, were to be saved (judging by communion table statistics) it was impossible that any more than one or two of the people I loved most would also be 'saved'. Salvation without them was a desolate prospect. I was not resigned to an oblivion or alteration[2] of human affections in the hereafter, such as churches envisage. Perhaps my obsession with the 'cause' of the unhappy, the unsuccessful, the oppressed comes ultimately from this. I preferred the multitude of my friends who [were] certain to be 'lost' to those few who were to be saved. In fact there was no-one of my own family who on form showed any potentiality[3] for salvation. I disliked many of the obvious 'elect' not because of their good fortune, but because most of them were unlovable people and I regarded their preoccupation with salvation much as I regard the careerist at present. God the

---

[1] As a means of referring to the Free Presbyterian Church and its members, the term has a pejorative colouring in line with MacLean's anticlerical stance at the time this letter was written.

[2] The word is difficult to read, and might just be 'alienation'.

[3] A conjecture. The ending of the word is unclear.

Father always seemed horrible to my inmost thought, the
Holy Ghost a cipher, and Christ's attraction was modified by
the early realisation that his earthly suffering was nothing,
because he was not properly human, and it was, at any rate,
an episode in his existence, and also he was 'coming to judge
the world at the last day'[4] when he would exhibit the 'wrath
of the Lamb'.

No Seceder minister showed the least trace of saint-like
qualities, but I occasionally heard hints from two of my
uncles that they had come into contact with a saint and a
hero – John Maclean.[5] The most intellectual of my relations
was a sceptic and Socialist (my uncle in Jordanhill, Alex
Nicolson). Apart from his dangerous opinions, he appeared a
better man than all my religious acquaintance. I never read
tracts in Gaelic (or Seceder tracts at all), but constant sermon-
ising made me very familiar with Seceder metaphysics and
imagery and vocabulary. I have retained this knowledge (in
fact, at present I think I could make a very fine Seceder
sermon if my tongue were loosened with a little strong drink).
The result was that I paid extraordinary attention to sermons
for my age and I always rejoiced when I heard arguments
from outsiders, such as some of my uncles, that the sceptic
scientists were right and that the Seceders were ignorant
obscurantists.

All the same, about the age of ten I used to be perturbed
at times by atmospheric conditions which I feared might
indicate an imminent judgement. The millennium, good ortho-
dox Secederism, was not a certain assurance against that. So
even before I went to Portree School, at the age of 12, I was
beginning to shed my Secederism. At Portree I first learned
properly about Socialism and became one immediately before
I was thirteen. But the great Socialists for some time
appeared to my inmost mind as splendid Titanic humanitarians fighting a battle certainly lost. God was on the other
side. At this stage the Titanic humanitarian was everything to
me, even if he were certain to be wrong. By far the greatest
intellectual stirring in my teens was my first reading of

---

[4] See Question 28 in the *Shorter Catechism*.
[5] For John Maclean (1879–1923) see note on III: 11–12 in the
'Commentary'.

Shelley's *Prometheus [Unbound]* and for years Shelley was
almost everything to me. His music intoxicated me (now I
find it pretty thin). Thus, from about the age of thirteen, my
Secederism was rapidly ceasing to be even a fear to me and
atheism was becoming not merely an attractive lost cause.

I had from the earliest days been greatly affected by the
old 17th century Gaelic songs my grandmother (who died in
1923) sang, but the Gaelic poetry of Watson's *Bàrdachd*
which we read at school (mostly clan poetry) affected me not
at all, or very little, except a few things such as William Ross
and one or two of Duncan Bàn. At the time I had no time
for the heavily adjectival stuff of which we got a plethora.
For instance I disliked 'Allt an t-Siùcair' (MacDonald)
though after my school days, in the university, I came to
realise the wonderful sensuous richness of it. I liked Virgil
and Horace (odes) very much. Not much the *Eclogues* but
the *Aeneid* and *Georgics* very much. But history and socialism
were my main interests and I think there was much of this
in my enthusiasm for Shelley. Keats I was more critical of,
but liked 'Hyperion' immensely, also the Milton I read. I
disliked Shakespeare except the great tragedies (and I disliked
much even of them) but I considered the sonnets the greatest
things in all English poetry. Of French poetry I did not read
enough to have any opinion at this stage.

At[6] the university for the first three years I kept much to
myself. I did not know Caird or Davie until my last year. I
went to the Labour club, disliked the minutiae of it, but had
a tremendous contempt for the 'bourgeois decadents' who
crowded the literary societies. I retained[7] my main likes but
now[8] read much Gaelic poetry, especially MacDonald and
MacIntyre, and all the rest from the early 17th century
onward, Mary Macleod particularly. Her music interested
me. From about 16 I had been writing verse, mostly in
English, but some in Gaelic and I had a suitcase (small one)
full of it. I never published it or showed it to anyone. About
the age of 20 or 21 I destroyed it all except 'Dàin do Eimhir'
I, written when I was about 19. Much of this contained

---

[6] Paragraph division in original.
[7] Word unclear. Could just be 'realised'.
[8] Word unclear.

competent exercises à la Eliot. I never did take much to Eliot,
but found that I was dropping into his style. (Most of the rest
of my early verse was bad Shelleyan-Keatsian-Words-
worthian). I always was fascinated by a few of the great
passages in the *Prelude* but not by the rest of Wordsworth. I
was also contrary. I refused to give Eliot the twaddling
homage of the university literary societies and to Donne I
gave a very qualified admiration (though I read all his verse).
I was not interested in his religious contortions but his style
struck something similar in myself. I think the twaddle of the
Grierson days, when no junior member of the University
English staff could speak about anything without mentioning
Donne, sickened me. I liked Marvell immensely, still do. At
present I rate Donne as a middling poet and find frigidity
where I used to find feeling and intellect suffused.

I had not read anything of Grieve until I met Davie and
Caird late in my fourth year. I immediately recognised the
lyrics of *Sangschaw* and *Penny Wheep* as supreme. I regarded
them in much the same way as I regarded the greatest things
of Blake's, things completely new and unbelievable. I still do
that. There is nothing on earth like the greatest of those
lyrics. I myself do not despair of yet being able if I choose[9] to
write poems in Gaelic like Yeats's middle and later stuff or
Shakespeare's sonnets, but Grieve's greatest lyrics are always
a miracle and mystery to me. Of course they don't influence
my own work. They are completely 'magic' and unable to be
emulated. I think you exaggerate Grieve's influence on my
style. He has very little and it is very superficial but he
constantly stirs me emotionally and intellectually. I am not
one of Hugh's sons in poetry. In fact I think the vast gulf of
difference between his mental set up and mine makes that
impossible. I am a man of obsessions, more like Yeats, whom
I despise. I don't think I have W.B.'s contemptible neuroses.

Where[10] the hell did you get the idea that Auden etc. have
meant anything to me? When I first read a little of the crowd
(about 1934) I was willing to agree that they were probably
good fellows but very poor poets. And now I think them
contemptible as fellows and as poets. I have never been able

---

[9] Possibly 'chose'.

[10] Paragraph division in original.

to memorise a single line of any of them and I take away poems by Yeats, Grieve and even Eliot and Pound whole. I think your finding of this influence in me is like your accusations of my socialism or communism as being of the Gollancz brand, which I think nonsense. I had exactly the same feelings at 13 as I have now. I was as much of a communist then. It is not an intellectual phase with me and what I read about it matters little.[11]

What I have of literary background is mainly Gaelic. MacDonald, Ross, MacIntyre, the old song stuff, Livingston slightly, Neil Macleod not at all. He is just a symbol in 'The Cuillin'. But Mary MacPherson a great deal. A huge deal of her stuff is just comical in its padding but there is a great deal of extremely moving clean-cut stuff. Strong, tender feeling. She has influenced 'The Cuillin' quite a lot, especially the expressions of blood kinship are not unlike things in Mary e.g. 'mo chàirdean is mo chuideachd fhìn iad'[12] etc., etc. In fact the most easily distinguished stylistic influences in 'The Cuillin' are those of MacDonald (e.g. the opening of Parts I and II) and those of Mary MacPherson appearing *passim*, in simple expressions of simple feeling.

I have already written a devil of a screed but I shall send more if you wish it later. As for tracts etc., I myself have never read any, but look at the *Free Presbyterian Magazine* (published weekly, I think by the *Northern Chronicle*, Inverness) and the *Shorter Catechism* in Gaelic. There is a memoir with sermons of Rev. Neil Cameron, the great pontiff of the Seceders. He died some years ago, a horrible person, but of a distinguished appearance and commanding personality (probably the *Northern Chronicle* does this too but I am not sure). Of course the Seceders have their theology and imagery in common with one wing of the Free Church (1843 onwards) who had Gaelic ministers like Kennedy of Redcastle, MacDonald of Ferintosh (the 'Apostle of the North'). I suppose sermons by those chaps in English and in Gaelic are somewhere preserved in book form. I shall try to think of some more and especially of particular books.

---

[11] One page and a half, of political rather than literary interest, is omitted here. The following paragraph division is original.
[12] See MacLean 1999: 80.

Dugald Buchanan 'Là a' Bhreitheanais' ('The Day of Judgement') gives a good idea of Seceder cosmic imagery. It is a very great poem.[13]

As to the Secederism, I did not substitute 'bourgeois' for 'devil' because even before I was thirteen my real sympathies were with the Devil. I was never a 'converted' seceder who had experienced 'conviction of sin, repentance into life, effectual calling, justification, adoption and santification'[14] as Muir probably was in some ways. I had experienced conviction of sin and still do, but not against a Seceder God or any other God but merely against my own aspirations. In my teens those were Shelleyan aspirations in the main. Before 12 or 13, when I was a 'Seceder', I was merely a child 'adherent', frequently experiencing what the Seceders call 'slavish fear' of the literal burning pit. So Portree school only confirmed a sort of anti-Secederism latent in my childhood and made it quasi-Promethean or Shelleyan. Yes, my Promethean view of Socialism is an inversion of the career of the 'saved' in the sense that it was a justification of the 'lost', 'damned' Promethean. I had to find a humanist, hence Promethean, substitute. I have never been on the side of the established angels. I was probably more like you in my teens than now, because in my teens my Socialism would have repudiated the 'class war' utterly. My later Communism or Socialism is probably a fortifying, or rather restatement, of the Promethean, non-class war, boyish socialism, in the light of my experience of the actualities of life.

I[15] shall deal with your points as they come. I took Honours English instead of history (at which I was better in school) because I hoped some day to write a book on Shelley. Hence, I think, my English verse. It became pseudo-Eliotan in my later years at the university (it had been even pseudo-Keatsian-Shelleyan-Wordsworthian for a while) because I fairly soon discovered (but did not admit to myself) a distaste for the unsubstantial diffuseness of Shelley. I liked Horace

---

[13] End of first letter. The remainder of the 'Autobiographical Sketch' is taken from the letter immediately following, starting halfway through the second paragraph on page 6.

[14] For the latter part of this quote see Question 32 in the *Shorter Catechism*.

[15] Paragraph division in the original.

in Latin, the odes especially. I came to like the language of
the great Shakespearean tragedies and Webster very much,
also the 'Jacobean grace', Ben Jonson, Suckling, etc., etc.
Curiously enough, the influence of Donne came very late,
and many years after I had read Donne. It is, I think, in
'Eimhir' II, written in my third year at the University, 1932. I
depreciated it in my letter so as to keep you from exag-
gerating it, but I hear it much in 'Reic Anama' ('Eimhir'
XIV), 'Eimhir' XLV, and even in LVII as you say. (By the
way I now see the germ of LVII was Yeats's 'Where had her
sweetness gone?')[16] Somehow I have come back to Donne,
after my natural rebellion against the sickening emphasis on
him in Edinburgh in Grierson's day.

As to innovation in Gaelic verse forms, I have not thought
of that, but I can think of no parallel for the rhythm of
'Eimhir' II, 'Eimhir' IV, 'Tràighean' ('Eimhir' XLII). Also
the 'Aigeach',[17] I think, is in a new stanza form, as [are]
many other lyrics (including LVII as Deorsa,[18] a connoisseur
in such [matters], has pointed out). Also, there are absolutely
new stanza forms in 'Craobh nan Teud' and, I think, in
'Coilltean Ratharsair'. The general form of 'The Cuillin',
which appears modified as the basis of many of the 'Eimhir'
lyrics (e.g. 'Coin is Madaidhean-allaidh' and 'Na Samhlaidhean') had been used by Livingston in his longer poems,
which I had not read when I wrote 'The Cuillin'. I misled you
in my reference to Eliot. I did take to him stylistically but
reacted against his attitudes or attitudinising. I would now
say Pound and Eliot I have always liked in one way or
another but not Auden, Day Lewis, Herbert Read. Naturally
I also liked much Hardy and Housman. But I cannot see
any of Eliot's influence on my Gaelic verse, nor Pound's.
Hardy and Housman are perhaps in 'Ban-ghàidheal'. But
you were right on Donne.

As to Grieve, I admit tremendous emotional and intellectual influence but not stylistic, except in superficial points

---

[16] See introductory note to poem LVII in the *Commentary*.
[17] See the extended passage in Part V of 'An Cuilithionn' (MacLean
1999: 96ff.) and footnote on p. 151.
[18] George Campbell Hay.

like perhaps 'mar chunnaic Marlowe' etc.[19] As to his
early lyrics, I'll not write like them. Who has and who will?
As Davie has pointed out, most of the great lyrics are on
'marginal themes', very foreign to my obsessions, but there
are many times when I think that in no language have I read
such completely magical breath-taking poetry. I liked
Verlaine very much but I fancy that in one or two places
Baudelaire has influenced me stylistically, the 'sous la griffe
effroyable de Dieu'[20] manner. Of course Yeats, but I don't
think stylistically except, as you have already pointed out, in
'Eimhir LI' 'My prudence said...'. I did not read Yeats at the
university at all and only read him in bulk about 1936, and
it is only in the last two years that his poetry has become one
of my obsessions. I now read and re-read him.

Did I tell you that in my last two years at the university I
had come to regard Shakespeare and Blake as the greatest
English poets? I still hold to that. For a third I think I would
now put Yeats. But I don't regard the greatest of his poetry
as [being as] great as the greatest of Grieve. I put Blake and
Grieve together, though they are very different. Don't worry
about the Gollancz remark. The Gollancz / Left Book Club
fortified a position I had already taken up, probably to a
greater degree than I care to admit. The Muir parallel I can't
agree to, as I was never a 'converted' Seceder by a long chalk.
I cannot really remember any time when I really accepted
Secederism. But I agree the Socialism was important in
casting out just what there was of Secederism.[21]

Finally as to the influences, the chief stylistically
are MacDonald, Ross, Iain Lom, Mary MacLeod, Mary
MacPherson, Livingston and 17th century songs. (By the
way, one of my aunts has even more of them than my
grandmother had.) The English and Lowland influences are
far [less important] stylistically. They probably are in something like this order: Donne, Hardy, Housman, Yeats,
Grieve, Wordsworth, and, perhaps more important than any
other English influence, Shakespeare's sonnets. As to 'foreign'
influences I think only Baudelaire and Virgil. For instance I
can hear the influence of Shakespeare's sonnets in 'Eimhir'

---

[19] See 'An Cuilithionn' Part II. (MacLean 1999: 80.)
[20] The quotation is not quite accurate. See note to XIX: 39–40.
[21] Two sentences omitted.

XXIII, the concert poem. It has rounded cadences that have come from God knows where. I have in one 'Eimhir' poem accurately, I think, enumerated the four chief emotional dynamics in my life: 'an t-adhbhar mòr agus a' bhàrdachd, / an t-Eilean àlainn 's an nighean ruadh'.[22] I am afraid the last has been far more important than you or anybody else has ever imagined. By far my greatest period was the last three months of 1939, when I saw her very often, and when I was exhilarated at what I thought was the beginning of the suicide of European capitalism.

This has again turned out to be a long selfish screed. I still hope you will write that critique. No one else can do it...

---

[22] XII: 3–4.

COMMENTARY

The following commentary is rather more than a series of explanatory notes about places and people whose names crop up in the poems. It is intended to accompany the reader through the sequence, indicating anticipations and echoes, recurring words and themes, so as to render more visible its gradually emerging shape. To this extent, the best thing would be to read it from beginning to end, in parallel with the poems, though hopefully it will also be of help when only single poems are consulted. Full use has been made of the standard reference works, both the *Micropaedia* and the larger version of the *Encyclopedia Britannica*, the *Dictionary of National Biography* (where the 'Missing Persons' volume proved particularly helpful), and *The Companion to Gaelic Scotland*. Unless otherwise indicated, English translations are reproduced from MacLean's 1999 collection.

MacLean's **metrical practice** in the 'Dàin do Eimhir' is relatively conservative. Generally speaking he eschews free verse, favouring a basic line of three or four stresses with a variable number of intervening unstressed syllables. Some thirty years afterwards he would write that

> ...however slack the rope of auditory shape may be, there nevertheless has to be some kind of tightrope onto which the poet goes. I am not prepared to allow to the word 'rhythm' the vagueness sanctioned by much contemporary theory in Britain, Europe and America. Metre does not make poetry, but I am not satisfied that poetry can exist without it.[1]

He makes abundant use of end-rhyme, as well as of rhyme between the final stressed vowel in a line and an internal stressed vowel in the line immediately following, which is known in Gaelic as *aicill*. Faithful to Gaelic practice, his rhyming takes no account of the following consonant or

---

[1] MacLean 1985: 113.

consonants. To this extent, it might be more precisely spoken of in English as 'assonance'. He on occasion rhymes closed and open forms of long 'o', but not closed and open forms of long 'e'.

In a letter to Douglas Young dated September 11th 1941, however, MacLean lays claim to his place as an innovator, acknowledging a kinship with Livingston,[2] while at the same time denying any direct influence:

> As to innovation in Gaelic verse forms, I have not thought of that, but I can think of no parallel for the rhythm of 'Eimhir' II, 'Eimhir' IV, 'Tràighean' ('Eimhir' XLII). Also the 'Aigeach',[3] I think, is in a new stanza form as [are] many other lyrics (including LVII as Deòrsa,[4] a connoisseur in such [matters] has pointed out). Also, there are absolutely new stanza forms in 'Craobh nan Teud' and, I think, in 'Coilltean Rath-arsair'. The general form of 'The Cuillin', which appears modified as the basis of many of the 'Eimhir' lyrics (e.g. 'Coin is Madaidhean-allaidh' and 'Na Samh-laidhean') had been used by Livingston in his longer poems, which I had not read when I wrote 'The Cuillin'.

Douglas Young had evidently compared MacLean's metrical practice in Gaelic with Gerard Manley Hopkins's in English, for in a letter dated March 30th 1943 MacLean writes:

> I am not sure of your 'sprung rhythm' remarks. In fact I don't think it 'sprung' at all, and I think you exag-gerate its looseness, but that is a minor matter. You know I don't think Gaelic metre (Scottish) has ever been

---

[2] The Islay born poet William Livingston (Uilleam Mac Dhunlèibhe, 1808–1870). There are two essays on him in *Ris a' Bhruthaich*: 'The poetry of William Livingston' and 'Clach air a' Chàrn – Uilleam Mac Dhùn-Léibhe'. See MacLean 1985: 134–161.

[3] 10 stanzas of this poem were published in 1940 in the periodical *New Alliance* (Vol. 1 No. 3 (May 1940): 5). Part V of 'An Cuilithionn', MacLean 1999: 98–104, has 9. The completest version, with 14 stanzas, is to be found in the original version of 'An Cuilithionn' in NLS Acc. 12022.

[4] George Campbell Hay (1915–1984), poet in Gaelic, Scots and English, dedicatee of MacLean's poem 'Craobh nan Teud' ('The Tree of Strings'). See Byrne 2000.

adequately dealt with, because no Gaelic poetry is
either purely 'syllabic' or purely stressed, the speech
stresses being preserved and strong in so-called syllabic
metres. You know I don't always mark the necessary
colloquial elisions when I write Gaelic. But that is a minor
matter.

Despite those last two sentences, in MacLean's poetry,
contrary to colloquial usage, a final 'schwa' syllable often
requires to be given syllabic value for purposes of scansion.[5]
The remarks made concerning 'An Cuilithionn' in his next
letter (dated April 9th 1943) are also illuminating as regards
the 'Dàin do Eimhir':

> I had thought that I had on the whole erred on the side
> of conservatism metrically, always remembering that I
> hate the heavily assonated and artificially 'stressed'
> Gaelic poetry of the 19th century and looked back
> towards the old syllabic metres with their dependence
> on speech stress, although I generally cut down the
> assonance very deliberately, but I don't think mine is at
> any time what the English mean by 'sprung' rhythm.
> At any rate my rhythms are never at any time anything
> as loose as Livingston's are normally...

Indications of metrical and rhyming patterns are given at
the end of the notes on individual poems, not least in the
hope that these may be both informative and valuable for
readers with little or no knowledge of Gaelic.

In estimating the number of 'real' stresses in a line, priority
has generally been given to those words which bear a stress
under normal linguistic conditions. It might, however, be
more appropriate to analyse MacLean's practice in terms
analogous to those of the English iambic pentameter, where
each line has five 'notional' stresses only four of which are
normally realised, and where unstressed syllables and particles can be 'promoted' to stressed status because of their
position in the line. Heretical as it may seem, an influence of
this sort cannot be discounted, given MacLean's profound
knowledge and appreciation of English poetry. But no con-

---

[5] I am indebted to Dr John MacInnes for this observation.

fident answers can be offered for such interrogatives until a
thorough and competent study of the prosody of MacLean's
poetry has been undertaken.

While MacLean's account of his own metrical practice is
convincing and fundamentally accurate, the same cannot be
said of the claims made regarding his **diction** in a letter to
Douglas Young dated April 20th 1943:

> As to your 'note on the making'[6] the only points I noted
> that might need adjusting are that you exaggerate the
> 'difficulty' of my Gaelic. Indeed I use hardly more than
> ['half' scored out] a dozen words at most that won't be
> at once understood by a crofter of average intelligence
> and knowledge of Gaelic. Hence you also exaggerate the
> 'atrophy' of the Gaelic of Gaelic-speaking Skye and my
> work of 'revitalisation' and on the score of language I
> certainly have not done 'something unattempted for
> generations in Gaelic'...

One detects a strain of idealism in MacLean's estimate of
the accessibility of his poetry, as well as a modest wish to
distance himself from Young's more outspoken words of
praise. John MacInnes has written that 'A large part of
Somhairle MacGill-Eain's greatness as a poet lies in his
restorative work: this can properly be celebrated as a triumph
of regeneration', insisting, on the next page of the same essay,
that

> Simply by reading an English translation, no one could
> ever guess at the nature of MacGill-Eain's Gaelic
> diction. There is nothing very difficult – nor, in purely
> linguistic terms, anything very egregious – in the
> English. By contrast the original Gaelic exhibits vir-
> tually an entire spectrum of language. Transparent
> simplicity is to be found side by side with a formidable
> density of verbal texture. A full linguistic commentary
> must await another occasion; for the moment it is

---

[6] As printed in 1943, Young's prefatory 'Note... on the Making of this
Book' includes no reference to the points raised in this letter by
MacLean.

enough to say that practically all the available registers
of Gaelic, ranging in quality from the demotic to the
arcane, are included at some point or another. There are
times, naturally, when the ordinary reader requires
industry combined with ingenuity to unravel the
meaning.[7]

Eimhir is the wife of Cuchulainn, the principal hero of the
Ulster Cycle in early Irish literature. The spelling Emer has
given rise to an erroneous contemporary pronunciation
without lenited 'm'. 'Tochmarc Emire' or 'The Wooing of
Emer', existing in several versions, the oldest of which
dates back to the eighth century, tells how her father,
Forgall Manach ('the wily') initially rejects Cuchulainn as a
suitor. Returning from his training in Scotland under the
female warrior Scathach, Cuchulainn slaughters Forgall's
followers, prompting him to commit suicide, before de-
parting triumphantly with Eimhir. 'Serglige Con Culainn',
known in English as both 'The Wasting Sickness of
Cuchulainn' and 'The Only Jealousy of Emer', tells of
Eimhir's plans to kill her rival for Cuchulainn's love, Fand.
Realising, however, the depth of Fand's attachment, she
resolves to give up her claim to the hero. Showing equal
magnanimity, Fand then returns to her own husband
Manannan, and the affair is magically forgotten.[8] The tale
is a compilation of different versions of a single story, from
which a certain clumsiness of narrative movement results.
Gantz describes it as 'part myth, part history, part soap
opera'. Bragela in Macpherson's *Poems of Ossian* (1760–3)
is based on Emer.[9] She also plays a major part in Yeats's
drama *The Only Jealousy of Emer* (1919), further redacted
in a prose version, *Fighting the Waves*, 'so arranged as to
admit of many dancers and to be immediately intelligible
to an average theatrical audience'.[10]

---

[7] Ross and Hendry 1986: 137–138.
[8] Sydney Goodsir Smith devotes the fifteenth elegy of his *Under the Eildon
Tree* sequence to this incident (Smith 1975: 173–174).
[9] McKillop 1998: 160–161, 338–339; Cross and Slover 1936: 153–171,
176–198 and Gantz 1981: 153–178.
[10] Yeats 1982: v.

I

The core of this poem consists of its three central sections (lines 5–17), written in Raasay in August or September 1931. It is a unique survival from the body of verse MacLean wrote in his teens. He wrote to Douglas Young from London on September 7th 1941: 'From about 16 I had been writing verse mostly in English but some in Gaelic and I had a suitcase (small one) full of it. I never published it or showed it to anyone. About the age of 20 or 21 I destroyed it all except "Dàn do Eimhir" I, written when I was about 19. Much of this contained competent exercises à la Eliot.'

Hendry sees the girl in this poem as 'a personification of the ideal object of desire, perhaps a symbol of his love for Raasay, for the Western Isles, his love specifically for a people, a culture, a way of life, a language which is disappearing'.[11] It can be read as part of a narrative, with a situation (Eimhir is indifferent to his love for her) and a setting (the speaker is steering a boat across the Sound of Raasay). The beloved is identified with her 'music' ('do chiùil', line 8). In lines 14–15, there is a brief flurry of activity which, however, cannot galvanize the overriding atmosphere of torpor and indolence. Editor's translation.

1   The opening and closing quatrains were added in December 1939, qualifying this unique survival from MacLean's *juvenilia* to stand at the head of the 'Dàin do Eimhir'. The beloved is addressed directly at the very start, identified by her hair, which will become a *leitmotif* of the sequence. The paired colour adjectives suggest a precise desire on MacLean's part to blur any distinctions subsequently implied between the different Eimhirs. See note to VI: 5–8 for a broader review of colour adjectives occurring in the sequence.

In a list of poems drawn up at the beginning of May 1941 (for which see also VI), a deleted version of this line reads 'A nighean ruadh a' chùil òir'. Whether this represents the original form, or was merely a slip of memory on the poet's part, is impossible to tell. The line is taken up and extended

---

[11] Ross and Hendry 1986: 21.

in the opening of IV ('A nighean a' chùil bhuidhe, throm-
bhuidh, òr-bhuidh').

2 Besides the motif of her hair, the added quatrains
introduce a concept crucial to the sequence, the 'tòir', a
pursuit or search. It is not entirely clear what the speaker is
seeking: Eimhir's love, an active expression for his political
commitment, or realisation as a poet. There is a possible
further ambivalence: has his search no hope of reaching her,
or is she diverting him from his true aims? (XIX: 26–28)
Cf. Yeats's 'Words':

> I had this thought a while ago,
> 'My darling cannot understand
> What I have done, or what would do
> In this blind bitter land.'[12]

5 The Sound of Raasay, whose width varies from 1 to 5¼
miles, lies between MacLean's native island and the east side
of Skye.
8 Here 'ciùil' (genitive of 'ceòl') echoes 'a' chùil' of the
opening line, as if music and head of hair were related
elements of the loved one's beauty.
10 At 443 metres, Dun Caan is the highest point on
Raasay, commanding fine views of the Hebrides, Wester
Ross and north west Inverness-shire. Its characteristic, sliced-
off top is visible from a considerable distance.
11 MacLean glosses 'sliabh' as 'moor grass (a sense not
found in lexica)' (letter to Douglas Young, February 22nd
1941).
17 The awakening battle reads like a hint of the two wars,
the Spanish Civil War and the Second World War, which will
constitute the historical backdrop to the sequence. It may
also be a reference to the conflict within the speaker.
21 The insertion of a single word 'glè' provides a sense of
closure, highlighting both the poet's isolation and his awareness of Eimhir's indifference to his suffering.

Five quatrains (though the second has an additional line)
with a basic pattern of four stresses per line (though even

---

[12] Yeats 1983: 90.

lines in the added stanzas tend to three). End-rhyme in all lines, changing with each quatrain.

II

Written in Edinburgh in May 1932, in its intellectual precision and punctiliousness, and its hair-splitting play with abstract concepts ('ciall', 'gràdh', 'tuigse', 'gaol'[13]), this poem betrays the influence of Donne and the English Metaphysical poets, so much in vogue when MacLean studied English Literature at Edinburgh University. He explained to Young in a letter dated September 11th 1941 that 'Curiously enough the influence of Donne came very late and many years after I had read Donne. It is, I think, in "Eimhir" II, written in my third year at the University, 1932.' The theme of internal division achieves a positive resolution, belied by what ensues in the remainder of the sequence. Such ill-placed optimism can seem an indication of immaturity. See XXIII for a further, unsuccessful attempt at synthesis. The poem outlines an internal dialogue, perhaps an instance of 'a' chòmhail / a th' agam rium fhèin' (XLVIII: 9–10)[14] and curiously reminiscent, in its way, of the *psychomachia* of medieval drama.

The **title** brings together two nouns, 'ciall' and 'gràdh', 'reason' and 'love' respectively, but in the vocative form (preceded by 'a' with no apostrophe), where they both function as endearments addressed to the loved one, an effect which cannot be rendered adequately in English.

2 Gaelic idiom is responsible for the misleading impression that reason can be reconciled with love.
4 It is as if the speaker ought to be able to read deeper truths in Eimhir's face. See the note to IX for discussion of MacLean's Platonism.
6 The reason for love is an untraceable third party, the original pair being constituted by the poet's eye and the loved one's face.

---

[13] Rendered on this occasion by MacLean as 'reason', 'love', 'intellect' and 'love' respectively.
[14] 'the meeting / that I have with myself'. Dwelly also gives the meaning 'interview' (s.v. 'còmhdhail').

7   Note the careful parallelism between this and the preceding stanza.

8   Division or 'roinneadh' is a major preoccupation of the sequence, which closes with the paradoxical awakening of 'seann roinneadh ùr 'nam fheòil-sa' (LX: 15–16).[15] See XVIII, XXII and the 'knife poem', XLV. Here the division has already occurred.

11–12   Division uproots the self, producing instability and a sense of homelessness or alienation.

15   MacLean's English version does not do justice to the ambivalences of the Gaelic, which could also mean 'a struggle took place with [against] my reason' but also, of course 'with [against] my beloved'.

18   Inability either to integrate psychologically or fully to reject his experience of love characterises the poet's situation throughout the 'Dàin do Eimhir'.

20   If the poet's intellect is on the 'elegant' side, is his love therefore inelegant, unaesthetic?

21   The remaining poems in the sequence will suggest that the 'còmhla bhaoth' is indestructible.

22   The intervention of 'mo thuigse' renders a synthesis possible, at least in prospect. It has a very different role in XXII.

Eight stanzas of three lines with between two and four stresses. End rhyme is replaced by the hypnotic effect of recurring terms such as 'ciall', 'gaol' and even 'taobh'.

III

The conflict between love and political commitment outlined in this poem underpins the entire sequence. Written in Portree in November or December 1936, the poem was inspired by 'a Skye girl, to whom [MacLean] had been strongly attracted in 1934–36, but the circumstances and his feelings had soon changed... [she] never had reason to suspect that MacLean had a strong, if transient feeling for

---

[15] 'an old new division... in my flesh. (Editor's translation.)

her'.[16] The much longer IV expands upon the basic conflict expressed here.

3 Though consistently translated 'suffering' by MacLean, 'allaban' is more commonly rendered as 'wandering, deviation'.

4 The word 'millean' recurs in the first star poem of the sequence, XVII (see also L). The wonders of the material universe are placed on the same level as Christ's life. Neither can compete with Eimhir's beauty.

5–6 The 'aisling bhaoth' referred to is presumably the Celtic Twilight debasing of Scottish Gaelic culture at the hands of a writer like William Sharp (who wrote under the pseudonym Fiona MacLeod, 1856–1905), and which can be traced back to the prose poems of James Macpherson (1736–96), which purported to be translations from the Gaelic originals of the legendary poet Ossian. For Derick Thomson 'The "Celtic Twilight" style derived from a false idea of Gaelic literature, which is objective, concrete and free from mysticism. In place of the robust heroes of Gaelic mythology and tales, "Celtic Twilight" gives us the rather wan and ethereal young men and women who appear in Pre-Raphaelite paintings.'[17] MacLean may also have in mind the versions of Gaelic folksongs prepared by Marjory Kennedy-Fraser (1857–1930), with the assistance of Kenneth Macleod, whom she had met in 1908, the first volume of which came out in 1909 as *Songs of the Hebrides*. In an essay first published in 1970,[18] he writes that 'In 1920 the "image" of Gaelic song was to almost all articulate Gaels only as mediocre Victorian Gothic is to the Gothic of the 12th or 13th centuries', and that 'The Celtic Twilight of the 1890s and its cultural product, the *Songs of the Hebrides*, were to the realities of Gaelic song poetry as Victorian Gothic is to the North French cathedrals'.[19] A scornful quatrain on Kennedy-Fraser is among the unpublished items transcribed by George Campbell Hay:

[16] Ross and Hendry 1986: 21–22.
[17] Thomson 1994: 265.
[18] In *Memoirs of a Modern Scotland* ed. Karl Miller (now MacLean 1985: 106–119).
[19] MacLean 1985: 107.

Soraidh le Nic Ualraig-Friseal,
bean uasal ise gun chron;
spoth i ar Ceòlraidh lùthmhor
's chuir i siùcair air an lot.[20]

In a congratulatory letter on MacDiarmid's translation of
the 'Birlinn' by Alasdair Mac Mhaighstir Alasdair, written
from Raasay on April 1st 1935,[21] MacLean revels to think
'What a confusion MacDonald and your translation must be
to our Twilightists and their latter-day successors!' He adds
that 'Very likely those who hailed Mrs Kennedy-Fraser's
fooleries as good poetic reproductions of their Gaelic originals will dislike your translations. They will also dislike
Alexander MacDonald if they care to read him.' Kennedy-
Fraser is further mentioned at the end of the satirical piece
'Road to the Isles', whose speaker promises that 'boillsgear
follais aig gach céilidh: / càrnar leam tùis mar dh'fheumar /
air altairean Khennedy-Fraser, / seinnear duanagan...'[22]
8 Though MacLean translates 'head', 'cuailean' properly
means 'hair'. He consistently avoids 'falt', preferring the
phonetically related terms 'cùl' and 'cuailean'.
11–12 Vladimir Ilich Lenin (originally Ulyanov) (1870–
1924) was the founder of the Russian Communist Party. He
inspired and directed the Bolshevik Revolution of 1917 and
ruled the new Soviet state until his death, though hampered
by serious health problems after 1922. The political philosophy he formulated, which went under the name of
Marxism-Leninism, was the governing ideology of the Soviet
Union and its satellite states until the crisis of the later
1980s.
It was he, along with Litvinov, who in 1917 named the

---

[20] NLS MS 26722, 51r. I am grateful to Dr Michel Byrne for bringing
these lines to my attention. They may be translated: 'Farewell to
Kennedy-Fraser, / an untarnished gentlewoman; / she gelded our vigo-
rous Muses / and put sugar on the wound.'

[21] The letter carries no indication of the year, which can, however, be
arrived at by deduction.

[22] MacLean 1943: 95. The lines are translated on p. 103 'I will shine at
every "ceilidh", heap incense, as is fitting, on the altars of Kennedy-
Fraser. I'll sing ditties...' This piece was among those included in *17
Poems for 6d.*

Scottish revolutionary John Maclean[23] as the first Bolshevik consul in Great Britain, based in Scotland. The poet felt a personal connection with this working-class hero and martyr, having 'occasionally heard hints from two of my uncles that they had come into contact with a saint and a hero – John Maclean' (letter to Young, September 7th 1941). MacLean's treatment of Lenin may well have been influenced by MacDiarmid's example. The older poet draws an explicit parallel between Christ and the Russian leader in his 'First Hymn to Lenin', expounds Lenin's achievements to a relative working in the mills in 'The Seamless Garment' and, in 'The Skeleton of the Future', evokes 'The eternal lightning of Lenin's bones'.[24] There is a reference to 'tuigse Lenin' (there translated 'the judgement of Lenin') in Part III of 'An Cuilithionn', next to 'taobh dearg Chrìosda', though the poet is less than sanguine about the possibilities for harmonising the two teachings: 'chan fhaicear an dithis còmhla / a dh'aindeoin farsaingeachd na mòintich; / chan fhaicear ann an aon àit' iad / ach air mullach lom nan àrd bheann'.[25]

MacLean confesses, in the letter mentioned above, that 'the great Socialists for some time appeared to my inmost mind as splendid Titanic humanitarians fighting a battle certainly lost. God was on the other side. At this stage the Titanic humanitarian was everything to me even if he were certain to be wrong.' While it is hard to conceive of Lenin as in any sense a loser, the words indicate an interest in the

---

[23] John Maclean (1879–1923), grandson of a crofter evicted from Mull during the Highland Clearances and of migrants to industrial Strathclyde, a schoolteacher who held open classes in Marxism and campaigned against military and industrial conscription during the First World War on a pacifist basis, was imprisoned for his beliefs in 1916 and again in 1918. While before the war his closest political contacts were with followers of Trotsky, his championing of soldiers' and workers' councils led to his appointment as first Bolshevik consul for Britain in the aftermath of the October Revolution. The battle for a distinctive Scottish Communist Party which he waged in 1920 was, however, lost to a coalition which, with Lenin's backing, formed the Communist Party of Great Britain. Maclean died of pneumonia in November 1923.

[24] MacDiarmid 1993: I, 297, 311, 386.

[25] 'the red side of Christ'; 'The two may not be seen together / for all the expanse of the morass / they are not to be seen in one place / except on the bare tops of the high mountains.' MacLean 1999: 90–91.

concept of the Christ-like heroic individual who can function as a saviour for humankind. Writing to Young on October 27th 1940, MacLean explains, in connection with the above-cited passage from 'An Cuilithionn', that 'I am not at all interested in "great minds" of the emotionless contemplative types, especially the scientist. Christ and Lenin to me are only almost random examples of great minds realising emotionally as well as intellectually the "miseries that will not let them rest".'

The poet was certainly more concerned with the fate of ordinary working people than with any cult of a great leader: 'I feel there is something which people like Muir, Grieve, seceder evangelists, myself etc. have experienced that neither you nor Davie nor MacIntyre[26] have experienced, which is poverty or nearness to it. Therefore it is not Stalin whom I am really thinking of, but the millions in Russia and elsewhere to whom he symbolises hope, no matter how many fine "bewildered patriots" he sends to Siberia, no matter how many Kulaks he has "liquidated". Hence Lenin, Stalin and Dimitroff now mean more to me than Prometheus and Shelley did in my teens.' (Letter to Douglas Young, September 11th 1941).

Coming after religion, the marvels of astronomy and cultural fashion, politics takes the crucial place in the list of concerns which Eimhir's beauty casts into shadow. MacLean makes no secret, here or in his correspondence with Young, about his admiration for the achievements of the Bolshevik Revolution. He perhaps had fewer opportunities than other Western intellectuals to acquire a balanced understanding of the grim realities of life in 1930s Russia. While he approved of Young's initiative in applying to MacCaig's Trust for a subsidy towards the cost of publishing his verse, MacLean doubted whether 'they would publish much of my stuff, because of religious and political objections which they, as trustees of such a fund, would have to face. And if such "objectionable" matter, that is, practically the whole of "The

---

[26] MacLean has in mind the poet Edwin Muir and the philosopher George Davie. Robert Douglas McIntyre (1913–1998), son of a United Free Presbyterian minister, was Chairman of the SNP 1948–1956, and President 1958–1980. He was his party's first MP, winning the Motherwell election in 1945.

Cuillin" were eliminated, there would be little left except the Eimhir poems, and perhaps not all of them'.[27]

See also XIV: 2–3, XXXII: 7, and 'An Cuilithionn' Part V ('...Lenin an Ruisia, / ceann-uidhe nan sàr-bhreith')[28] and *passim*.

Three quatrains with a rhythm similar to ballad metre. End rhyme in the second and fourth lines of each stanza, with *aicill* in ll. 1–2 and 7–8. At the end of line 9, 'sgleò' echoes the rhyme of 'sgeòil' and 'òir' in the previous stanza.

IV

Written in Mull in March or April 1938, this poem is one of the pillars holding up the larger scale structure of the sequence. Joy Hendry states without qualification that 'The woman in "Gaoir na h-Eòrpa" ("Dàn" IV) is an Irish woman whom [MacLean] met in Edinburgh while attending a Celtic Congress in August 1937'.[29] Nessa Ní Sheaghdha (or O'Shea, later Mrs Doran) was working in the National Library of Scotland on texts subsequently published as *Leabhair ó Láimhsgríbhnibh* by the School of Celtic Studies of the Dublin Institute for Advanced Studies. Although MacLean felt 'irresistibly drawn' to her, he 'could never make any kind of advances', being 'under the mistaken impression that one of his greatest friends, who was responsible for the poet first meeting the woman in question, wanted to marry her himself'.[30]

Eimhir is addressed directly for the first time since I, in a series of questions to which the use of parallelism gives an effect of *crescendo*. III acknowledged her pre-eminence calmly, in an almost intimate tone. Here she is called upon to

---

[27] Though it would appear to have been written at a single sitting, the letter from which these lines are taken carries two dates: December 1st 1940 and, rather puzzlingly, February 1941.
[28] '...Lenin in Russia, / where great judgements go.' MacLean 1999: 104–105.
[29] According to Dr John MacInnes, it was Angus Matheson who introduced the two, on the platform at Waverley Station.
[30] Black 1999: xxxiii, Nicholson 1986, Ross and Hendry 1986: 22.

give her opinion as to whether it can be justified or not. The
poem contains the first references in the sequence to the
political situation on mainland Europe.

MacLean expressed on more than one occasion his
contempt for W. H. Auden and the English poets associated
with him (see notes to XV). Writing to MacDiarmid from
North Africa on February 23rd 1942, he comments that
recent work by Sydney Goodsir Smith, in both English and
Scots, 'marked a very great advance on his earlier stuff which
was so influenced by the contemptible verse of the Auden
clique and the (to me) unsuccessful aspirations of Dylan
Thomas and his followers of the surrealist or near-surrealist
type'. During the voyage out, he had found time to send
Goodsir Smith himself a detailed evaluation of the latter's
collection *Skail Wind.* 'I know you will not mind my
suggesting', he writes, 'that here and there in your earlier stuff
I saw the cloven hoof of Auden or Spender', adding that
'Poetically I am often jealous of Grieve, Yeats, Lorca, Valéry
and D. H. Lawrence but not of Eliot, Auden, Spender who
have neither great moral passion nor great sensibility but are
competent "mocking birds" '.[31]

Yet there may have been a greater similarity between
Auden's concerns and his own, during the run up to the
Second World War, than MacLean was willing to acknowledge. Anthony Hecht has written of the 'dilemmas' which
'are blown through' Auden's 1937 collection *On This Island*
'on a steady and ominous wind', dilemmas which he articulates as follows, and which have an unmistakable
pertinence to poem IV, as well as to the 'Dàin do Eimhir'
sequence in general·

How may one hope to enjoy, or even entertain the
possibility of, personal happiness in a world filled with
omens or actual instances of horror and danger? What,
indeed, is the proper relationship, if any, between one's
private and intimate life as a lover or a friend, and one's
social and civic life as a citizen, both of a nation and
of what may loosely be called Western civilization? The
answers to these questions were easy if one was, on the
one hand, a left-wing political activist, or, on the other,

---

[31] National Library of Scotland MS 26153 f8.

a poet in the Romantic tradition, but what if one were both?[32]

1 The accumulation of adjectives (for which see also note to 3) emphasises the abundance and heaviness of Eimhir's hair. Gaelic tradition in Scotland and Ireland is so rich in precedents for concentrating on this aspect of a woman's beauty, almost a commonplace of amorous poetry, that to single out any one example risks misleading. These lines from Uilleam Ros's song 'Oran air gaol na h-òighe do Chailein', which happen also to contain the compound 'òr-bhuidhe', are however typical:

> Bha falt cama-lùbach, bòidheach,
> Bachlach, òr-bhuidhe, 'na dhuail,
> Cas-bhuidhe, snìomhanach, fàinneach...[33]

2 The two elements, both auditory, competing for the poet's attention are her 'fonn' and the (presumably inaudible) 'gaoir'. Eimhir is singing. In I: 7 the poet spoke of her music.

3 Writing to Douglas Young on September 7th 1941, MacLean explains that while at school 'I had no time for the heavily adjectival stuff of which we got a plethora. For instance I disliked "Allt an t-Siùcair" (MacDonald) though after my school days, in the university, I came to realise the wonderful sensuous richness of it.' In a study of Mac Mhaighstir Alasdair's nature poetry,[34] Derick Thomson takes a more sympathetic view of the strings of adjectives which were a recurrent feature of Gaelic poetry until the 18th century and even after.

According to Angus MacLeod, though Mac Mhaighstir Alasdair 'has been blamed for starting this itemising characteristic of Gaelic poetry', such 'stringing of adjectives was in vogue long before his day'. MacLeod attempts to justify the practice as follows:

---

[32] Hecht 1993: 48.
[33] Calder 1937: 30, there translated as 'Her hair cross-looped, pretty, / Crook-like, golden, in curl, / Crisp-yellow, twisted ringlets...'.
[34] See Derick Thomson 'Mac Mhaighstir Alasdair's Nature Poetry and its Sources' in Thomson 1990: 99ff.

The restriction of the old bardic metres compelled the
bards to compress ideas within narrow limits; and the
simple device of expressing a thought by adding -*ach* to
a substantive was not without its temptations... This
piling of adjectives no doubt produces many tedious and
unmusical verses; certainly, it is often difficult to show
in English any differentiation between successive
epithets. But Gaelic poetry was composed for Gaelic
speakers, in the Gaelic manner, as in the Gaelic idiom...
when skilfully executed, each stroke adds some detail,
and is not mere repetition... One might raise similar
questions after an examination of the intricate designs
and elaborate decorations that adorn the pages of the
Book of Kells...[35]

MacLean himself was not above deploying the convention
(of which the accumulation of abstract nouns in the closing
lines of 'An Cuilithionn' may well be an extension[36]), here
and at XIV: 13, XV: 6–7 or XXII: 21–22.
4 The rest of the poem contradicts or corrects this
statement.
5 The parallelism of this and the following stanza ('An
tugadh... bhuamsa') is taken up in the fourth ('An cuireadh...
bhuamsa').
7 Though no names are given, it is tempting to read 'a'
bhrùid 's am meàirleach' as a reference to Hitler in
Germany and Mussolini in Italy. The definitive victory of
Franco and the nationalists in Spain did not take place until
about a year after this poem was written. In his memoir
of the poet, J. B. Caird interprets the line as referring quite
simply to Hitler.[37]
15–16 The October Revolution in Asturias, northern Spain,
broke out late in 1934 in response to the entry into the
government of the right-wing CEDA (Confederación Española
de Derechas Autónomas). Headed by the well-organised local
miners (among the best paid workers in Spain), it was
initially successful, until the Madrid government summoned

---

[35] MacLeod 1933: 28.
[36] MacLean 1999: 130.
[37] Caird 1995: 197.

Generals Goded and Franco to suppress it, with the help of
Moroccan and Foreign Legion troops. The brutality of the
reprisals which followed made civil war inevitable.[38]

MacLean evokes 'tuiteam nan Asturaidheach 'nan glòir'
in 'An Cuilithionn' Part II, addressing the rebels in terms not
dissimilar to those used here:

> A Dhia, nach fhaicinn cruas an dùbhlain
> air mill a' Chuilithinn a' tùirling!
> O fheara 's fheàrr air clàr an t-saoghail,
> ged a tha ur dìol-sa aognaidh,
> thug sibh nàire do na gruaidhean
> a dh'fhairich móralachd ur cruadail
> 's a dh'fhuiling cluinntinn mu 'r diachainn
> fo fhòirneart, cealgaireachd is briagan.[39]

17ff.   In this and the final stanza it is almost as if the poet
placed kisses and locks of hair in the pans of a balance,
weighing them against the other issues that demand his
attention. Note the parallelism of 'Dè bhiodh pòg... mar ris
gach' and 'Dè gach cuach... ris gach'.

18   Christ's precious blood was shed to save humanity,
as the blood of the Spanish miners has been shed in the
cause of justice and equality. 'Braon' / 'bruan' / 'bròn' is
another of the series of phonetically similar and often
semantically related word chains MacLean sets echoing
throughout the sequence (in this case see further XLII and
XLV).

19–20   This is a vague reference. But it is worth remembering that the date of the poem corresponds more or less to
the offensive launched by Franco's nationalists against
Republican positions on the Aragon front on March 7th.
Support from the air was crucial. Seventy miles were gained
in eight days, and positions which the Republican army had
held since August 1936 collapsed. Though Franco's troops

---

[38] Thomas 1977: 136ff.
[39] 'the fall of the Asturians in their glory... O God, that I would see the
steel of their challenge / descending on the masses of the Cuillin! / O best
men on the board of the earth, / though your dispensation is death-chill,
/ you brought shame to the cheeks / who felt the majesty of your
hardihood / and suffered to hear of your extremity / under violence,
deceit and lies.' MacLean 1999: 80–81.

did not push forward, the road to Barcelona was open, and a victory seemed near.[40]

21 'Cuach' forms a series with 'cùl' and 'cuailean' (see note to line 18, also note on III: 8).

24 Members of the Clan Macleod were shipped in significant numbers to North Carolina as slaves in the wake of the Battle of Worcester in 1651. But the facts indicate that the incident referred to here did not result in any of the people abducted reaching America. The man at the centre of the 'Soitheach nan Daoine' affair[41] was Norman Macleod of Unish in Berneray, tacksman to Macleod of Dunvegan. He connived with the owners of *The William*, from Donaghadee, in County Down, to have some 100 people forced on board at Loch Bracadale in Skye and Finsbay in Harris, in the spring of 1739. When the ship docked at Donaghadee for repairs on October 20th, there were 96 prisoners in the hold, some of whom escaped, only to be recaptured with considerable brutality. Rumours in the surrounding countryside led to all of them being freed and brought before the magistrates, though they were unable in the event to return home and settled instead in the north of Ireland. Warrants were issued for the arrest of Macleod of Unish and the ship's captain, William Davison. Neither was ever caught. The affair caused considerable embarrassment to both Alexander Macdonald of Sleat and Norman Macleod of Dunvegan, in spite of the fact that their involvement could never satisfactorily be proved.[42] MacLean named the culprits in four lines excised from the published version of 'An Cuilithionn':

> mallachd Dhé air Fear Dhùn-bheagain
> agus air Dòmhnallaich Shléibhte
> agus air Tarmad Uinis
> sgiobair soitheach nam brùidean![43]

---

[40] Thomas 1977: 797ff.

[41] MacLean refers to it as both 'saothach' (an alternative form of 'soitheach') and 'long' in 'An Cuilithionn' (MacLean 1999: 68, 104, 114).

[42] See two articles on the affair by Norrie Maclennan in the *West Highland Free Press* 12th and 19th May 1989.

[43] An early draft of the poem can be found in NLS Acc. 12022, where these lines are translated: 'God's curse on the Laird of Dunvegan / and on MacDonald of Sleat / and on Norman of Unish / the skipper of the brutes' ship'. They come between lines 13 and 14 in Part VI of the published version (MacLean 1999: 106–107).

Tales of people from the islands being carried as slaves to north America are extant, but have not been substantiated. MacLean may have had one of these in mind when he informed Douglas Young (letter of August 19th 1940) that the 'emigrant girl passage is quite original, based only on the story that such a girl, kidnapped from Gesto shore, was responsible for the rhymed list of Skye names of which I have two lines in "The Cuillin"...'.[44] MacLean additionally told Douglas Sealy that, when asked the time by a Highlander in the King's army in America, unable to answer in either English or French, the girl was able to communicate with him in Gaelic.[45] The girl has a monologue at the opening of Part VI of 'An Cuilithionn':

> Bha mi 'n Geusdo a' buain maoraich
> an uair a ghlacadh mi 's mi 'm aonar.
> Dh'fhuiling mi daorsa nan stràc,
> an dubh-chosnadh is grian le àin
> a shearg m' fheòil air mo cnàmhan...[46]

Gesto is at the northern end of Loch Harport in Skye.

Six quatrains with final rhyme, 'ò' in stanzas 1, 2 and 6, 'è' in stanza 3 and 'ua' in stanzas 4 and 5. The internal rhymes and high level of assonance within lines suggest an echo of 'amhrán' style.[47] Four stresses per line.

---

[44] The lines in question are 'Beinn Thota-Gormuil nam fear sgiamhach, / Beinn Dubhagraich, m' ionam 's mo chiall'. ('Ben Thota-Gormuil of the handsome men, / Ben Duagraich, my dear dear love!') MacLean 1999: 70–71.

[45] Ross and Hendry 1986: 59.

[46] 'I was in Gesto gathering shellfish / when I was seized, being alone. / I suffered slavery with strokes, / the "black labour" and a sun with a heat / that withered my flesh on my bones...' MacLean 1999: 104–105.

[47] I am indebted to Dr Michel Byrne for this observation.

V

Young wrote to MacLean from Old Aberdeen on February 11th 1941 that he

> had some things in your poems to be explained to me. I copied them all, to get a good legible text (forgive me! but your handwriting plus an unfamiliar language and strange notions is too much even for my not unnimble brain). On returning here I had your stuff bound with Deòrsa's, also my own in a separate volume. The binder was told to do yours in sky-blue with the title *Dàin le Deòrsa is Somhairle*, which made a pretty pattern in gold on the blue; and mine in bright scarlet with the title *Antrin Blads* ('Occasional Leaves'). Of course, he did them the other way about, so you and Deòrsa are the 'antrin blads'. But perhaps the symbolism is alright; we are all the voice of Scotland.

There follows a list of places in the text Young has had difficulty in understanding, and he continues:

> I think that is all I noted meantime of places where I couldn't even read the original. There will be a score or so, no doubt, where I have miscopied and not had enough grammar to correct wrong forms myself. I still know the declensions etc. very poorly.

He is concerned that the material should be lodged in safe hands, given the wartime conditions:

> I am anxious, doubtless unnecessarily, but I have a Fife canniness, to have these things put in order against the eventuality of an utter chaos in which we all might go to hell. I shall tonight give Macdonald[48] your own book of mss. to keep; he is an accurate scholar, to judge from his edition of the Gaelic Homer, and would edit it properly if it was left to him. When my bound copy of yourself and Deòrsa is fully corrected and amplified, I

---

[48] John Macdonald (1886–1970), Lecturer and then Reader in Celtic at the University of Aberdeen, 1922–1956, and first editor of *Scottish Gaelic Studies*.

thought of committing it to John MacKechnie,[49] although he is liable to have his papers searched by the
police (his Iain Lom was purloined and some valuable
researches lost); or J. L. Campbell,[50] whom I once knew
slightly and have corresponded with; or Carmichael
Watson,[51] whom I don't actually know...

It was thanks to what came to be christened the 'Red Book'
that fully 27 years later, on April 3rd 1968, Young was able
to reply as follows, from his home at Makarsbield, Tayport,
to a request from MacLean:

> In the matter of Gaelic manuscripts, in which Tayport
> is unexpectedly rich, I have your 'Dàin do Eimhir'
> bound in red boards with George Hay's stuff. I have
> snipped out and enclose the texts of those 'Dàin' that I
> copied, but which are not in your Maclellan print of
> 1943: V, VII,[52] XII, XVI, XXVI, XXXVI, XXXIII early
> version, and XLI. XV became one of the 'Dàin Eile'. I
> never had XL, and you told me you had forgotten what
> it was. I never had XLVI and XLVII. So I think that
> accounts for them all.

Young's transcripts constitute the only surviving copies
known to the editor of V and the early version of XXXIII, as
well as of all but the first lines of XII and XXXVI. Although
they do contain grammatical errors (in XVI he inverts the
position of 'dè' and 'de', has 'bhithinn-se' for 'bhithinn-sa',
and replaces 'tabhartas' with 'tachartas', no doubt influenced
by the preceding line), comparison with the typescript copies

---

[49] Revd John MacKechnie (1897–1977), minister in Glasgow and Reader
in Celtic at the University of Aberdeen. Author of *Catalogue of Gaelic
Manuscripts* (1973). MacLean wrote to Young on March 27th 1943 that
'The more I see of the Gaelic text [of the 1943 volume] the more I like its
correctness and for it I have nothing but gratitude to MacKechnie and
yourself'.

[50] John Lorne Campbell of Canna (1906–1996), indefatigable collector of
Gaelic oral tradition, author and editor of many works on aspects of
Scottish Gaelic language and literature.

[51] James Carmichael Watson (1910–1942) succeeded his father in the
Chair of Celtic at the University of Edinburgh, and edited volumes 4 and
5 of *Carmina Gadelica*, material his grandfather had collected (see note
to LIX).

[52] This poem carries the number VI in the present edition. See note on
the following poem.

of XXVI and XLI conserved with MacLean's letters to
Young indicates that he was a reliable transcriber. The transcripts are at present enclosed in a folded sheet annotated
by Donald Archie MacDonald in April 1997, where he
puzzlingly describes them as autographs by MacLean.

The survival is all the more striking given that, writing
on May 3rd 1941, MacLean had instructed Young to destroy
his copies of five poems, among them V, XVI and XXVI.
Writing from Raigmore Hospital, Inverness on April 20th,
1943, he expressed his surprise that V still figured in the
Gaelic text of the sequence. Young hastened to assure him
the next day that the item

> was marked by me as not for publication, and I don't
> know how it got in. I would have excised it when
> reading proofs, but I only got proofs the day or so
> before I heard of your return, and in fact did not
> seriously read them, much less correct them.

What prompted MacLean to seek out these poems? Had the
issue of *Lines Review* which was to give such generous
coverage to his work, and which appeared in 1970, bringing
XL, XLVI and XLVII into print for the first time, already
been mooted? Is this why he began drafting a revised version
of XVI, making annotations in pencil on the transcript
Young had sent him? And if he had really mislaid XL, XLVI
and XLVII at this stage, where did he succed in tracking
down copies of them?

The translations of V and XVI which MacLean promised
Young in a letter dated April 15th 1942 are untraced. V is a
nightmare for the translator, with its semantic concision, its
use of a range of abstract nouns for qualities or mental
processes, and its fondness for paradox. It is the first of four
items written in September 1939 and marks the entry of the
Scottish woman, the 'nighean ruadh', into the sequence of
love poems. Hendry writes that, having known her 'briefly
when she was in her teens', MacLean 'began to feel strongly
attracted in August or September, and by December 1939
had committed himself by declaring his love for her'.[53] The
'chance meeting' which 'brought back the old passion' and
led to 'An Cuilithionn' being 'completely interrupted' (letter

---

[53] Ross and Hendry 1986: 25.

to Young of March 30th 1942) occurred in late May or June.

1   The long vowel is an idiosyncracy, the standard form being 'eire'.
6   The line could be metrically improved by the introduction of a relative 'a' after 'bhon'.
18   Cp. XIX: 26.
24   Cp. I: 2, 4 and XIX: 25–28.
25–26   A reference to the imminence of MacLean's departure to fight in the Second World War. Commitment no longer hangs in the balance (as in the poems concerning Spain (e.g. IV and XXII)) but has become an inescapable reality. MacLean told Young (letter of October 1st 1940) that

> You see I am not a pure conscript. I am afraid I did not tell you that I asked the Edinburgh Corporation to release me for military service in September 1939. I did that because I took it to the C[ommunist] P[arty] line then. At that time I did respect the political line of the C[ommunist] P[arty]. I am afraid I don't now.

30–32   The parallellism of the three closing lines indicates a simplification in both syntax and thought, with the fourfold occurrence of the 'ao' vowel bringing a fine sense of closure.

The underlying pattern is of two anapaests per line with alternate feminine and masculine endings. Consistent *aicill* in each couplet. Even lines rhyme within each stanza.

VI

Writing on May 3rd, MacLean instructed Young to put VI among the 'Dàin Eile', 'as in the list'. The list referred to survives in two copies, one of which was sent to John Macdonald. Of the 17 items it contains, all but three can be excluded, given that they figure independently in the 'Dating Letter'. 'Clach air càrn' is cited as an independent item in a letter to Young of February 22nd 1941. The two remaining poems, which interestingly come at the end of the list, are 'Trì Slighean' (here restored to its rightful place as XV in the sequence) and 'An Dùn-Èideann 1939'. When Young returned his copy of the latter poem to MacLean in April 1968, it was marked VII. The number given in MacLean's letter is, however, preferred here. Young would appear never to have possessed a copy of the one item missing in this edition. As a result confusion between VI and VII was possible.

The poem depicts one woman taking the other's place in relative tranquillity, a perspective which is belied by the impassioned lyrics MacLean would continue to dedicate to the Irishwoman, until possibly as late as the first half of December. This may have motivated the removal of VI to the 'Dàin Eile' in the 1943 volume. MacLean's translation is reproduced from a letter to Young dated April 15th 1942.

1–2 The reference to slaughter in Germany and France should not be taken literally. Not until May 10th 1940 did German troops break through the Netherlands and Belgium to attack France.

3 The 'bòrd' is unlikely to have been in a private house. Perhaps the poet had in mind a favourite pub, or even a restaurant.

6–7 In the light of these lines it is worth turning attention to the application of colour adjectives to Eimhir, and specifically her hair, in the course of the sequence. She is 'ruadh' at V: 1, 17 and 25, VI: 6, XVI: 38, XXVI: 1 and LX: 1, 13 and 15, all items which there is no difficulty in assigning to the Scottish woman. At XIX: 25 and XXI: 7 she is 'buidhe', a term linked with the Irishwoman, and introduced in IV:1, where Eimhir's hair is 'bhuidhe, throm-bhuidh, òr-bhuidh' (see also line 21). 'Geal', on the other hand, has a more neutral application (XVI: 38, XVIII: 37, XXII: 7, XXIII: 27, XXXIV: 2), as does 'òr' (III: 8, XLIX: 8). The single recurrence of 'bàn' at XXIII: 9 can hardly function as evidence for the addressee of this item (see note on this poem), while the composite 'ruaidh òir' in the lines added to I in 1939 probably represents a wish on the poet's part to blur distinctions and propose Eimhir as a unitary figure.[54]

---

[54] The variant 'òr-laist' (for 'òr-bhuidh') occurs in the *17 Poems for 6d* version of IV: 21, as well as in a line from 'An Cuilithionn' Part II: 'mar chiabhan òr-laist ceann mo luaidhe' ('...like the clustered gold-lit hair of my beloved', MacLean 1999: 78–79), which has the interesting manuscript variants 'chuachan' (for 'chiabhan') and (for the whole line) 'mar chuachan fuilt na h-ighne ruaidhe' ('like the curly hair of the red (-haired) girl' (editor's translation) (NLS Acc. 12022).

Two quatrains with end-rhyme in the even lines and consistent *aicill*.

VIII

In the sequence as first printed, this item follows directly on IV. MacLean offered the Irishwoman a respective apology in 'A' Mhalairt Bhreugach'[55] for, as it were, 'recycling' poems written with her in mind:

> Gabh mo leisgeul, a luaidh,
> gun tug mi uair do 'n téile
> an dà dhàn dhiag a rinn mi dhutsa:
> bu ghoirt 's bu ghiar a feum-se.[56]

Which twelve poems did MacLean have in mind? The 1943 volume features thirteen items between IV and XXII. There are at least three possible explanations: (i) the poet was mistaken in his count; (ii) IV was not included as its writing preceded by more than a year the Scottish woman's first appearance in the sequence, and it therefore did not belong to the period of 'mixed allegiances'; (iii) one of the poems published in 1943 in fact 'belonged' to the Scottish woman. The war in Spain would appear to be linked with MacLean's passion for the Irishwoman (XV: 12–13, XVIII, XXII). This could also be true of poems foregrounding Yeats (VIII, X, XX) or with a strongly Celtic colouring (XIII). It may, however, never be possible to come up with a precise attribution for each single poem.

In the present item, Fimbir quotes Yeats to the speaker, but the lines involved are deceptive. Beauty, it seems, can mask a political affiliation, symbolised by the helmet of steel, which is opposed to the poet's own (as became increasingly true of Yeats in the latter part of his life). The contrast with the Platonism of the next poem could hardly be stronger. The epigraph comes from 'In Memory of Eva Gore-Booth and

---

[55] 'The False Exchange,' MacLean 1999: 192–195, where it forms part of the section entitled 'An Iomhaigh Bhriste' ('The Broken Image'), written between August 1941 and April 1944.

[56] 'Accept my excuse, dear, / that I once gave to another / the twelve poems I made for you: / her need was sore and sharp.'

Con Markiewicz', dated October 1927 and first published in
The Winding Stair and Other Poems. The two women were in
fact sisters. On meeting the latter, Yeats had noted 'some
small' physical resemblance and 'a very exact resemblance in
voice' to Maud Gonne.[57]

There is a parallel implication of the beloved's potential
for political betrayal, or at the least vacillation, in this passage from Part VII of 'An Cuilithionn':

> Chaidh mo ghaol liom air a' bheinn
> fiach an cluinneadh i an t-seinn
> a bha air stùcan nan ceum gàbhaidh;
> chual is leth-thuig i 'm mànran
> agus air ball bha cruth na biataich
> air a bòidhche ghil chianail
> agus 's ann tholl i mo chliathaich.[58]

6 The particular (inauspicious) significance seemingly at-
tached to Monday (see XXII: 8) could derive from the phrase
'gu là luain', 'a day that will never come', but MacLean
may also have been influenced by the song 'Mo nighean donn
a Còrnaig' (see note to XIII: 5) or by similar verses in other
songs he knew. Ronald Black considers that the choice of day
may merely reflect the facts.

7 Hendry writes that MacLean viewed the Irishwoman as
'a pious Catholic, from a pious family, and... conservative in
politics'. She notes that 'during the Spanish Civil War,
MacLean was very negative about Catholicism because
he believed most Catholics were pro-fascist, supporting
Franco'.[59]

8 According to MacLean, ' "àlainn" in Gaelic is the most
high-sounding of all synonyms of "beautiful", something like
"lovely" in early Yeats. In ascending order the Gaelic words
for it are "brèagha", "bòidheach", "eireachdail", "àlainn".'
(Letter to Douglas Young, August 19th 1940.)

---

[57] Yeats 1991: 161, 278.

[58] 'My love went with me on the mountain / so that she might hear the
singing / on the peaks of the dangerous steps; / she heard and half
understood their melody, / and at once the form of the vulture / took her
fair sad beauty / and she holed my body.' MacLean 1999: 122–123.

[59] Ross and Hendry 1986: 22.

Two quatrains resembling ballad metre. In each, lines 1, 2 and 4 have final rhyme, while the closing vowel of 3 is echoed internally in line 4 (*aicill*).

IX

This is the first of the series of poems written in Hawick during the last two months of 1939, which extends as far as XXXVI. In his 'Dating Letter' to Douglas Young (March 30th 1942), MacLean assigns poems IX-XVI to very early November. There was to be a second burst of creativity in the spring of the following year.

The beauty of Eimhir's face is a manifestation of the beauty of her soul, and the poet proudly asserts the immortality of the praise which he is planning. The pairing of face and soul in this epigrammatic quatrain is the first striking instance of the Platonism which underpins MacLean's sequence.

In the *Republic* Plato made no secret of the suspicion with which he regarded poetry, since it was for him little more than the imitation of an imitation. Aristotle, however, did his best in the *Poetics* to regain lost ground by claiming value for poetry as the imitation of a divine archetype. The theory of platonic love elaborated by Neoplatonic philosophers such as Plotinus, on the basis of the *Symposium* and with an input from Oriental mysticism, became a powerful force in the literature of the Renaissance, with the aid of the 15th century Latin translation of Plato's works by Marsilio Ficino. In terms of this theory

> physical beauty was an outward expression of the inward grace and spiritual beauty of the soul, and this spiritual radiance was an extension of the effulgent beauty of God Himself. The Platonic lover therefore paid devotion and adoration to a physical beauty of his mistress only in so far as that beauty reflected her soul...[60]

---

[60] Cuddon 1998: 674.

Not just Shakespeare in his sonnets, but the Metaphysical poets too and, given the renewed fascination of the Romantics with Neoplatonism, Shelley, Blake and Wordsworth all show a debt to such theories, in greater or lesser measure. All are cited, at one stage or another, as influences by MacLean. Yeats mentions his enthusiasm for Plato and Socrates while still a schoolboy, though he did not engage seriously with texts by Plato and Plotinus until after completing the first version of *A Vision* in 1926.[61]

MacLean's Platonism is evident in his fondness for pairing 'aodann' and 'spiorad' ('face' and 'spirit') or their analogues, as well as in the notion that the fundamental components of his poetry are drawn from Eimhir. The Platonic theory of beauty holds that

> the beauty of the body is a result of the formative energy of the soul. According to Ficino, the soul has descended from heaven and has framed a body in which to dwell. Before its descent it conceives a certain plan for the forming of a body; and if on earth it finds material favorable for its work and sufficiently plastic, its earthly body is very similar to its celestial one, hence it is beautiful.[62]

Harrison cites Spenser's 'An Hymne in Honour of Heavenly Beautie' as an instance of such an approach:

> Which powre retayning still or more or lesse,
> When she in fleshly seede is eft enraced,
> Through euery part she doth the same impresse,
> According as the heavens haue her graced,
> And frames her house, in which she will be placed,
> Fit for her selfe, adorning it with spoyle
> Of th'heauenly riches, which she robd erewhyle.[63]

In the sequence, it is as if Eimhir's soul were capable of informing and moulding in its likeness not only her body but also the poetry of the man who loves her (see, for example, XXVII).

---

[61] See Brian Arkins' treatment in Baldwin and Hutton 1994: 279–289.

[62] Harrison 1903: 112–113.

[63] Lines 117–123, in Spenser 1912: 591.

As well as to Platonism MacLean is indebted to Petrarchism, which conventionally viewed the beloved as

> a lady of great beauty and spotless virtue, and of a correspondingly great cruelty. Hence the subjects of the Petrarchian love poem were either the praise of the mistress's beauty or an account of the torment of the soul caused by her heartless indifference.[64]

Stylistically, the characteristic markers of Petrarchism were 'the use of antitheses, puns, and especially of conceits'.[65] If the influence of Platonism and Petrarchism lends MacLean's poetry an attractive aura of archaism, the same can be said of Eliot and Pound, similarly drawn to earlier idealisations of love in, for example, Dante, Guido Cavalcanti and the Italian 'stilnovisti'.[66] When Socrates argues in the *Phaedo* that

> the soul, when using the body as an instrument of perception, that is to say, when using the sense of sight or hearing or some other sense (for the meaning of perceiving through the body is perceiving through the senses) – were we not saying that the soul too is then dragged by the body into the region of the changeable, and wanders and is confused; the world spins round her, and she is like a drunkard, when she touches change?[67]

one cannot help recalling MacLean's words, in the above-mentioned 'Dating' Letter' to Douglas Young:

> I try to avoid writing anything now as it reminds me of the *joie-de-vivre* I had during the last two months of 1939, and makes me feel that all my best stuff is the product of a drunkenness that won't return and that if I can write any more it will only be the dreich poetry of 'wisdom'. I liked my drunken idolatry...

---

[64] Harrison 1903: 105.

[65] Harrison 1903: 126.

[66] For Platonic influences on these poets, see the chapters 'Plato and Eliot's earlier verse' by Dennis Brown, and 'The *Cantos* of Ezra Pound: "to build light"' by A. D. Moody in Baldwin and Hutton 1994: 298–307, 308–318.

[67] *Phaedo* 79, quoted in Harrison 1903: 48.

Such distrust of sensory data, however, also alerts one to a dissonant, more modern strand in the poetry which cautions against our too glibly labelling MacLean a Neoplatonist. While the Irishwoman conformed to the Petrarchan ideal, the Scottish woman and the 'wounded Eimhir' who represents her in the sequence most definitely did not. In LVII, the Platonic notion of transcendence, of beauty as having its truest being on another, immaterial sphere, is rejected in favour of immediate sensory perception. The speaker refuses to acknowledge any reality beyond it, and the Platonic hierarchy of substance and shadow is reversed, privileging the latter over the former.

Two rhyming couplets with four stresses in each line.

X

Experience is seen as the fuel of poetry. Though he may lack their talent, the speaker's material would be sufficient for a number of poets like Yeats or Ross. The lyric proceeds by accumulation ('labhar... teud-mhodhanach... caoin, uiread... uimhir... uiread... uiread' and so forth). Editor's translation.

11 Is there a further instance of Platonism in the suggestion that poets of yearning are confined to the earthly sphere ('a-bhos') and may never penetrate beyond it?

12 The first mention in the sequence of the Gaelic poet who was such an important model for MacLean, eager to find 'a symbol for Gaelic poetry and for a life determined by a grand and tragic romantic passion'.[68] An interesting sidelight on the respect in which the poet was held in MacLean's Raasay comes in the anecdote included in an essay first published in 1970, where he tells of 'an old woman of impeccable Free Church antecedents' who 'once said of the Psalmist: "David, the dirty blackguard, what was he compared with William Ross!"'[69]

---

[68] Mac Síomóin in Ross and Hendry 1986: 113.
[69] MacLean 1985: 111.

Born in Skye in 1762, William Ross was educated at Forres, where he acquired some knowledge of the Classics, and lived most of his life in Wester Ross, dying of a consumptive condition in 1791.[70] The tale of his unhappy love affair is summarised by John Mackenzie in *The Beauties of Gaelic Poetry*:

> It is not to be wondered at, that a being so highly gifted as was Ross, should be extremely susceptible of the influence of the tender passion. Many of his songs bear witness that he was so. During his excursions to Lewis, he formed an acquaintance with Miss Marion Ross of Stornoway (afterwards Mrs Clough of Liverpool,) and paid his homage at the shrine of her beauty. He sung her charms, and was incessant in his addresses... But still he was rejected by the coy maid; and the disappointment consequent on this unfortunate love affair, was thought to have preyed so much on his mind, as to have impaired his health and constitution, during the subsequent period of his life.[71]

In its fullest form, however, the legend is found in the 'Short Memoir of the Life of William Ross' prefixed to Calder's edition of his songs:

> He was all his life a traveller not merely in his packman days but when settled as schoolmaster in Gairloch... In a tour which he made to Stornoway, while yet heart-whole, he met Marion Ross, perhaps a kinswoman of his own, and fell in love with her. From his songs one would conclude that the passion or infatuation was only on his own part, not on hers; but friends of his, it is affirmed, declared that he told them of an engagement between himself and Marion at which she invoked fire from heaven to consume her if she proved unfaithful... Not long afterwards she married a sailor, a sea captain named Clough, and went to Liverpool, his port, and took up her abode there. She had compared the rural schoolhouse, the hens on one side and the cow on the

---

[70] Thomson 1989: 209ff.
[71] Mackenzie 1904: 277.

other, with the comforts and attractions of a great city, and she chose the latter. But time and experience raised doubts in her mind as to the wisdom of her choice, and her thoughts turned to Ross, her constant lover. It is generally believed that when her husband was away on a long voyage she wrote to Gairloch suggesting that Ross should meet her; and, preposterous as the suggestion was, he fell in with it, and undertook the long and toilsome journey, till he reached Stirling. Here he paused, and common-sense came to his aid. Did he actually, he asked himself, propose to take another man's wife and appear with her before the world? And this in Gairloch of all places? The idea would not bear examination. He therefore retraced his steps, and, in the course of his long journey homewards, had to spend a night in the open before he could reach the shelter of his father's cottage. Bruised and broken in body and spirit he took to bed for the last time... When the unhappy Bard was breathing his last breath, his wraith winged its way to far off Liverpool to make claims on Marion which she could not refuse, the fulfilment of her promise to wed, or the end which she had invoked heaven to send upon her if she proved unfaithful. She was at the moment, with the help of her maid, dressing herself in white in preparation for a ball she was about to attend. A knock was heard at the door which blanched her face with fear. The maid answered, and announcing that a tall young man in Highland dress was waiting, she heard her mistress whisper, "William Ross". Marion herself then went to the door, but no one was to be seen. At that instant the flame of the candle she held in her hand was blown inward and lit her flimsy garments, and her screams soon ceased in the agony of death.[72]

Derick Thomson is at pains to insist on the broad range of Ross's surviving work (he is reputed to have destroyed a number of his songs), pointing out that only three specifically concern Marion Ross. As she moved to Liverpool with her

---

[72] Calder 1937: xxvi–xxviii.

sea-captain husband in 1782, the affair ended before Ross
was twenty, some nine years before his death.

The clearest statement of the parallelisms between Ross's
situation and MacLean's comes in the poem 'Uilleam Ros is
mi fhìn' ('William Ross and I'):

> Chan eil mise càirdeach idir
> do dh'Uilleam Ros ged leig mi orm
> gu bheil mo chàs-sa mar a chàs-san,
> 's mi 'g iadach ris na briathran geàrrte
> ceòlmhor as mìorbhail 'na bhàrdachd.
>
> Esan a' bàsachadh 's a' chaitheimh,
> a' fàgail gaoil is "gàir nan òg"
> is a Mhór a' dol thar sàile,
> a' falbh an aoibhneas a h-àilleachd
> le fear eile is 'ga fhàgail.[73]

The Irishwoman, too, was to cross the sea and become the
wife of another man. There is a double parallelism between
Ross and MacLean. Both experience rejection in love, and
both are poets capable of giving lasting expression to their
torment. In 'Craobh nan Teud', Ross is paired with the French
poet Charles Baudelaire ('Ros is Baudelaire an cràdhlot').[74]
When, in a paper read to the Gaelic Society of Inverness
some 40 years later, MacLean observes of Ross's 'Òran eile'[75]
that the 'sublimation of sexual love has been responsible for
much of the world's greatest poetry and notably when the
sexual love is crossed with tragedy',[76] one cannot help noticing
how applicable these words are to his own achievement in the
'Dàin do Eimhir'

---

[73] 'I am not at all related / to William Ross though I pretended / that
my case is like his case, / being jealous of the musical chiselling / of
words, which is a marvel in his poetry. // He dying of consumption, /
leaving love and the hubbub of the young, / and his Marion going over
the sea, / going away in the joy of her beauty / with another man and
leaving him.' MacLean 1999: 188–189. The words 'gàir nan òg' occur in
line 4 of the final verse of the 'Òran eile, air an aobhar cheudna' (Calder
1937: 174).

[74] MacLean 1999: 52–53. 'Ross and Baudelaire in misery.'

[75] For which see further XXXI.

[76] MacLean 1985: 132.

William Butler Yeats (1865–1939), who spent some two
thirds of his life outside Ireland, was nonetheless the dominant figure of the Irish Literary Revival. Moving from an
initial adherence to the modes and tones of the so-called
Celtic Twilight, he achieved in his mature work a robust
and passionate eloquence rarely equalled in English in the
course of this century. While the history, folk traditions and
troubled politics of his country, along with the profound
interest in the occult which accompanied him throughout his
adult life, are fundamental to his poetry, it would be unthinkable without the influence of his obsessive and
unrequited love for the patriot, actress and feminist Maud
Gonne (1866–1953). Yeats owes to this troubled passion his
place alongside Ross and Blok in MacLean's trinity of luckless poets (see XX: 17ff.). Caird writes that MacLean was
'particularly moved' by 'Yeats's despairing love for Maud
Gonne and the magnificent lyrics in which he expressed it',
anticipating as these did 'the anguished lyricism of some of
his own love poetry'.[77] Yeats wrote of his first meeting with
Maud Gonne on January 30th 1889 that he

> had never thought to see in a living woman so great
> beauty... A complexion like the bloom of apples and yet
> face and body had the beauty of lineaments which Blake
> calls the highest beauty because it changes least from
> youth to age, and stature so great she seemed of a divine
> race. Her movements were works of grace and I
> understood at last why the poet of antiquity, where we
> would but speak of face and form, sings, loving some
> lady, that she seems like a goddess.[78]

He proposed to her two years later. In the meantime she
had had a son, who died before his second birthday, by the
French Boulangist Lucien Millevoye, who was to give her a
daughter three years later. An affair with Olivia Shakespear
could not prevent Yeats's passion returning with all its force
when he visited Maud Gonne in Paris in December 1896. In

---

[77] Caird 1995: 199.
[78] Yeats 1972: 40, quoted in Jeffares 1996: 50, to which the reader is
referred for a more detailed account. There is an invaluable chronology of
the relationship in MacBride White and Jeffares 1992: xiii–xvi.

1902 she took the title role in his play *Cathleen ni Houlihan*, a part written with her specifically in mind. The effect of her performance was such that years later the poet would ask himself 'Did that play of mine send out / Certain men the English shot?'[79] In 1903 she was received into the Catholic Church and married John MacBride (see XIII: 3), who had fought alongside the Boers against Britain and who was one of the few participants in the Easter Rising of 1916 to have the benefit of military experience. The French courts granted the couple a legal separation in 1906. In 1916 Yeats proposed once more, and it was not until after Maud Gonne's daughter Iseult had also refused a proposal that he finally contracted marriage to George Hyde Lees, on October 20th 1917. If the Scottish poet's love for Eimhir represents a dangerous deviation from a chosen political affiliation, Yeats saw political involvement as ultimately damaging to the woman he loved. This is borne out by lines from 'The Circus Animals' Desertion' ('I thought my dear must her own soul destroy, / So did fanaticism and hate enslave it'[80]) and by a further passage from the *Autobiography*:

> I told her after meeting her in London I had come to understand the tale of a woman selling her soul to buy food for a starving people as a symbol of all souls who lose their peace, or their fineness, or any beauty of the spirit in political service, but chiefly of her soul that seemed so incapable of rest.[81]

A considered and compassionate verdict on Yeats can be found in MacLean's poem 'Aig Uaigh Yeats' ('At Yeats's Grave'), where he tells the Irishman: '...tha leisgeal air do bhilean, / an leisgeal nach do mhill do bhàrdachd, / oir tha an leisgeal aig gach duine'.[82]

Lines of three (occasionally four) stresses each. There are two rhymes in the poem, 'à' in lines 1–2 and 5–8, and 'o' in lines 3–4 and 9–12.

---

[79] See 'Man and the Echo' from *Last Poems*, Yeats 1983: 345.
[80] Yeats 1983: 347.
[81] Yeats 1972: 47.
[82] '...there is an excuse on your lips, / the excuse that did not spoil your poetry, / for every man has his excuse.' MacLean 1999: 260–261.

XI

Another epigrammatic quatrain. The mention of Edinburgh is the first clear indication of a metropolitan setting for at least some poems in the sequence.

The metrical pattern is the same as in VIII.

XII

For the survival of this item, see note to V. The quatrain bears a distinct resemblance to the close of XV. MacLean told Young in a letter dated September 11th 1941 that 'I have in one Eimhir poem accurately, I think, enumerated the four chief emotional dynamics in my life', and quoted the last two lines of this poem, adding that 'I am afraid the last has been far more important than you or anybody else has ever imagined'. Editor's translation.

1 '...thug mi luaidh' can also mean 'I praised' or 'I mentioned'.
2 A compressed line of difficult interpretation. Alternative readings could be 'four allegiances which called forth different virtues' or 'four to which I gave allegiance with varying success'.
3 It is common in Gaelic to refer to Skye simply as 'the Island'.

Four lines of basically four stresses. End rhyme in ll.1, 2 and 4 and *aicill* in ll. 3–4.

XIII

Though Bertran de Born (1150-ca.1215) is slipped unob-trusively into MacLean's list of unfortunate lovers, this poem was clearly inspired by Pound's 'Na Audiart'[83] (included in *Personae* (1908, 1909, 1910)), loosely based in its turn on de

---

[83] See Pound 1975: 17–18.

Born's 'Dompna, puois de mi no us chal' ('Lady, since you don't care for me').[84] Where Bertran had written of a 'domna soiseubeuda' or 'composite woman', MacLean adumbrates a composite poetry which will embody the virtues of different European traditions. De Born's notion can be traced back to an anecdote in the Elder Pliny, telling how the Greek painter Zeuxis put together a portrait of Helen by combining the finest qualities of five naked girls.[85] The idea that terrestrial beauty is of its nature imperfect, and that true beauty can only be attained by selecting and reassembling, is of course Platonic in nature. The poem is evidence of MacLean's debt to the Modernist poetry of Pound and Eliot, which he consciously rejected as a model during his university years. He would later write that 'I am greatly attracted by Pound's Provençal versions, whether they are relatively genuine or not. I consider him now the best of all those post-war English or Anglo-American poets. His virtuosity is, I think, richer and more varied and more satisfying than the meagre mosaic[k]ed whinings of Eliot and the flat slicknesses of Auden etc. etc.' (letter to Douglas Young, February 22nd 1941).

At the same time, the opening paragraph of XIII may usefully be compared with the fourth section of the 'Ora nam Buadh' (or 'Hymn of the Graces', see LIX) in Carmichael's version, with its mention of Helen of Troy and, near the end, Queen Maeve:

> Is tu gleus na Mnatha Sithe,
> Is tu beus na Bride bithe,
> Is tu brigh nn Moire mine,
> Is tu gniomh na mnatha Greig,
> Is tu sgeimh na h-Eimir aluinn,
> Is tu mein na Dearshul agha,

---

[84] See Whyte 1996 for a detailed account. Regarding Audiart, MacLean refers Douglas Young to 'the poetry of Bertrans de Born troubadour Englished by Pound' (February 22nd 1941).

[85] Pliny the Elder, *Historiae Naturalis* XXXV, 36. Pliny speaks of the city of Girgenti, though the painting in question was destined for Croton, and does not name Helen at this point. Domenico Beccafumi (1486–1551) painted a fresco of this scene in the Palazzo Bindi Sergardi at Siena.

Is tu meanm na Meabha Laidir,
Is tu taladh Binne-bheul.[86]

Two transcripts of this poem are appended to a letter to
Douglas Young dated May 25th 1941. The earlier of the two
carries deletions and makes it possible to recover previous
readings in several places.

1   Deirdre is the tragic heroine of the Ulster Cycle, with a
role similar to Helen of Troy in ancient Greek tradition. Her
story, *Longes Mac nUislenn* ('The Exile of the Sons of Uisliu'
or Uisneach), has survived in versions which can be dated,
on internal evidence, as far back as the eighth or ninth
centuries. Included in both the Book of Leinster (compiled
after 1150) and the Yellow Book of Lecan (compiled around
1390), it constituted one of the 'Three Sorrows of Story-
telling', and was a prologue tale to the major Irish epic *Táin
Bó Cuailnge* ('The Cattle Raid of Cooley'), serving to explain
why Fergus Mac Roig, Cormac the son of Conchobar and
other Ulster heroes find themselves at the rival court of
Queen Medb of Connacht when the epic starts.[87]
      The elements of her story can be briefly summarised. While
still inside her mother's womb, Deirdre utters a cry which
prompts Cathbad the druid to foretell both her great beauty
and the destruction she will bring about. Refusing to have
her killed, Conchobar King of Ulster arranges to have her
brought up in secrecy, planning to make her his companion
in due course of time. But with a mixture of threats and
flattery she persuades Naoise, eldest of the sons of Uisneach,
to run away with her. No longer able to find refuge in
Ireland, the couple, along with Naoise's two brothers, eventually go into exile in Scotland, until they are lured back by a
treacherous invitation from Conchobar, for which Fergus
and Conchobar's son are among the guarantors. The sons of

---

[86] 'Thine is the skill of the Fairy Woman, / Thine is the virtue of Bride
the calm, / Thine is the faith of Mary the mild, / Thine is the tact of the
woman of Greece, / Thine is the beauty of Emir the lovely, / Thine is the
tenderness of Darthula delightful, / Thine is the courage of Maebh the
strong, / Thine is the charm of Binne-bheul.' Carmichael 1928: I, 8.
[87] Caerwyn Williams and Ford 1992: 130–131, MacKillop 1998: 117ff.

Uisneach are killed and, a year later, Deirdre succeeds in putting an end to her life.[88]

Deirdre's story features prominently in Anglo-Irish literature of the 19th and 20th centuries, making her perhaps the best-known of all figures from Celtic mythology. It was reworked in dramatic form by Yeats and Synge, by James Stephens as a novel and by Lady Gregory as part of her retelling in 'Kiltartanese' of the Irish mythological cycles.[89] It also survived until modern times in remoter districts of Ireland and Scotland. On two successive days in March 1867, Carmichael transcribed, from the lips of a cottar and a smith on the island of Barra, versions of the story of Deirdre and of 'Laoidh Chlann Uisne' ('The Lay of the Children of Uisne') which he then published (after some touching up) as a combined volume.[90]

2 'At the head of Glen Etive is a plain called "Dail-an-eas", dale of the waterfall... A gentle declivity looks down on the waterfall, and on the clear crystalline water running on the boulders, and away down between the mountains and down the course of the loch. A spot upon this declivity is called "Grianan Dearduil", "Grianan Dearshula" – the sunny bower of Dearshula. The remains of some building are indicated in the green grass of the slope. The old people of the place had a tradition... that the sunny bower of Dearshula was thatched without with the long-stalked fern (royal fern) of the dells and the red clay of the pools, and lined within with the pine of the mountains and the down feathers of birds. Here the deer of the hill could be shot from the window and the salmon of the stream could be fished from the door of the bower. The spot is most beautiful and the prospect most magnificent.'[91]

Carmichael gives Dearshula as the commonly used form of Deirdre's name in local oral tradition. A poem from the 15th century Glen Masan manuscript, set in the mouth of Deirdre, has the verse:

---

[88] See Cross and Slover 1936: 239–247, also Gantz 1981: 256–267.
[89] See 'Fate of the Sons of Usnach' in Gregory 1970: 92–117.
[90] See Carmichael 1914.
[91] Carmichael 1914: 139.

> Glend Eitci! O'n Glend Eitci!
> Ann do togbhus mo chét tig;
> Alaind a fidh iar néirghe
> Buaile gréne Glend Eitchi...[92]

See also note to XXIII: 16.

3   Maud Gonne (for whom see note to X: 12) married Major
John MacBride (1868–1916) in Paris on February 21st 1903.
The pair had one child, named Sean, but separated after only
two years. The event prompted a bitter quatrain from Yeats,
which remained unpublished in his lifetime:

> My dear is angry that of late
> I cry all base blood down
> As though she had not taught me hate
> By kisses to a clown.[93]

Though not involved in planning the Easter 1916 uprising,
MacBride lost no time in joining the insurgents. He was
court-martialled and shot by a firing-squad.

5   A version of this song, with the refrain 'Mo nighean donn
a Còrnaig / Gu robh thu buidhe bòidheach / Mo nighean
donn a Còrnaig' was among those collected by K. C. Craig
from Màiri Nighean Alasdair and published in 1949.[94] The
Cornaig girl was killed by her brothers to prevent her
marrying a man they did not approve of. They left her dead
on the moor, and the speaker laments that he could not have
been there with a bare sword to try his strength on them.[95]

---

[92] 'Glen Etive! / There I raised my first house, / beautiful are its woods
in the morning, / Glen Etive, the fold of sunlight...' Quoted in Ross and
Hendry 1986: 64. For the original, see Cameron 1894, II: 467.

[93] Yeats 1972: 145.

[94] See Craig 1949: 108. MacLean later expressed the view that this version
contained 'disturbing accretions' in its words (1985: 121).

[95] An English translation by MacLean of one version of this song can be
found in NLS Acc. 12022. It reads as follows: 'My brown-haired girl from
Cornaig / you were golden beautiful / my brown-haired girl from
Cornaig. / It was an evil tale I heard / on Monday after Sunday. / When
the rest went to the sermon / the hunters went to the moorland. / And
your hair was trailing and your finely spun shirt in shreds, / and your
smooth white breasts / dripping blood together / my golden heavy-haired
girl / sleeping on the moorland. / It is a bad morning's work for me /
to be putting the men in order, / and it is a bad evening's work for me /
to be preparing your burial. / And the ale that went for your wedding /

An earlier version of this line (see 'Copytexts and Variant Readings') cited the heroine of Alasdair Mac Mhaighstir Alasdair's 'Moladh Mòraig'.[96] Writing to Young on February 22nd 1941, MacLean had glossed 'MacDhomhnaill' (see line 35) as 'Alexander Mac Mhaighstir'.

6 The note prefaced to 'Òran an Amadain Bhòidheich' [sic] in Sinclair's *An t-Òranaiche* explains how, when a young man fell in love with his father's milkmaid, a girl named Mairearad or Margaret, his mother, knowing the girl had gone to wash herself in the river, tricked him into shooting her by claiming to have seen a fine white swan swimming at the place. The song is said to have been composed as a consequence of the shooting.[97] In a letter to Douglas Young dated February 22nd 1941, MacLean names the Handsome Fool as the author, the song as 'A Mhairead òg', and refers to its English version by Marjory Kennedy-Fraser, the 'Mull Fisher's Song'. In a paper on 'Domhnall Donn of Bohuntin', however, read after the war to the Gaelic Society of Inverness, while considering this to be 'by far the most famous poem' attributed to the 17th century scion of the Keppoch MacDonalds, MacLean writes that 'two songs have been inextricably confused' in Sinclair's version, one by Domhnall Donn, the other 'ultimately a variant of the international folk tale used in "The Swan Lake"'. According to a different tradition, the girl in the song was the poet's 'illegitimate daughter, who visited him in prison'.[98]

7 Tómas Láidir (Thomas the Strong), also known as Thomas Costello (which may mean 'of the shapely feet'), famed in Ireland for his deeds of physical prowess, fell in love with Una MacDermott. His love was returned, but her father disdained him as a suitor and, although Tómas was able to come to her sick bed, a foolish vow prevented him returning when she summoned him, and she died as a consequence. In the song entitled 'Una bhán' he made to her, she is referred

---

at your funeral was drunk. / I wish to God that I was at grips / with the young men who did the evil deed. / With a long naked sword / I would try the strength of my fists on them.'
[96] For a recent edition see Mac Mhaighstir Alasdair 1996: 56–74.
[97] Sinclair 1879: 522.
[98] MacLean 1985: 211, 232–233.

to as 'blossom of the amber locks' ('a bhláith na ndlaoidh
ómra'), having 'ringletted *cooleen* upon which grew the
melted gold' ('cúilín fáinneach air ar fhás suas an t-òr
leaghtha'), terms which notably resemble the depiction of
Eimhir in MacLean's sequence although, as stated in the note
to IV: 2, such descriptions are commonplace in love poetry
of both the Irish and Scottish Gaelic traditions.[99]

An earlier version (see 'Copytexts and Variant Readings')
placed this and the following line after line 12.

8 For Eimhir, wife of Cuchulainn, who gives her name
to MacLean's whole sequence of poems, see the note at the
beginning of this commentary. Cuchulainn, the greatest
hero in early Irish literature, dominates the Ulster cycle
and *Táin Bó Cuailnge*. Originally named Sétanta, he gained
his nickname (the 'hound of Culann') when, aged 7, he
smashed a guard dog belonging to Culann the smith
against a doorpost. The boy agreed to serve as the dead
animal's substitute until a whelp could be raised to take its
place.[100]

Gràinne, Diarmad and Fionn Mac Cumhaill are the principal characters in 'Tóraigheacht Dhiarmada agus Ghráinne'
('The Pursuit of Diarmad and Grainne') which, though it
must date back at least to the tenth century, has survived
only in an Early Modern Irish redaction. Gràinne, promised
in marriage to Fionn, forces Diarmad, who is a member of
Fionn's warrior band, to elope with her. Its theme, 'the
tragedy of a young girl betrothed to an old man and of the
conflict between passion and duty on the part of her love',[101]
is basically that of Deirdre's story.[102]

9–10 In Scene xviii of Christopher Marlowe's *Doctor
Faustus*, Helen of Troy enters the stage a second time, after
Faustus has begged Mephistophilis to let him enjoy her
embraces. Faustus greets her with the famous words: 'Was

---

[99] Hyde 1969: 46–61.
[100] MacKillop 1998: 102ff. For 'The Boyhood Deeds of Cu Chulainn'
(which form part of the *Táin*) see Cross and Slover 1936: 137–152 and
Gantz 1981: 134–146.
[101] Caerwyn Williams and Ford 1992: 130–131.
[102] MacKillop 1998: 230, Cross and Slover 1936: 370–421, Gregory
1976: 269–309.

this the face that launch'd a thousand ships / And burnt the topless towers of Ilium?'[103] Yeats had asked of Maud Gonne 'Was there another Troy for her to burn?'[104]

11–12 For William Ross's unhappy love affair, see note to X: 12.

13 MacLean's idea of the relationship between the troubadour Bertran de Born and Lady Audiart comes from Pound, who chose the Provençal phrase *Que be-m vols mal* as epigraph for his poem, which opens 'Though thou well dost wish me ill / Audiart, Audiart'. Pound's longest De Born poem, 'Near Périgord', includes a summary of 'Dompna, puois de mi no us chal'.[105]

14 Maebhe or Medb, whose name means 'she who intoxicates', is the principal antagonist of Cuchulainn in *Táin Bó Cuailnge* and the architect of his eventual downfall. It is she who sets the action moving in the initial pillow-talk, when she discovers that her husband possesses a white-horned bull she cannot match. She also spurs on Cuchulainn's friend Ferdiad to confront him in a series of one to one combats. When she and the hero come face to face, she is menstruating, and he mockingly spares her. Referred to as 'Medb of the friendly thighs', she claimed to require the attentions of 32 men if she was to be satisfied in bed.[106]

20 Rather than designating a specific metre, 'Dàn Dìreach' indicates the strictness with which rules of rhyme, consonance and alliteration are observed in syllabic verse composed in Classical Gaelic roughly between the end of the twelfth century and the beginning of the seventeenth.[107]

23 For a similarly eclectic approach, drawing together the qualities of different national traditions, see 'Craobh nan Teud' lines 49–56.[108]

28 Before becoming identified with Scandinavia and speci-

---

[103] Marlowe 1965: 139.

[104] 'No Second Troy', beginning 'Why should I blame her that she filled my days / With misery...' in Yeats 1983: 91.

[105] See Pound 1975: 57ff.

[106] MacKillop 1998: 288–290.

[107] See Knott 1994: xi, 2ff.

[108] MacLean 1943: 64. These lines are omitted from the 1999 reprinting of the poem.

fically Norway, 'Lochlann' was simply a mysterious realm
from which dangerous invaders originated.[109]
34   For MacBride see note to line 3, and for Naoise to line
1 (also XXIV: 5–6).
35   See notes to lines 5 and 6.
37   For Cuchulainn, Fionn and Diarmad, see note to line 8.
43–44   In an earlier version the order of these two lines was
reversed (see 'Copytexts and Variant Readings').

Lines of varying length, between two and four stresses,
rhyming most frequently in pairs, though the rhymes at 15,
19, 37, 41 and 45 embrace four lines, and at 29 six (if
'ioghnadh' is incorporated).

XIV

The second poem in the 1943 volume to have a title. The
theme of the poet selling his soul in order to gain Eimhir's
love returns in the brief quatrain XXXVI and in XXXVIII,
where the very idea is described as blasphemous. The casu-
istical nature of the argument, and the poet's aggressive
display of intellectual brilliance, again reveal a debt to the
English Metaphysicals. This is one of a group of poems in
which MacLean explicitly acknowledged the influence of
Donne (letter to Douglas Young of September 11th 1941).

2   The bondage to which MacLean refers is presumably the
victory of capitalism and the consequent enslavement of the
industrial working classes. See IV: 24 and XXXII: 4.
9   Concerning his own translation of a passage in 'The
Cuillin',[110] MacLean told Douglas Young (May 12th 1941):
'Somehow I had thought that "deifir" meant "defiance" whereas, of course, it means "hastiness"'. That the same misunderstanding applies here is evident from a letter written
later in the same year (November 9th): 'In Dàn XIV you can
leave "deifir" in and translate "hastiness". That is dishonest
but convenient.'

---

[109] MacKillop 1998: 268.
[110] Presumably II, 48 (MacLean 1999: 78).

10   This line leads the reader to anticipate a retraction. But the blasphemy here could be as much his failure to respect Eimhir as a swerving from political commitment, and it paves the way for further assertion of his readiness for self-betrayal.

Four five-line stanzas with three or four stresses per line and consistent end-rhyming. The first two stanzas both have rhymes in 'ao'.

XV

Young added in pencil, between XIV and XVII in his copy of the list of poems already mentioned in the note to VI, 'N.B. XV Trì Slighean *not* placed here'. It appears in the 1943 volume as XVIII among the 'Dàin Eile'. The implication that it originally formed part of the 'Dàin do Eimhir' sequence is unmistakable. Writing to MacDiarmid from Hawick on January 10th 1940, MacLean tells him that the poem on p. 5 of *17 Poems for 6d* (a joint effort with Robert Garioch) is 'a slight thing but technically it satisfies me. It is really one of 40 poems I have written for a woman whom I call Eimhir in the booklet.' The poem in question is 'Trì Slighean',[111] further evidence that the item originally formed part of the love sequence. It is therefore inserted at this point in our edition.

Like X and XX, XV is concerned with poetics, with the kind of poetry MacLean would like or is able to produce. The three paths of the title are, to follow MacDiarmid's example; to follow that of the English poets of the 'MacSpaunday' group; and the path MacLean follows almost against his will, dictated by a range of personal and political loyalties.

---

[111] MacLean is referring to the first edition of the pamphlet, where the Gaelic text appeared without accent marks. In the second, corrected edition, 'Trì Slighean' appears on page 8, while page 5 is occupied by one of Garioch's poems. A copy of the first edition, with manuscript corrections by MacLean, may be consulted as National Library of Scotland MS 26630.

Hugh MacDiarmid is, along with Mac Mhaighstir Alasdair, one of the dedicatees of 'An Cuilithionn', Part V of which closes with a Gaelic adaptation of 'If there are bounds to any man' from *Second Hymn to Lenin and Other Poems* (1935).[112] The poet, whose real name was Christopher Murray Grieve (1892–1978), launched and spearheaded the Scottish Renaissance Movement, aimed at regenerating Scottish literature on a basis of independence from the English tradition, with due weight being given to the two 'indigenous' languages, Scots and Gaelic. From 1922 onwards he was prodigiously active, editing *The Scottish Chapbook* (1922–23), *The Scottish Nation* (1923) and *The Northern Review* (1924), producing two volumes of Scots lyrics, *Sangschaw* (1925) and *Penny Wheep* (1926) as well as the long poem in Scots *A Drunk Man Looks at the Thistle* (1926), while also evaluating the current state of Scottish literature in *Contemporary Scottish Studies* (gathered together in 1926) and indicating the way forward in *Albyn, or Scotland and the Future* (1927). From this point on MacDiarmid became increasingly marginalised in political,[113] cultural and eventually even in geographical terms. From May 1933 he resided in a sort of internal exile on the Shetland island of Whalsay.

George Davie introduced MacLean to MacDiarmid in Rutherford's Bar, off South Bridge in Edinburgh, in May 1934. The two worked together on English versions of Gaelic poems, including Mac Mhaighstir Alasdair's 'Birlinn of Clanranald' and Duncan Bàn Macintyre's 'Praise of Ben Dorain'. MacLean visited MacDiarmid on Whalsay in the first week of August 1935, making a trip to West Linga with the poet and his son. Though MacLean noted that his physical and emotional condition was poor, he found that 'there was nothing wrong with him mentally'. Nonetheless, on August 17th MacDiarmid was admitted to the Royal Hospital in Perth for psychiatric treatment. In a letter dated January 26th 1937, MacLean extended a warm invitation to MacDiarmid to visit Raasay, and in September the older poet

---

[112] MacLean 1999: 64–65, 104–105; MacDiarmid 1978: I, 555.

[113] Due to his Communist sympathies, he was expelled from the National Party of Scotland in May 1933, while the Communist Party of Great Britain expelled him for 'nationalist deviationism' in November 1936.

made a trip to the islands in the company of W. D. MacColl. They spent one night on Raasay with the MacLean family, then spent the weekend in Portree with the poet before travelling on to Barra to visit Compton Mackenzie.[114]

MacLean had been introduced to MacDiarmid's poetry by Davie and James Caird while still at Edinburgh University. He expressed on numerous occasions throughout his life the intense admiration and even reverence he felt for the older poet's early lyrics. In a letter to Young of September 7th 1941 we read that

> I immediately recognised the lyrics of *Sangschaw* and *Penny Wheep* as supreme. I regarded them in much the same way as I regarded the greatest things of Blake's, things completely new and unbelievable. I still do that. There is nothing on earth like the greatest of those lyrics... Grieve's greatest lyrics are always a miracle and mystery to me... They are completely 'magic' and unable to be emulated.

A distancing had, however, already taken place, as is evident in these lines from a letter to Douglas Young written on November 23rd of the preceding year:

> I am afraid that something or everything has gone out of Grieve's poetry. I suppose it indicates that Grieve's political "line" is what I had taken it to be but Grieve's Anglophobia strikes me as a bit hollow. That may be because for a long time I have not paid much attention to his politics. As early as the *Drunk Man* I had resented

---

[114] Letter in Edinburgh University Library MS 2954.13, Bold 1988: 323, 330, 332, 345. MacColl, described by Bold as 'a Gaelic revivalist who, like MacDiarmid, had been expelled from the National Party of Scotland in 1933', kept MacLean informed of Douglas Young's fortunes in 1942 and was one of those who prepared English versions for the 1943 volume (not utilised in the event). Writing to MacDiarmid from Egypt on February 23rd 1942, MacLean comments that 'When I was in London in July and early August and again in September [1941] I had news of you from MacColl with whom I had some very pleasant meetings', adding towards the end of the same letter that 'I learned much from my delightful meetings with MacColl whom I got to know properly. My friendship with him I consider, along with my friendship with you, as one of the two or three greatest things in my life.' See also note to XXVII: 1.

an arty attitude to politics, and I gave up paying much
attention to his utterances on politics when he began to
use *The Voice*[115] largely to fulminate against his literary
enemies in imaginary quarrels.

Of the *Golden Treasury of Scottish Poetry* which MacDiarmid
edited, and which contained translations on which the two
poets had collaborated, MacLean claimed to be 'much
disappointed with it as I expected from reports... By the way
what a bad judge he evidently is of his own poetry' (letter to
Douglas Young, December 7th 1940).[116]

MacLean's translation is reproduced from a letter to
Young dated April 15th 1942.

7–8 'Where the hell did you get the idea that Auden etc.
have meant anything to me? When I first read a little of the
crowd (about 1934) I was willing to agree that they were
probably good fellows but very poor poets. And now I think
them contemptible as fellows and as poets. I have never been
able to memorise a single line of any of them and I take away
poems by Yeats, Grieve and even Eliot and Pound whole. I
think your finding of this influence in me is like your accusations of my socialism or communism as being of the
Gollancz brand, which I think nonsense.' (Letter to Douglas
Young of September 7th 1941.) Earlier in the same letter
MacLean had written: 'I think you exaggerate Grieve's influence on my style. He has very little and it is very superficial
but he constantly stirs me emotionally and intellectually.'

MacDiarmid expresses a contempt analogous to MacLean's
in his 'British Leftist Poetry, 1930–40', which begins 'Auden,
MacNeice, Day Lewis, I have read them all, / Hoping against
hope to hear the authentic call' and ends 'You cannot light

---

[115] The *Voice of Scotland* was a quarterly magazine aimed at offering a
platform for 'Scottish Republicanism and the Leninist line in regard to
Scotland of the late John Maclean, and the detailed analysis of Scottish
issues in the light of dialectical materialism'. The first issue was dated
June–August 1938 (Bold 1988: 372–3, quoting a letter of MacDiarmid's
to Neil Gunn dated May 9th 1938).

[116] Though it would appear to have been written at a single sitting, this
letter rather confusingly is also marked '(Feb.)'. The date 1941 has
subsequently been added in pencil.

a match on a crumbling wall'.[117] J. B. Caird says of his discussions with MacLean, at the time of their first acquaintance
in Edinburgh, that while they included 'the emerging
MacSpaunday group', the poet's 'crofter radicalism, nour-
ished on memories of the Battle of the Braes and Glendale,
was poles removed from the affected English public school
communism of these gentlemen'.[118]

For T. S. Eliot (1888–1965) and Ezra Pound (1885–1972)
in relation to MacLean, see further the 'Introduction' and the
notes to poems I and XIII. The poets Wystan Hugh Auden
(1907–1973) and the Ulsterman Louis MacNeice (1907–1963)
were contemporaries at Oxford University and, with Stephen
Spender and Cecil Day Lewis, members of the group
laughingly nicknamed MacSpaunday by its detractors. The
critic and poet Sir Herbert Read (1893–1968) was Professor
of Fine Art at Edinburgh University at the same time as
MacLean studied there. His poetry was strongly influenced
by Imagism, and his experiences on active service in the First
World War are reflected in his earlier collections.

10   The idea that Eimhir has diverted the speaker from his
true purpose will recur in XIX: 27–28.

11–13   Cp. XII 3–4. The specification 'two years' and the
reference to Spain indicate that MacLean has the Irishwoman
in mind.

Thirteen lines of three or four stresses, rhyming in pairs
except for the first three.

XVI

Dr Michel Byrne, of the Celtic Department at the University
of Glasgow, very kindly drew my attention to a transcript
of this poem made by George Campbell Hay, included in a
notebook among his papers in the National Library of
Scotland. A transcript of it was also among the items Young
sent the poet on April 3rd 1968 (see note to V). After receiving this copy, MacLean made alterations in pencil which

[117] MacDiarmid 1993: II, 1060.
[118] Caird 1995: 198.

indicate he was working towards a revised version of the lyric, never completed. In both copies the first 16 lines form quatrains, the remainder octaves, lines being run together on three occasions. In this edition the text is presented in octaves throughout. MacLean himself may have been undecided, or at least inconsistent, in the presentation. Running to 40 lines, XVI is the largest single recovery in the present edition and, like V, a significant addition to the canon of MacLean's poems.

Lines 37 and 39 are quoted, along with English translations, in a letter to Douglas Young of February 22nd 1941. MacLean's versions of them have been incorporated into the editor's translation. In a letter to Young dated April 15th 1942, MacLean promises to 'send versions of Dàin V and XVI and the other four short pieces as soon as I can', which are so far untraced.

If the poem refers to a specific incident, it could be that Eimhir remained unexpectedly close to him throughout a social gathering (lines 1–2, 11, 15–16) during which the poet painfully witnessed her being the subject of mocking laughter (lines 13–14). He insists at the close of the poem on the illusory nature of the exultation caused by her behaviour (lines 33–34, 39–40).

9 The image of the Wheel of Fortune, which with its turning brings the helpless individual good or bad luck, is medieval in origin, and chimes in with the archaising tendency evident throughout the sequence. See also lines 27ff. and especially 29–32, where the poet emphasises the bad luck he is subject to. The image also occurs in Part VI of 'The Cuillin'.[119]

18 In 1968 or after, 'a' ghàire' was altered to 'an ànraidh' ('of storm, distress, misfortune').

22 The sense of 'shaoil mi' is difficult to interpret. The idea may be that Eimhir surprisingly found herself at the poet's side, where he had so often fantasised about her being. Altered in pencil in 1968 or after to 'le d' fhaoilteachd chòir àghmhor' ('with your honest, pleasing welcome').

---

[119] See ll. 218 ff. (MacLean 1999: 116–117).

24 The laughter with which she gifts the poet is contrasted with the mocking laughter to which her beauty was subjected in the previous stanza. In 1968 or after, the line was altered to 'ròs aoibhinn do ghràidh dhomh?' and then 'do ghràidh-sa?' ('the pleasant rose of your love [for me]?').

25–32 Annotation in pencil: 'added in Dec. 1939'. One wonders if the reference in this stanza to a disastrous fall coming after good fortune may have been prompted by the tragic news MacLean received on Tuesday December 19th (for which see 'Introduction'). Was this also the time poem I got its opening and closing stanzas? The new line replacing 32 in pencil, ('᾽s tu bris' deleted and altered to) ' 's thusa briste gu h-iomlan',[120] dispels any doubt that the 'nighean ruadh' of this poem is, indeed, the Scottish woman.

33 Campbell Hay transcribes the line without 'leam', then adds the word in the margin, in small brackets and with a question mark. But the insertion is unnecessary, and absent from Young's transcription.

37 The reference to Eimhir's shadow (her 'faileas') interestingly anticipates a word that will be crucial in XVIII.

39–40 A nicely ironic touch closes the poem (and anticipates XXI). Nothing could be further from her thoughts than the lot of Scotland's poets (or specifically of MacLean, and the role she herself might be destined to play in the manifestation of his poetical abilities).

Five octaves (but see note above). All lines have stress on the penultimate syllable and the metre of individual lines has an underlying pattern of amphibrachs ('A nighean, a nighean', 'bu mhiann leam air t nigeal') Stanzas 2, 3 and 5 have the same end-rhyme in all even numbered lines. In the remaining stanzas, even numbered lines rhyme in pairs. There is *aicill* in a majority of couplets.

XVII

The galactic imagery deployed here anticipates the sequence of poems starting at L, in the course of which Eimhir herself

---

[120] 'and you broken completely' (editor's translation).

becomes a star. At this stage the vastness of the universe merely serves as a foil to highlight the twin wonders of her face and their love.

In his 'Dating Letter', MacLean makes no mention of poems XVII-XXII, merely stating that 'By the 13th Dec[ember] I know Eimhir XXIII was written, sometime between the 10th and the 13th'. Writing to Young on December 7th 1940, he does, however, allow that 'It will be enough for you to refer to [the "Dàin do Eimhir"] by my own (chronological) numbers', while on May 3rd 1941 he gives permission for the 'Dàin' to 'be published without numbers but in the order of the old numbers which is merely chronological'. On this basis, there is every reason for assigning poems XVII-XXII to November and early December 1939, notwithstanding their overwhelming preoccupation with the Irish, rather than the Scottish woman.

2 Note the verbal anticipation of this and the next line in XI: 4 ('baile lòghmhor, geal-reultach').
3–4 The sequence of adjectives paradoxically juxtaposes positive and negative qualities.
5–6 Fullness and knowledge are set against emptiness and ignorance. If a mind does control the motions of the universe, it is inaccessible to us and probably indifferent. See L.

Three quatrains with basically three but occasionally two or four stresses per line. End-rhyme in couplets in the first two, with one end-rhyme throughout the last quatrain.

XVIII

At 86 lines, this is the second longest item in the sequence, and the third to bear a title. LVII has 120 lines, and functions as a structural counterweight to XVIII. The contrast with the preceding poem could hardly be stronger. John MacInnes has written that Sorley MacLean

> would not be the kind of poet that he is, if he had ignored the impassioned eloquence of the Church; it is almost as certain that he would be a different kind of

poet if he had rejected the conscience-searching that the teachings of the Church invite... In the most general terms, Maclean's debt to the Church is in confidence of language; the unconfined deployment of an enormous range of vocabulary, abstract and concrete... The sermons of the Evangelicals... whose ministers and lay members came almost entirely from the common people, were enormously vital and passionate and drew on every available linguistic register of Gaelic... It was a theatrical display... The Evangelicals were never guilty, in this sense at least, of talking down to their audiences. The point made earlier about difficulty and obscurity is equally applicable here... this magniloquent prose, or poetry, or whatever it is, settled easily into the patterns of Maclean's verse. It is demonstrably there in 'Prayer'...

This influence, according to MacInnes, is not exclusively or even primarily linguistic, but intellectual and ideological:

To do justice even to this [the influence of Free Presbyterian eloquence] would require an analysis of the connection, and disjunction, between the Marxist view of history and the world view, in the Gaelic Evangelical context, of history and its meaning, as that has been interpreted in Christian thought. From childhood Maclean was accustomed to hearing discussions on these subjects – and he heard them in his native Gaelic. It is impossible to over-emphasise the unparochial nature of such views, even when they involve a tunnel-vision of history. Sorley Maclean was not the only Free Presbyterian Marxist in Raasay... if Sorley Maclean had been born in 1811, instead of 1911, would he have become not a Gaelic poet but one of the leading figures in the Evangelical Movement? Would the tremendous passion and anguish of his poetry have flowed instead into the channels of 'the peasant religion'? And if so what kind of prayers and sermons would he have delivered?[121]

For Terence McCaughey 'stretches of Sorley MacLean's

---

[121] MacInnes 1981: 16–17.

poetry are richly furnished with the terminology of that
Protestantism in which he was reared and by which he has
been surrounded for a great part of his life'.[122] 'Ùrnaigh' is
clearly a case in point. MacLean himself told Young that

> I never read tracts in Gaelic (or Seceder tracts at all)
> but constant sermonising made me very familiar with
> Seceder metaphysics and imagery and vocabulary. I
> have retained this knowledge (in fact, at present I think
> I could make a very fine Seceder sermon if my tongue
> were loosened with a little strong drink). (Letter of
> September 7th 1941.)

John MacInnes speaks of the 'authentic pyrotechnics' with
which MacLean here exploits the linguistic and intellectual
inheritance of Free Presbyterian sermons, whose ' "sometimes
racily colloquial" speech could move imperceptibly into the
arcane language of theological disputation', or else 'with
disconcerting abruptness from the flamboyant to the austere'.
According to MacLean, if even 'only a moderate fraction'
of 'the almost wholly extempore and unrecorded sermons
and prayers of ministers and "men" to whom all poetry and
song except the Psalms of David was one of the more seduc-
tive vanities of this vale of tears' had been recorded, then
'Scottish Gaelic would have a great 19th-century prose'.[123]

For MacInnes, XVIII 'moves in an indirect way which is
peculiar to the genre it imitates' and he characterises it as 'a
genuine prayer of the unconverted, no less authentic for being
a sceptic's prayer, which constantly turns aside and returns
as obsessively in a hopeless search for one fixed point of
human experience'. If 'at one level it is incoherent', the poem
is 'deliberately so' because 'belief in the eternal truths is
impossible: they cannot be accepted, but neither can they be
rejected...'. It is characteristic of such extempore prayers to
'use gnomic statements and biblical quotations to give
structural strength'.[124]

---

[122] Ross and Hendry 1986: 127. I am indebted to McCaughey's essay in
the notes to lines 16, 18, 22, 56 and 69.
[123] MacLean 1985: 108.
[124] MacInnes 1981: 16.

The poet here undertakes a stringent examination of conscience, using vocabulary derived from a Christian religious tradition in a context that is declaredly atheist (witness the original reading of lines 1–2). The provocative denomination 'prayer' is symptomatic. This is a kind of laying bare, and images of flaying recur throughout the poem, along with the fundamental idea of an irreconcilable division between what the poet ought to be and what he is.

Concerned about his brother's reaction, MacLean asked Young (July 30th 1942): 'What others besides Dàn XVIII did John object to?' And, earlier in the same letter:

> As for my stuff, I am rather disturbed by John's attitude to the publication of my godless stuff [sic]. It means of course that for various reasons John is terribly afraid of its effect on my mother and father who are Seceders of a kind. My mother, I know, will be especially worried by a new manifestation of my godlessness at this time.

1–2   For MacInnes, the poem 'opens abruptly, as extempore prayers frequently do, with a conclusive statement... as if it had been preceded by vehement but silent spiritual wrestlings'.[125]

In an airgraph dated June 1941, Young told MacLean how 'I had everything set weeks ago to start printing when your brother John threw a spanner in the works by flatly forbidding the atheistic stuff like Dàn XVIII'. Writing on May 2nd 1943, the poet informed him that 'I have altered the first two lines,.. by putting "dìon" "refuge" for "Dia" and "m'iarrtas" "my asking" for "Crìosda". All very disingenuous but it will remove the very worst nightmare to my mother.' Thus he arrived at the version of the opening as it has appeared in all printed texts until now:

> A chionn nach eil dìon ann
> agus a chionn nach eil m' iarrtas...[126]

On April 20th he had written, from Raigmore Hospital: 'I myself am afraid those two lines... will give [my mother] a

---

[125] MacInnes 1981: 16.
[126] 'Because there is no refuge / and because my desire...'

nervous breakdown. The effect of the last verse I do not fear so much, as she certainly won't bother reading the piece to the end!' Young replied (April 25th) that 'I am more and more convinced that you must change the first two lines of "Ùrnaigh", not only because it would give pain to some, but also because your propositions are too dogmatic anyway. The end of the first stanza must be kept though.'

The original reading is restored here not only because the changes were made in response to external pressure, but also to preserve the careful framing effect with the last stanza, where 'diathan' and 'Crìosda' recur in rhyming position. The translation is taken from National Library of Scotland MS 14978.

6 The city of Barcelona was occupied on January 26th, 1939, sealing the collapse of resistance to Franco's troops in Catalonia. Madrid fell on March 27th, and by the end of the month Alicante and Valencia, Almería, Murcia and Cartagena had been occupied. Thus the final objectives of the nationalist troops were attained. The United States recognised Franco's nationalist regime on April 1st.[127]

16 There is a clear element of self-projection in the speaker's portrayal of Cornford as having to banish any thought of the woman he loved, if he were to serve his chosen cause effectively. Son of the Professor of Ancient Philosophy at Cambridge University and of the poet Frances Cornford, John Cornford (1915–1936) (also named Rupert, in memory of Rupert Brooke) was a great-grandson of Charles Darwin. He refused to join the Officer Training Corps, and at the age of fifteen was already writing poetry under the influence of Eliot, Graves and Auden. A member of the Young Communist League, he went up to Cambridge in 1933 at the age of 17 and became a full member of the Communist Party of Great Britain in March 1935. At the outbreak of the Spanish Civil War, he left Britain without bidding farewell to his family, and was rumoured to have been the first Englishman to join the International Brigade in the fight against Franco. Severely injured in the battle for Madrid, he wrote many of his finest poems, including 'Heart of the Heartless World' (see note to lines 19–20),

---

[127] Thomas 1977: 873, 913, 915.

during the last weeks of his life. The precise date and circumstances of his death in the shambolic battle near Lopera are
not known.

John MacInnes writes that the formula 'Bha seo aig...'
(more common in the frequentative 'Bhiodh seo aig...') 'often
prefaced some dictum or maxim enshrining a basic truth of
the spiritual life'.[128] Following on from MacInnes, Terence
McCaughey comments that it traditionally refers to 'some
memorable insight or saying of a godly person from the
Evangelical past', adding that 'Such a godly person would, of
course, belong to that small group of "Members", or
communicants, who would actually partake of the Sacra-
ment', a group which, in this poem, includes Cornford,
Dimitrov and Connolly, all belonging to 'the secular Elect
among whom the "unregenerate" might pray eventually to be
found'.[129] In the same volume, MacLean confirms these
insights when he tells Donald Archie MacDonald how, on
the Friday of the communion celebrations which took place
once (sometimes twice) each year, the contributions from a
range of preachers

> would vary from a purely theological discussion, to a
> giving of their own particular experience and of course
> you would hear so much, even long quotations trans-
> mitted orally from people as far back as Maighistir
> Lachlainn, Maighistir Ruairidh, Céit Mhór Loch Carann,
> 'Blind Munro', the woman called Bean a' Chreideamh
> Mhóir, and so on. And, as I use in one of the poems, you
> would hear a phrase like 'somebody had this', meaning
> that some point had come home to him and he had
> illustrated and so on...[130]

18 The 'latha-traisg' is 'the Fast-Day which is normally
held on a Thursday' and 'precedes and helps to prepare
communicants for the sacramental celebration on the
following Sunday... The Fast-Day then... has become the
purifying time of self-denial in Spain, during which John
Cornford was prepared for the sacrifice of his life'.[131]

---

[128] MacInnes 1981: 16.
[129] Ross and Hendry 1986: 128.
[130] Ross and Hendry 1986: 217.
[131] Ross and Hendry 1986: 128–129.

MacLean told Donald Archie MacDonald, in the interview cited above, that 'The Thursday was the Fast-day: there would be a sermon in the morning: two sermons', although he had no memory 'whatsoever of fasting, of actual fasting', or of traditions concerning this.

19–20 The human being is afraid of losing the one he loves, but the hero knows that to experience any kind of fear is unacceptable. A more or less direct translation of the lines 'I am afraid to lose you, / I am afraid of my fear' in Cornford's poem 'Heart of the heartless world', of which MacLean would later publish a Gaelic version.[132]

21 The speaker moves directly from Cornford to himself, the transition made all the starker by the fourfold repetition of the word 'eagal' ('fear'). This and the next stanza give an impression of what the remainder of Europe (Britain included) can expect from the definitive victory of Fascism, which appears unavoidable at this point. MacLean dedicated a whole poem to 'Cornford', in which he forms, with Virginia Woolf's nephew Julian Bell and the homosexual poet Garcia Lorca, a trio of fallen heroes, comparable to that formed by the poets presiding over the Eimhir sequence.[133]

22 Cf. the second part of *Jeremiah* 12, 5: 'agus ann am fearann sìth, ged robh agad dòchas, ciod a nì thu ann an onfha Iordain?' ('and if in the land of peace wherein thou trustedst, they wearied thee, then how wilt thou do in the swelling of Jordan?') See also note to line 69.

34 The possibility of ridding himself of his feelings for Eimhir is characterised in turn as uprooting, purifying and flaying.

38 MacLean deploys in this poem in the sense of 'flay' a word whose precise meaning is 'scald with boiling water in order to remove the hair', as with the hide of a pig. The normal Gaelic term for 'flaying' would be 'feannadh'.[134] The term 'faileadh', which returns obsessively in the remainder of the poem (see lines 47, 55, 60, 70 and 71), like a lash with which the speaker can sting himself, one capable of tearing the skin from the flesh it hides and protects, does, however,

[132] Cornford 1986: 40, MacLean 1999: 304.
[133] MacLean 1999: 44–47.
[134] I am indebted to Dr John MacInnes for this observation.

rhyme with 'faileas' ('shadow', returning at 75 and 82 and anticipated at 3), thus forming one of those clusters of phonetically related terms for which MacLean shows such fondness (phonetical similarity being exploited as a basis for semantic enrichment). For the link between flaying and shadow, one could cite the apostle Saint Bartholomew, so often depicted carrying his detached skin like a shadow of himself. In the 1943 volume, both terms are (mis)spelt with 'broad l' ('faladh', 'falas' and related forms).

40 Two further heroes against whom the speaker can measure himself and be found wanting. Georgi Mikhailovich Dimitrov (also 'Dimitroff' in MacLean's English versions) (1882–1949), a printer and trade union leader, played an important part in founding the Communist party of his native Bulgaria and in 1921 joined the executive committee of the Communist International. He was its secretary-general from 1933 to 1945. The revolt which he organised in Bulgaria in 1923 was put down with ferocious reprisals. Resident in Berlin from 1929, he was among those accused of plotting the burning of the Reichstag on February 27th, 1933, and gained acquittal, famously triumphing over his Nazi prosecutors at the trial. He then moved to Moscow, and was responsible for the consolidation of a postwar Communist regime in Bulgaria, in which he assumed the office of prime minister. In Part VI of 'An Cuilithionn', Clio, the muse of history, proclaims that

> Bha mi 'n Leipzig le ùidh
> nuair sheas Dimitrov air bialaibh cùirt...
> Chunnaic mi 'n chaoir bheò uile
> spiorad beadarrach an duine,
> anam aigeannach a' churaidh,
> eanchainn eagarra nam mullach,
> aigne sìor-bhuadhach an duine,
> cridhe geal-ghathach an t-saoi.[135]

See also Part VII of the same poem: '...chunnaic mise

[135] 'I was in Leipzig, with eager hope, / when Dimitrov stood before the court... / I saw in one living flame / the surging spirit of man, / the spirited hero soul, / the exact brain of the summits, / the ever triumphant irrepressible spirit, / the white-darting philosophic heart.' Maclean 1999: 116–117.

leumraich / air sliabh a' Chuilthinn le éibhneas / ri faicinn Dimitrov...'[136] Cornford names him in 'Full Moon at Tierz':

> Three years ago Dimitrov fought alone
> And we stood taller when he won.
> But now the Leipzig dragon's teeth
> Sprout strong and handsome against death,
> And here an army fights where there was one.[137]

Born in Edinburgh in 1868, James Connolly helped found the Irish Socialist Republican Party shortly after arriving in Dublin in 1896 and, while in New York between 1903 and 1910, was one of the organizers of the Industrial Workers of the World. At Clonmel with James Larkin in 1912 he founded the Irish Labour Party and it was he who led the Irish labour movement to oppose the Allied war effort when the First World War broke out. If it had not been for Connolly's insistence, plans for a revolt centred on the General Post Office in Dublin on Easter Sunday 1916 might have been dropped. After its failure, severely wounded and affected with gangrene, he was executed by a British firing squad. See further 'An Cuilithionn' Parts V, VI and VII.[138] Caird writes that both he and the poet were 'interested in and sympathetic to Irish nationalism'. While 'Pearse and Connolly played a prominent part' in their discussions, it was Connolly 'the socialist' who 'above all appealed to Sorley's imagination, an appeal that has lasted'.[139] The poet's major tribute comes in the later poem 'Ard-Mhusaeum na h-Eireann' ('The National Museum of Ireland'), inspired by the bloodstained shirt exhibited there, worn by Connolly at the time of his execution.[140]

42 This understanding of irrevocable division is a prelude to the choice facing the speaker at 44, one in which he will take the losing part.

45 Note the careful chiasmus or mirror structure of this

---

[136] '...I saw a leaping / on the Cuillin mountain for joy / to see Dimitrov...' MacLean 1999: 120–121.

[137] Cornford 1986: 38–39, cited by Sealy in Ross and Hendry 1986: 57.

[138] MacLean 1999: 102–103, 112–113, 124–125.

[139] Caird 1995: 198.

[140] MacLean 1999: 258–259.

line: 'bàs... bheatha... beatha bhàsail'. Eternal life awaits the Calvinist Elect, but the concept is not used here in a Christian sense. Such redeployment of religious terminology also typifies MacDiarmid's practice in his poetry of the 1920s and 1930s.

48   The speaker's mistake would appear to have been that he dared to feel love for a human individual rather than a sublimated love for mankind as a whole, which would have manifested itself in political commitment, heroic action, and death for the sake of the cause. MacLean wrote to Young from Catterick on June 21st 1941 that 'To be a revolutionary one ought to have no children, parents or any close relatives, in fact no ties at all except with other revolutionaries...'

50   It is history that is pregnant with new life, not Eimhir.

56   The ideal hero is characterised in terms drawn from religious discourse. Cf. *John* 13, 10: 'Thubhairt Ìosa ris (.i. ri Peadar), An tì a tha air ionnlad, chan eil feum aige ach a chasan ionnlad, ach tha e gu h-iomlan glan'. ('Jesus saith to him, He that is washed needeth not save to wash his feet, but is clean every whit.') The term 'glan' has already occurred in lines 36 and 37.

61ff.   Repetition of the term 'guidhe' produces a sense of being trapped.

66ff.   The poem moves towards a conclusion. This stanza echoes and compresses lines 21–30.

69   Cf. *Jeremiah* 12, 5: 'Ma ruith thu leis na coisichean, agus gun do sgìthich iad thu, cionnus idir a nì thu strì ri eachaibh?' ('If thou has run with the footmen and they have wearied thee, then how canst thou contend with horses?')

74–75   Having articulated a confident position, the speaker then interrogates it again. Can his love really be described as surrender, faintness or shadow? For 'aomadh' see XIV: 8; for 'fannachd', line 73 of this poem, and for 'faileas' the note on line 38 above. See note to IX for the Platonic idealism underlying this challenge.

76   The speaker is divided within himself, and rejects external help in clarifying the point. All that remains is for him ruefully and resentfully to iterate his divided state.

78   The answer to Question 31 in the Gaelic *Shorter Catechism* explains that ''Si a' ghairm èifeachdach, obair Spiorad Dé; [l]eis am bheil e dearbhadh oirnne ar peacanna agus ar truaighe; a' soillseachadh ar n-inntinn le eòlas air

Criosd; ag ath-nuadhachadh ar toile; agus an lorg sin g'ar deanamh deònach agus comasach air Iosa Criosd a dhlùth-ghabhail thugainn, mar a ta e air a thairgseadh dhuinn gu saor anns an t-soisgeul.'[141]

'I was never a "converted" seceder who had experienced "conviction of sin, repentance into life, effectual calling, justification, adoption and sanctification" as [Edwin] Muir probably was in some ways' (letter to Douglas Young, September 11th 1941).

'Dùrachd', which MacLean translates 'sincerity', is rendered 'diligence' in the English answer to question 90 in the *Shorter Catechism*: 'That the Word may become effectual to salvation, we must attend thereto with *diligence, preparation*, and *prayer*, receive it with *faith and love*, lay it up in our *hearts*, and practise it in our lives'.[142]

81–84 Gods are a fantasy of human longing, and Christ was merely human. The only possible entity that can be blamed for the poet's state is a vaguely conceived Nature.

85 MacLean's rhyme ('shlàn' / 'sgàinte') juxtaposes the opposing concepts of unanimity (health) and dividedness (splitting), the desired but unattainable condition being emphasised in the phonetically related adjectives 'shoilleir', 'shingilte'.

Seventeen stanzas of five lines, with the exception of the concluding one, which has six. The first three and the last two lines in each stanza rhyme with one another. Basically four stresses per line.

XIX

The weighing up of accounts in this lyric, which is particularly rich in intertextual references and echoes,

---

[141] See Domhnullach 1903. 'Effectual calling is the work of God's Spirit, whereby, convincing us of our sin and misery, enlightening our minds in the knowledge of Christ, and renewing our wills, He doth persuade and enable us to embrace Jesus Christ, freely offered to us in the Gospel.' (Lawson s.d.)

[142] 'Chum 's gu'm bi am focal èifeachdach chum slàinte, feumaidh sinn aire a thoirt da le *dùrachd*, ulluchadh, agus *urnuigh*; a ghabhail thugainn le creidimh agus gràdh, a thasgaidh 'nar cridheachaibh, agus a chur an gnìomh 'nar caithe-beatha.' (Editor's italics.)

anticipates the provisional sense of closure offered by the following poem. MacLean's beloved Shakespeare sonnets may have prompted his confident claim to have conferred immortality on Eimhir, while Horace, Baudelaire and the Metaphysicals all contribute to the closing stanza.

The 'Dàin do Eimhir' are not just a narrative of frustrated love, but also a conscious record of the realisation of a literary vocation. In a letter to MacLean dated December 8th 1941,[143] Young says of the sequence that 'Over ten years the dominant thought is of course the infatuation with the face of Eimhir, as a second thought the feeling of revolution; as a third thought the self-consciousness of being a poet...'

The echoing of Màiri Mhòr at the close of the fourth stanza can hardly be accidental. Both poets had an innate talent brought to fruition by their experience of grief.

On May 3rd 1941 MacLean ordered Young to destroy his copy of XIX (as well as of V, XVI and XXVI), while on March 27th 1943 he referred to 'Eimhir XIX which you remember I kept changing my mind about so often but at last agreed to have included', unhappy to see it among the items selected for translation into English. The poem was not reprinted in the poet's lifetime. The translation is reproduced from the 1943 volume, where it appears as prose.

9–10 Immortality enters the poem as a gift the speaker has conferred on his beloved, sharply contrasting with the pain she has caused him. Now the balance shifts, for without her he would never have managed to attain, far less make a gift of, immortality. It was she who gave his poems their 'drithleann' or 'radiance' and whetted his spirit to the necessary keenness. Who then do the poems belong to? And who is indebted to whom?

15–16 The note of masochism here is unmistakeable, and is reiterated in lines 23–24, where the speaker insists he would choose repeated wounding rather than spiritual calm.

18 'Tir na h-òige' (more usually 'Tir nan Òg'), the land of eternal youth, is the best known of the otherworlds of Celtic mythology, often imagined to be off the west coast of Ireland.

---

[143] A typescript copy is to be found in the same box as MacLean's letters to Young.

There the hero Ossian spent 300 years with Niamh of the Golden Hair without experiencing sickness or physical decay.[144]
26–28 MacLean's love of paradox emerges again. Though Eimhir has diverted him from his true path, if he achieves his aim, it will be thanks to her. The word 'tòrachd' recalls 'tòir' in the sequence's opening poem (I: 2). His aim here is to realise his literary ambitions. Political commitment, or the lack of it, is not at issue. Could a possible interpretation be that Eimhir has diverted him from the kind of poetry his political convictions prompted him to write ('An Cuili-thionn') towards poetry of a very different nature, exacted from him through intensity of suffering, almost against his will (the 'Dàin do Eimhir')? The clear echoes of V: 18, 24 in these lines are indicative of how identical notions are evoked by 'different' Eimhirs.
30 The rather vague formulation may conceal a reference to Parnassus, the poets' grove on Mount Olympus in Greece.
31 A further definition of Eimhir's role in his poetry. She is its 'grìosach' or 'fire' (more exactly, 'burning embers').
32 There may be a conscious echo of the famous lines from 'Eilean a' Cheò' by MacLean's beloved Màiri Mhòr nan Òran here: ' 'S e na dh'fhuiling mi de thàmailt / A thug mo bhàrdachd beò.'[145]
33–36 MacLean told Young that while at school he 'liked Virgil and Horace (odes) very much' (letter of September 7th 1941), reiterating in the preface to his collected volume his 'considerable love of Horace'.[146] So there may be a conscious echoing of the last ode of Horace's third book here:

> Exegi monumentum aere perennius
> regalique situ pyramidum altius,
> quod non imber edax, non Aquilo impotens
> possit diruere aut innumerabilis
> annorum series et fuga temporum.[147]

---

[144] MacKillop 1998: 358.

[145] See Meek 1998: 110.

[146] MacLean 1999: xiii.

[147] *Odes* III xxx 1–5: 'I have achieved a monument more lasting / than bronze, and loftier than the pyramids of kings, / which neither gnawing rain nor blustering wind / may destroy, nor innumerable series of years, / nor the passage of ages.' Cf. Horace 1983: 164.

There are of course direct reminiscences of Shakespeare's
Sonnets, which MacLean spoke of as 'perhaps more
important than any other English influence' (letter to
Douglas Young, September 11th 1941). See, for example,
Sonnet 18:

> But thy eternall Sommer shall not fade,
> Nor loose possession of that faire thou ows't,
> Nor shall death brag thou wandr'st in his shade,
> When in eternall lines to time thou grow'st.
>   So long as men can breath or eyes can see,
>   So long lives this, and this gives life to thee.

Or Sonnet 81:

> Your monument shall be my gentle verse,
> Which eyes not yet created shall ore-read,
> And toungs to be, your beeing shall rehearse
> When all the breathers of this world are dead...

Or again, Sonnet 107 ('And thou in this shalt finde thy
monument, / When tyrants crests and tombs of brasse are
spent.')[148]

37–38 Hendry writes that mention of a wedding in XXII
preceded MacLean's actually receiving news, in December
1939, of the Irishwoman's intention to marry. For problems
with her dating, and with her claim that poems IV to XXII
'are not ordered chronologically',[149] see note to XVII.

39–40 The last quatrain is a bitterly ironic recasting of the
carpe diem topic, which would be well known to MacLean
from his reading of the English Metaphysical poets. The tag
has, of course, a Horatian origin.[150] Convention dictated that
a female addressee should be reminded of the physical decay
awaiting her beauty so as to convince her to yield without
further delay. See Marvell's 'To His Coy Mistress':[151]

---

[148] MacLean may well have been familiar with Baudelaire's ironic
application of the convention in 'Je te donne ces vers afin que si mon
nom...' ('These lines I give to you...') (Baudelaire 1997: 104–105).

[149] Ross and Hendry 1986: 24.

[150] *Odes* I xi 7–8.

[151] 'I liked Marvell immensely, still do.' (Speaking of his university days
in a letter to Douglas Young dated September 7th 1941.)

> ...then worms shall try
> That long-preserved virginity:
> And your quaint honour turn to dust;
> And into ashes all my lust.
> The grave's a fine and private place,
> But none, I think, do there embrace.

The spectacle of Eimhir's putrefying corpse is evoked for her delectation somewhat in the spirit of Baudelaire's 'Une Charogne':

> – Et pourtant vous serez semblable à cette ordure,
>   À cette horrible infection,
> Étoile de mes yeux, soleil de ma nature,
>   Vous, mon ange et ma passion! [...]
>
> Alors, ô ma beauté! dites à la vermine
>   Qui vous mangera de baisers,
> Que j'ai gardé la forme et l'essence divine
>   De mes amours décomposés![152]

While Baudelaire addresses a woman with whom he may well be enjoying a physical relationship, MacLean now knows that Eimhir can never be his. What matters is the certainty that her beauty will survive longer as enshrined in his verse than it will in the flesh. She is more truly and lastingly herself in her verbal manifestation than in physical reality, though the degree of relief offered by the prospect of such vicarious possession is questionable. Douglas Sealy has written of the 'spiritual affinity between MacLean and Baudelaire'[153] and, in a letter to Douglas Young (September 11th 1941), MacLean admitted that 'in one or two places Baudelaire has in-

---

[152] Poem XXIX in *Les Fleurs du Mal*. See Baudelaire 1997: 76, where these lines are translated as '– And yet, someday, you too will come to this, / Angel of light, and love, and lust – / Undressed, unloved, unloveable, unmissed; / A stench. A pile of dust. [...] But don't forget to tell the fervent worms / That kiss away those lips of yours, / I keep the sacred essences and forms / Of my corrupt amours!'
[153] Ross and Hendry 1986: 53–54.

fluenced me stylistically, the "sous la griffe effroyable de Dieu" manner'.[154]

Five eight-line stanzas with either two or three stresses, frequently tending to an underlying anapaestic rhythm with closing feminine rhyme. Even-numbered lines have end rhyme, on 'ò' throughout the first four stanzas. Internal rhyme is deployed with increasing consistency as the poem progresses. Dr Michel Byrne points out that this is one of very few among the 'Dàin' which could be sung to a traditional tune, as it tends very closely to standard Gaelic song form.

XX

Another poem in which the political theme is dormant. It marks a kind of closure by enumerating (at line 3) the poems written up to this point. Maybe this betrays MacLean's realisation that his infatuation with the Irishwoman could lead nowhere. On the other hand, he may have contemplated rounding off a much shorter version of the sequence here. With the mention of Alexander Blok in the closing line, the trinity of unhappy poets presiding over it is complete. Editor's translation.

2   What matters here is the harmonising of art and love. Political commitment is forgotten, and images of splitting and division disappear for the time being.
3   Only 14 of the 19 poems MacLean had so far completed were to see publication in the 1943 volume, one of them (XV

---

[154] MacLean is quoting, not quite accurately, the conclusion of poem XCI of *Les Fleurs du Mal*, 'Les petites vieilles': 'Où serez-vous demain, Èves octogenaires, / Sur qui pèse la griffe effroyable de Dieu?' ('Where will you be tomorrow, ancient Eves, / Now that His monstrous claw is set to fall?' Baudelaire 1997: 238–239). The poem in question expresses a mixture of repelled fascination and compassionate identification with the socially derelict and marginalised. Perhaps MacLean comes closest to this in 'Ban-Ghàidheal' ('A Highland Woman') (MacLean 1999: 26–29), though his sober nobility of tone establishes an unmistakable distance from Baudelaire.

'Trì Slighean') among the 'Dàin Eile'. The line indicates a clear awareness of the sequence as a structural unit.

5–6   For the pairing of 'aodann' and 'spiorad', compare XIV: 18, 20 ('àilleachd', 'spiorad'), XXXIV: 1–2 ('aodann', 'spiorad') and XXXVII: 2, 5 ('aodann', 'anama'). The note to IX discusses MacLean's Platonism in detail.

7ff.   Like the main body of XIII, these lines constitute a poetics, an open avowal of the kind of poetry MacLean would like to write.

16–17   The words 'singilt' and 'fillte', which denote the tragically unattainable in the closing lines of the last two stanzas of XVIII, return here in a more promising context.

18–19   The potentially celebratory tone of this lyric comes adrift in its closing lines, where the speaker identifies himself with those poets who carried the cross and experienced the suffering of unsatisfied passion. For Yeats and Ross, see note to X: 12.

The Russian Symbolist poet Aleksandr Blok (1880–1921) was the son of a law professor. His maternal grandfather was rector of St Petersburg University. Strongly influenced by the philosophy of Vladimir Solovyev (1853–1900) (which so fascinated MacDiarmid in the early 1920s), Blok was rhythmically innovative in his work, which is characterised by an outstanding musicality. His first, idealistic collection, the *Verses to a Most Beautiful Lady* (1901–02), takes a strongly Platonic approach to love and eroticism. In 1903 he married Lyubov' Mendeleyeva, daughter of the famous chemist, in whom many, not least Blok himself, were tempted to see the embodiment of the sublime figure of his poems. Subsequent disillusionment led Blok possibly to celebrate a prostitute in his poem 'The Stranger', a Scots version of which is incorporated into the text of MacDiarmid's poem *A Drunk Man Looks at the Thistle* (1926).[155] In Blok's case, differently from MacLean's, we have some indication of how the woman in question responded to the poet's idealisation of her. In a letter of January 1902, Lyubov' told Blok that

I can no longer remain in the same friendly relationship with you as before; up till now I was completely sincere

---

[155] See MacDiarmid 1993: I, 88–89. For a Scots adaptation of a lyric to the Most Beautiful Lady see 90–91.

in it, I give you my word. But now, if I were to keep
it up any longer, I should have to begin pretending.
Suddenly, quite unexpectedly and for absolutely no
particular reason on your side or mine, it became quite
clear to me to what extent we are alien to one another,
how little you understand me. You look on me as
though I were some kind of abstract idea; you have
imagined all kinds of wonderful things about me and
behind that fantastic fiction which existed only in your
imagination you have failed to notice *me*, a live human
being with a living soul... I am a live human being and
that is what I want to be, even with all my faults.[156]

Quite probably it was MacDiarmid's enthusiasm which first
brought the Russian poet to MacLean's attention. Though
Blok welcomed the Bolshevik Revolution, the incomprehen-
sion with which his work was treated, combined with the
harsh material conditions obtaining in post-revolutionary St
Petersburg, hastened the poet's death. MacLean's close friend
Sydney Goodsir Smith made a Scots version of Blok's most
celebrated poem, 'The Twelve', which ends with the am-
bivalent image of Christ hovering above a band of Red Army
soldiers who are busily pillaging St Petersburg during a
snowstorm.[157] In Part VI of 'An Cuilithionn' Blok keeps
company (rather incongruously) with Lenin, Marx and
Nietzsche.[158]

Lines varying between three and four stresses, with end
rhymes in the following pattern: 'à' (1–6), 'uai' (7–8), 'io / ia'
(9–10), 'oi' (11–13), 'i' (14–17), 'o' (18–19). All except the last
pair of rhymes are feminine.

---

[156] Pyman 1979: 96. It appears that Blok 'would not (or could not)
consummate his marriage to Lyubov Dmitrievna Mendeleeva... yet he
willingly sought out the company of St Petersburg prostitutes...' See
Bethea 1994: 185.

[157] Smith 1975: 109–118 (originally published in 1959).

[158] MacLean 1999: 114–115.

XXI

The possibility that the lyrics he has written may have gained him an honoured place among Scottish poets cannot compensate him for having failed to secure Eimhir's attention. Editor's translation.

6 At IX: 4, the poet had defied death to label his words as 'arraghloir'. Here he repeats the slander and makes it his own.
7 A direct citation of XIX: 25.
8 She is the content of his poems. It is her beauty for which he has found an equivalent in Gaelic, yet she is excluded from his audience. Platonic theory implied that Eimhir's soul was responsible for the beauty of her face. MacLean suggests that his poems are a further manifestation of the same entity. (See note to IX).

Eight lines rhyming in couplets and having *aicill* on 'à' throughout. Basically three stresses.

XXII

For Douglas Sealy, this poem combines 'a Baudelairean sophistication with the directness of the Gaelic songs' and he compares its 'quatrain form, the outwardly dry tone, and the divided self in conversation' to the Frenchman's 'Tout entière'.[159] XXII offers a dialogue where the speaker is divided against himself MacLean devises an intellectual double-bind which, while altering biographical reality, gives memorable and dramatic form to an underlying tension of the sequence. In order to deserve Eimhir's love, he would have had to immolate himself fighting in Spain, but would thereby have lost any possibility of enjoying her. Failing to enlist has equally meant losing her.

On May 3rd 1941 MacLean wrote to Young that 'XXII

---

[159] Ross and Hendry 1986: 55; Baudelaire 1997: 108–109 (poem XLI in *Les Fleurs du Mal*, translated in the bilingual edition as 'Total Harmony').

of the Eimhir poems I desire to include though before I
wanted it cut out' and, on December 18th of the same year, 'I
have not yet changed the last verse of Eimhir XXII. As it is,
it now appears to me lamentably crude and stupid and I leave
it entirely to yourself whether to include the poem or not.
My own preference would be for its exclusion.' There is no
clear indication as to whether the lines in question were
indeed modified.

2   The dialogue has a liminal setting, at the edge of the sea.
4   The distance which his reason (here 'tuigse') maintains,
though at his side, symbolises the impossibility of integrating
it with other elements in his personality.
5ff.   His reason addresses him in tones of challenge and
defiance, verging on contempt. Sealy cites the words of an old
song as a possible influence:

> 'S olc an sgeul a chuala mi
> Di Luain an déidh Dhi Dòmhnaich,
> Sgeul nach bu math lium e –
> Mo leannan dol a phòsadh.[160]

11   The speaker refuses to show surprise or alarm, or to
rebel against his fate. He claims to find the situation emi-
nently 'reasonable'.
17   The heroism of those who opposed Franco is again
described in Christian terms.
20   The word 'dàn' carries of course the double meanings
of 'fate' and 'song'. Therefore Eimhir might also be the one
new prize of song.
21–22   These lines are an echo of XV; 6–7 (' an t-slighe
chrìon ud, / thioram, ìseal, leantainn tìorail...'). There they
refer to a choice of poetics, while the choice here lies between
heroism and death on the one hand, and a safe life with
unrequited love on the other.
24   MacLean glosses 'beithir' as 'dragon or thunderbolt',
the overall meaning being 'something like "fire-dragon"'
(letter to Douglas Young, May 26th 1940).

---

[160] 'I heard bad news / on the Monday following the Sunday, / news that
brought me no pleasure – / my sweetheart was going to be married.'
(Sealy's translation.) Ross and Hendry 1986: 55. The song is in Craig
1949: 109.

25ff.   For Sealy, the 'final verse affirms an heroic resolution, but the phrase "If I had the choice again!" betrays a subconscious fear that one's second choice might be no different from the first. There are no second chances in life. It is this hint of uncertainty behind the resolution that gives the poem much of its poignancy.'[161] See note above for MacLean's intention to modify the last verse.

27   A puzzling line. One might expect a leap to either heaven or hell, whereas the speaker envisages abandoning both for an unspecified destination. Ronald Black suggests interpreting 'whether my life were a heaven or a hell...'.

28   The poem ends with a talismanic word in the sequence, 'slàn', meaning both 'whole' and 'healthy' (as well as 'saved' in the religious sense).

Seven quatrains with basically three stresses per line, end-rhyme in the second and fourth lines (the second quatrain also rhyming first and third) and frequent, but not consistent, use of *aicill*.

XXIII

Despite its length and its importance for the sequence (as the point where the Scottish woman appears definitively to oust the Irishwoman from MacLean's imagination), this item has received relatively little attention. Though he spoke to Young of 'the Beethoven poem which is almost my own favourite' (letter of August 19th 1940), MacLean did not reprint it until the 1989 collected edition.

The practice of concert-going and the associated Viennese classical music tradition had not previously figured in Gaelic poetry. MacLean deliberately pairs Gaelic and non-Gaelic elements, in a challenging and potentially dissonant fashion (see lines 15–16, 19–20, 23, 51–52). While redolent of the Modernist determination to redefine existing canons, the strategy also shows his wish to restore Gaelic culture to its rightful place among more fully developed European traditions.

---
[161] Ross and Hendry 1986: 56.

MacLean was remarkably precise about this poem in the 'Dating Letter': 'By the 13th December I know "Eimhir" XXIII was written, sometime between the 10th and the 13th.' On Saturday December 9th, the Reid Symphony Orchestra, conducted by Adrian Boult, performed Beethoven's 8th Symphony as part of a concert which comprised works by Wagner (the *Mastersingers* overture), Dvorak and Elgar (the *Enigma Variations*). The *Scotsman* reviewer regarded the Beethoven symphony as 'perhaps the best thing of the afternoon. The playing of the *Allegretto* movement, in particular, deserved high praise.' The orchestra was composed of members of the University Music Faculty. This was the last in a series of three Saturday afternoon concerts, given at the unusually early time of 2.30 pm because of wartime lighting restrictions. The only other Beethoven item featured in the short season was his *Egmont* overture.

It is hard to connect lines 1 and 2 of this poem with what is perhaps the most lightweight and lighthearted of Beethoven's symphonies. The English of lines 11 and 47 (first published in 1989) implies the presence of a choir, as if the 9th and not the 8th were being performed, and indeed, the optimistic and humanitarian sentiments of Schiller's 'Ode to Joy', set to music in its final movement, would certainly have appealed to MacLean's instinctive socialism. Nonetheless, in an autograph translation from c.1943,[162] 'còisir' (line 11) is rendered 'orchestra'. Where the word occurs again (line 47), MacLean has deleted the latter part of the line so energetically as to make a hole in the paper, substituting 'stood in the great choir'. The Scottish woman was a violinist[163] and would appear to have played in the first violin section of the orchestra during the previous season.[164] There is therefore good reason to believe that she was in the orchestra on December 9th, that the poet was in the audience, and that the occasion provided the basic inspiration for XXIII.

---

[162] Preserved in National Library of Scotland MS 14978.

[163] Information from the poet's daughter.

[164] See programme for concert of March 9th 1939, preserved in the Reid Music Library, University of Edinburgh. The programme for the concert of December 9th has not been preserved. Beethoven's Choral Symphony had been given at the last concert of the 1937–38 season, though there is no indication that MacLean attended this.

In two stanzas from 'Craobh nan Teud' (written at some point between November 1939 and the early months of 1940) the beloved is depicted as playing a stringed instrument:

> Chunnaic mi a' chraobh ag éirigh,
> 'na meanglannan an ceòl leugach,
> mo ghaol geal fhìn a' gluasad theudan,
> bàrr-gùc air iomhaigh an éibhneis.

> Chunnaic mi a' chraobh an céin thir
> 's a ceòl cianail 'na phéin dhomh,
> mo ghaol geal fhìn 's a meòir air teudan;
> bu luaineach òr-ghuth glòir an éighich.[165]

XVIII emphasised division, and XXII made wholeness seem an impossible task. XXIII tells of a vain attempt at synthesis. The return of the opening lines, like a refrain, at the beginning of the seventh and the last stanzas underlines the speaker's inability to transform the given situation.

MacLean told Young (letter of September 11th 1941) that in this poem he could 'hear the influence of Shakespeare's Sonnets' (which he believed to be 'perhaps more important than any other English influence' on him), adding that 'It has rounded cadences that have come from God knows where'. He originally believed it to be 'very untranslatable' (letter to Young dated April 20th 1943).

1 By 1802, when he wrote the letter to his brothers known as the Heiligenstadt Testament, the symptoms of Beethoven's deafness had become unequivocal. The composer was tempted to take his own life, becoming more and more of a recluse, though his deafness would not become total until 1819. His surly and irascible temperament was a further factor in his increasing isolation as his life drew to a close.
6 Though more than a century has passed since the composition of the music, the art deployed in it continues to

---

[165] 'I saw the tree rising, / in its branches the jewelled music, / my own fair love moving strings: / the image of joy blossoming. // I saw the tree in a distant land / and its far sad music sore for me, / my own fair love with her fingers on harp strings, / restless the gold voice of their crying speech.' MacLean 1999: 52–53.

be new, unprecedented. The composer became deaf: the audience is struck dumb by his music.

8   The word 'gathadh' implies that the music is also a source of pain. Compare XXXV: 13 ('gathadh ùrlair ciùil Maoil Duinn'[166]).

9   It is unlikely that the occurrence of the adjective 'bàn' in this line is a reference to the Irishwoman (see 'Introduction' and note to VI: 6–7).

14   The key term 'tòrachd' (Beethoven's music is in search of joy – a possible reference to the last movement of the 9th symphony?) evokes the Greek virgin huntress Diana, who in turn evokes Deirdre (the object of a hunt on the part of her rejected suitor Conchobar).

15   Diana is the classical Italian goddess of wild nature, hunting and the moon. She was soon identified with the Greek goddess Artemis. MacLean mixes Greek and Italian in line 20.

16, 19   See notes to XIII: 1 and 2. The notes to Carmichael's version of the legend include the following passage:

> Loch Etive is in Argyll, a land greatly studded with fresh-water lakes, and as greatly severed with salt-water lochs. Loch Etive runs in from the sea for twenty-four miles, lying between hills all the way... It is the most varied, the most storied, the most stormy, and the most beautiful loch in Scotland. Its two divisions differ greatly. Lower Loch Etive is wider and more varied, expanding here and there into broad bays, and projected into here and there by long peninsulas. On each side, between the edge of the water and the base of the mountains, runs a belt of arable land, irregularly broad, studded with trees and fields, houses and churches. In Upper Loch Etive the bases of the towering mountains on each side descend immediately down to the water. They continue thus for twelve miles to the head of Loch Etive, and for six miles more to the head of Glen Etive. Loch and glen resemble a huge, deep railway cutting, through which the winds blow up or down during the years and the ages... The district of Loch Etive is

---

[166] 'the piercing music of Maol Donn's theme'.

deeply identified with Deirdire and the sons of Uisne. The old people who lived on the sides and at the head of Loch Etive, in the glens which run back, some of them for miles, among the mountains, spoke much of Deirdire... Alas, hardly one of these native people is now left on the land – all having been cleared away.[167]

A poem from the 15th century Glen Masan manuscript, set in the mouth of Deirdre, cites Glendaruel, in Kilmodan parish in Cowal, Argyllshire, as one of her places of exile in Scotland:

> Glend Daruadh! O'n Glend Daruadh!
> Mo chen gach fer da na dúal;
> Is binn guth cuaich ar craib cruim
> Ar in mbinn os Glend Daruadh.[168]

MacLean returns to this material in 'An Ceann Thall', where he mentions 'ceathrar ainmeil a' bhròin' who 'chaidh air tìr an Gleann Eite'.[169] See further the short poem 'Conchobhar', which also links the two places: 'Chan fhàg mi san aon uaigh iad / fad fìn-shuaineach na-oidhche... b' fhaide 'n oidhche na 'n Gleann Da Ruadh, / bu luasgan cadal Gleann Eite...'[170]

22 A further Platonic equivalence. Eimhir's physical beauty is identified with the content, the import of the music.

23 The pibroch tune 'Maol Donn' ('the brown polled cow'), known in English as 'MacCrimmon's Sweetheart', is attributed to one of the famed MacCrimmon family of pipers (see note to lines 39–40, also XXXV: 13).[171]

---

[167] Carmichael 1914: 136 137.

[168] 'Glen Da Ruadh! / My love to everyone who inherits it; / sweet is the cry of the cuckoo on the bending branch / on the summit above Gleann da Ruadh.' Quoted in Ross and Hendry 1986: 64 from Cameron 1894, II: 467–468. For an earlier stanza about Glen Etive from the same poem, see note to XIII: 2.

[169] '...the famous quartet of sorrow' who 'went ashore in Glen Etive'. MacLean 1999: 196–197.

[170] 'I will not leave them in the same grave / for the whole long night... / the night would be longer than in Glen Da Ruadh, / sleep in Glen Etive was unrest...' MacLean 1999: 48–49.

[171] Ross and Hendry 1986: 63. Haddow 1982: 119 suggests that the original Gaelic title may have been 'Mo Ghaol Donn'. Ronald Black disagrees, citing a reference to his wife as Maol Meidhe in 'M' anam do sgar riomsa aréir' by Muiredhach Albannach.

25   The opening returns, with a different sequel, yet this stanza, like the first, groups its material in two strongly contrasting couplets.

26   Here, as at III: 3, MacLean renders as 'suffering' a word more frequently glossed as 'wandering' or 'deviation'.

28   Now it is the girl who is 'ùr' rather than Beethoven's art, as if she were absorbing its qualities through a kind of osmosis (cf. line 6). There may also be a reference to the Scotswoman having replaced the Irishwoman as the addressee of MacLean's love poems.

29ff.   The elements whose synthesis the speaker vainly attempts to achieve are art, political catastrophe, human beauty and human suffering.

35   The word 'brèine' recurs significantly in XXXIV, where it denotes the degradation of the bourgeoisie in capitalist societies.

39–40   According to differing accounts, the MacCrimmon family arrived in Skye from Harris, from Ireland or from Cremona in Italy (though this may well be little more than a fanciful interpretation of the patronymic). They were hereditary pipers to the Macleods of Dunvegan from the sixteenth until the early nineteenth century. Patrick Mòr (1595–1670) was the greatest composer of the line. According to tradition, the piper had gone to church with his eight sons, one year after seven of them had been buried in Kilmuir churchyard (see line 51). Only Patrick Òg survived. They may have died of smallpox, which reached Skye on a visiting ship.[172] This is the traditional account of what led him to compose his 'Cumha na Cloinne' or 'Lament for the Children'. The tragedy is also referred to in MacLean's poem 'Craobh nan Teud': 'A chlann marbh san teasaich dhòbhaidh / agus Pàdraig Mór gu ceòlmhor'.[173] Legend attributes to him a love affair with the poetess Màiri Nighean Alasdair Ruaidh. His tunes are characterised by 'length of melodic line', and the 'Lament for the Children' has been claimed to contain 'the longest and best line of melody in European music'.[174]

---

[172] Haddow 1982: 94.

[173] MacLean 1999: 52 ('His children dead in the raging fever / and Patrick Mór in his music').

[174] MacNeill and Richardson 1996: 21–22, Thomson 1994 s.v. MacCrimmons.

MacLean commented to Young (letter of March 30th 1942) that

> I always hanker after a restrained, calm manner that would express depth and not fire, a manner that would belie an intensity of matter, something that would suggest or be in some way like the greatest of Mozart and of the MacCrimmons, and I look with disgust at some of my own too patent subjectivity... when I think what kind of poem I should ideally like to write, it would be one not like anything I know in Shakespeare, Blake, Yeats or Grieve [Hugh MacDiarmid] but rather like "Cumha na Cloinne" or "Maol Donn" or one or two things I heard in Mozart...

Further mentions of the MacCrimmons and of the 'Maol Donn' pibroch can be found in 'An Cuilithionn', Parts II, V ('stoirm / is glaodhaich gairm / duis fhoirmeil bhrais / o Phàdraig Mór / 's o Phàdraig Og: / an gaol 's am bròn / 's a' phròis mhór ait') and VI,[175] as well as in the extended poem 'Craobh nan Teud'.[176]

41   Patrick Mòr's success in immortalising the deaths of his sons supports the possibility of a synthesis between art and human pain, which is immediately dashed by the thought of the countless individuals whose sufferings and death have not been so celebrated.

45   In certain versions of her tale, Deirdre is so distressed by the killing of Naoise that she throws herself upon his grave and dies.

52   Note the insertion of the politically loaded term 'daorsa' (IV; 24 and XXXII: 4).

53   The second recurrence of the opening lines does not this time lead to a stanza equally shared between the positive and the negative. The flawless quality of Eimhir's beauty is almost blasphemous, inhuman for its apparent indifference to the realities of human suffering, with which it cannot be reconciled.

---

[175] 'the storm / and shouting cry / of stately impetuous drone / from Patrick Mor / and Patrick Og, / love and grief / and great joyous pride'. MacLean 1999: 78–79, 98–99, 110–111.

[176] MacLean 1999: 48–57. For the longer original version see MacLean 1943: 62–68.

Fourteen four-line stanzas with lines of three and four stresses. The second and fourth lines have feminine rhymes, while there is frequent but not consistent *aicill* within couplets.

XXIV

For another disagreement about the nature of beauty, see VIII with its epigraph from Yeats. Here the roles of Eimhir and the speaker are reversed, and he maintains the stance articulated at the close of XXIII.

5–6 More fully, the line asks whether Deirdre would have said these words to Naoise when they landed as fugitives on the west coast of Scotland. (See notes to XIII: 1 and 2 and XXIII: 16.)

Effectively free verse, with 'à' rhyme in lines 2, 4 and 6 and 'ao' rhyme in 3 and 5.

XXV

MacLean had come to admire the work of Shelley in his teenage years, and he may well have had the English Romantic poet's verse drama *Prometheus Unbound* at the back of his mind when writing this lyric. He told Young (September 11th 1941) that

> Portree school only confirmed a sort of anti-Secederism intent in my childhood and made it quasi-Promethean or Shelleyan... my Promethean view of Socialism in an inversion of the career of the "saved", in the sense that it was a justification of the "lost", "damned" Promethean. I had to find a humanist, hence Promethean subsitute.

Prometheus functions as a type of the hero who sacrifices his own interests to those of humanity as a whole. In that case, this lyric is yet another rejection of political commitment and its attendant sacrifice in favour of love, beauty, and the art they can inspire. The opening of Part VII of 'An Cuilithionn' refers initially to Aeschylus for 'aogas / suinn-dé-duine crochte màbte / air Caucasus nan sgurra gàbhaidh'.[177] Shelley is not named until the beginning of the following paragraph. Note the play on the phonetically similar 'milleadh' and 'meallaidh', contrasted in meaning, while the word for 'theft' appears as two variants ('goid' and 'gad'). Editor's translation, but see the note to lines 3–4.

3–4 MacLean's own translation of these peculiarly compressed lines is incorporated here, from a letter to Douglas Young of February 22nd 1942.
6 Another reference to the emergence of a 'new' Eimhir, the Scottish woman who succeeded Nessa Ní Sheaghdha as the focus of MacLean's affections, and to the burst of poetry she inspired?

Six lines with three stresses each (except for line 4). Lines 2, 4 and 6 have end rhyme, while the second two couplets have *aicill*.

XXVI

Published here for the first time. A typed copy is included in a letter to Douglas Young of April 15th 1942. One reason for leaving it out of the printed volume may have been its vaunting of a potential superiority to William Ross, while XXXI merely implies parity. The translation is MacLean's, given in the same letter.

4 For William Ross see note to X: 12. A possible alternative translation of the latter part of this could be 'William Ross with his store/abundance [of songs]'.

Four-stressed lines with 'ò' end-rhyme.

XXVII

A further poem insisting that the qualities of his art are drawn from Eimhir's face. See note on IX for an extended discussion of MacLean's Platonism. Editor's translation.

---

[177] 'the likeness / of hero-man-god hanged, lacerated / on Caucasus of the dangerous peaks'. MacLean 1999: 120–121.

1   The identity of the critic concerned (if indeed a specific person is intended) is uncertain. In a letter dated from Ardlogie, Leuchars on December 8th 1941, Douglas Young asked MacLean if he had W. D. MacColl in mind.[178]

3   The choice of words establishes links with preceding and following lyrics in the sequence. Cf. XIX: 8 'goirt drithleann na glòire' and XLIV: 8 'caoir na cèille buadhmhoir'. See also line 5.

5   For 'mealladh', see XXV: 5 ('gad meallaidh bho do shùilean'). Note the careful parallelism of these lines. In XXIII: 22 her face was identified with the joy ('aoibhneas') of the music. Here the joy ('èibhneas', an alternative form of the same word) of MacLean's own art has its source in her face. Cf. Shakespeare's Sonnets 103 ('For to no other passe my verses tend / Then of your graces and your gifts to tell') and 78:

> Yet be most proud of that which I compile,
> Whose influence is thine, and borne of thee:
> In otheres workes thou doost but mend the stile,
> And Arts with thy sweete graces graced be.
> But thou art all my art, and doost advance
> As high as learning, my rude ignorance.

Seven lines with mainly three stresses, rhyming *aabbccb*.

XXVIII

In response to Douglas Young's curiosity about this and the following poem, MacLean wrote (March 30th 1942) that

> As to "Samhlaidhean" and "Coin" this is all I can say. On Tuesday 19th Dec 1939 (I remember the date because I travelled home to Raasay on Christmas Day 1939, which was Monday) I got a letter that meant for me the end of my period of great activity in poetry. All Tuesday I was depressed and wrote nothing but about 2 or 3 a.m. on Wednesday 20th I got up out of bed and

---

[178] Typescript copy in NLS Acc. 6419 Box 38b. For W. D. McColl, see Bold 1988: 345 and introductory note to poem XV.

very quickly wrote down "Samhlaidhean" and "Coin", of which, as far as I remember, I have never changed one word from that first writing down. It seems to me that I composed them simultaneously in a troubled sleep.

It is probable that the letter in question contained a revelation of the Scottish woman's physical condition and of the limitations this would place on any relationship with MacLean.

The two poems have in common a haunted, visionary, even nightmarish quality. Here MacLean's poems figure as ghosts, while in XXIX they are wolves and mad dogs engaged in a symbolic hunt. He believed the metrics of this and the following poem to be related (but not indebted) to the experiments of the 19th century Islay-born poet Uilleam MacDhunlèibhe (William Livingston (1808–1870)) (letter to Douglas Young of September 11th 1941).

The translation is reproduced from the 1943 volume, where it appears as prose.

1   From poems XL, XLV and XLVI it is clear that the Scottish woman, who stands behind the figure of Eimhir at this point, had claimed she was incapacitated and therefore unable to have a physical relationship with the poet. This line could therefore be interpreted in a direct, sensual way as well as more Platonically.

7ff.   The consistent use of syntactical parallelism produces a ritualistic, almost liturgical effect, while also making the lines flow in a fashion appropriate to the movement of fleshless ghosts. 'Gabhaidh iad' is followed by 'falbhaidh iad' (12), 'chithear iad' (14), 'tachraidh iad' (16), 'ni iad' (18), 'seasaidh iad' (20, 23) and again 'falbhaidh iad' (25). Note also the lesser parallelism in the sequence of verbal nouns: 'ag iargain', 'ag èigheach' (7), 'a' sìor rànaich' (9), 'a' sìor iargain' (10), 'a' sìor dhèanamh luaidh' (11).

13   For History, cf. XVIII: 50. MacLean's poetic ambition comes to the fore here and in the following poem. History (the victories of Fascism throughout mainland Europe) made major claims on his poetic talent, though in the end they were to yield to the claims of love.

22ff.   It is tempting to compare the 'bàrd gun aighear' with the 'chòmhlan gun tost, / gun fhurtachd, gun fhoighidinn, gun fhois'[179] mentioned in X, whose members include Yeats and William Ross. This is a nocturne, a poem filmed in black and white. Line 24, in particular, offers a striking contrast with the abundance of colour adjectives used to describe Eimhir elsewhere in the sequence.

25 There is an implication of transcendence in this final couplet, though the rising sun cannot restore vitality to the lifeless bodies of the poets.

Lines of three or four stresses, with feminine end rhyme on 'ao' (1, 5–7), 'à' (2–4, 7–15), 'oi' (16–19), 'ai' (20–22), 'ua' (23–24) and 'è' (25–26).

XXIX

Like XXVIII, this poem was the result of a process as close as MacLean ever came to automatic writing (with the possible exception of the final section of 'An Cuilithionn'). The ethereal, plangent quality of 'Na Samhlaidhean' gives way to a frenzied and bloodthirsty chase, the kind of un-resolved pursuit which is a not uncommon element of dreams. The use of parallelism and listing gives the poem an obsessive intensity and speed, as MacLean redeploys the rich Gaelic vocabulary of landscape and hunting to portray a psychologi-cal state. The dogs and mad wolves are his unwritten poems, and there can be no doubt that, were they ever to catch up with their prey, the deer that stands for Eimhir's beauty would be torn to pieces.

2 It is unclear whether these are poems the speaker still intends to write, or poems that will never now be written. Eimhir is unattainable in his dream of the hunt. The letter MacLean mentioned to both Young and Hendry had, it would appear, rendered the Scottish woman unattainable in a different, more carnal sense.

7 Four lines of the strictest syntactical parallelism. See also 12 and 18, 13 and 14.

---

[179] 'the band lacking stillness, / lacking succour, patience or rest' (editor's translation).

16, 20   Note the recurrence of the words 'tòir', 'tòrachd', for a pursuit that is ruthless and life-threatening.
21   Inner and manifest beauty, 'anam' and 'aodann', are paired Platonically as the reader has come to expect.

Lines with four or three stresses rhyming in groups of two or four. Note the double rhymes in 9–10: 'caol-ghleann', 'gaoth-bheann'.

XXX

'When I got up on Wednesday [20th December 1939] I felt more serene and that day I wrote Eimhir XXX-XXXV and perhaps XXXVI as well.' (Letter to Douglas Young, March 30th 1942.) This and the next five, or even six poems, were written in a calmer frame of mind, but still in the aftermath of the letter from the 'wounded Eimhir' with its tragic revelation (see XL and note to XLVI: 9–10). The light-hearted treatment of the conflicting claims of love and political allegiance in **XXX** belies the circumstances of its composition. For Mac Síomóin, MacLean here 'gives a new twist to an old love convention wherein the beloved is preferred even to God by replacing the latter with the State, in this case a fantasised Scottish Republic'.[180] Were the utopian Scotland here envisaged ever to become a reality, love for Eimhir would lead the speaker to flout its ideology. Such a potent brew of nationalist fervour and Bolshevik enthusiasm is rare in 20th century European poetry.

1   MacLean is responsible for introducing this coinage to Gaelic poetry. See also 'An Cuilithionn' Part VI.[181]
3ff.   The fourfold repetition of 'Alba', followed by three lines beginning 'gun', another three 'Alba's and then the conditionals 'bhristinn... bhristinn... dh'èighinn' create an effect of speed and splendidly prepare the irreverent conclusion of the poem.

---

[180] Ross and Hendry 1986: 114.
[181] MacLean 1999: 116.

7–9   Compare the lines in 'An Cuilithionn' Part II (where 'Alba gheal' is also ' 'na brochan brèine'):

> Seo latha eile air na sléibhtean
> is Alba mhór fo bhinn bhéistean,
> a mìltean bhochdan air an spùilleadh,
> air am mealladh 'nan cuis-bhùrta,
> air am briagadh, air an ungadh
> aig maithean is bùirdeasach dhiadhaidh
> tha deanamh bùirdeasach de Chrìosda.[182]

12   The implication may be that the poet would break the traditions of masculine succession to the throne.

Lines of three or four stresses, two-thirds of which have final rhyme in 'ao'.

XXXI

A further stage in the speaker's ongoing dialogue or rivalry with William Ross, implying a degree of parity between the two, not just in the pain of their loves, but in poetic achievement. An interesting comparison is offered by the rather more chastened lines from Part III of 'An Cuilithionn', where MacLean speculates as to the circumstances in which he might have equalled the work of that poem's dedicatees, MacDiarmid and Mac Mhaighstir Alasdair, but is content to remain at the level of Mary Macpherson ('Màiri Mhòr').[183]

The translation is reproduced from the 1943 volume, where it appears as prose.

3   Iain Crichton Smith has produced a fine English version of Ross's 'Òran eile air an aobhar cheudna'.[184] In his essay

---

[182] 'our choice Scotland a porridge of filth'. 'Another day upon the mountains / and great Scotland under the doom of beasts: / her thousands of poor exploited, / beguiled to a laughing-stock, / flattered, doctored and anointed / by the nobles and godly bourgeois / who make a bourgeois of Christ.' (MacLean 1999: 82–83).

[183] MacLean 1999: 90–91.

[184] See Thomson 1989: 215–216, Gaelic original in Calder 1937: 172–174. Watson 1995: 362–365 prints the original and Iain Crichton Smith's translation side by side.

'Old Songs and New Poetry', MacLean considers it 'one of
the very greatest poems made in any language in the islands
once called British', while doubting whether 'I nor anyone
else can ever hope to persuade the non-Gaelic world that
William Ross's last song is comparable in quality to the best
of Shakespeare's Sonnets'.[185] In a list of tunes for Gaelic
songs which 'seem like exhalations from the words, as if the
very words created the tunes' he cites 'the version of Ross's
"Òran eile" as sung by my father'.[186] For Thomson, it is the
'barest, most desolate of his love-songs, the one most firmly
pruned of extraneous ornament... without bravado... short,
and tightly reined, so that the emotion which sets it in
motion is kept compact and compressed'.[187] Did such
starkness bring it close to the ideal MacLean expressed in the
poem immediately following this one?
5   Notice the dual, paradoxical implications of control and
restraint in 'sgaoil' and 'shriante'. For all the undeniable
sincerity of these lyrics, they are reined in, controlled by art.
6   All the preceding lines have 8 or 7 syllables, while this
one has 5. Such compression heightens the impact of this new
metaphor for MacLean's lyrics.

Basically three stresses. End rhyme in even lines, and *aicill*
in lines 3–4 and 5–6.

XXXII

It is possible that the images of lopping and mutilation which
emerge in this poem (recurring in XL, XLV, XLVI and XLVII)
were prompted by the contents of the letter the poet received
on December 19th 1939 (see note to XXVIII). His aspirations
here bring to mind the doctrine of Socialist Realism, which was
to dominate aesthetic discourse in the Soviet Union and its
satellite states from 1932 to the 1980s, with its hostility towards
'bourgeois' or 'formalist' inclinations to foreground aesthetic
considerations. The citing of the Communist martyr Liebknecht, whom MacLean pairs with Ernst Thaelmann in a
passage from 'An Cuilithionn' (see note below), is appropriate

---

[185] MacLean 1985: 111, 114.
[186] MacLean 1985: 120.
[187] Thomson 1989: 214.

in such a context, though the poet's concern with the plight
of the masses brings him closer to the critical realism of 19th
century Russian authors than to the rigidly optimistic and
idealised approach demanded by Stalin's regime.

In terms of the 'Dàin do Eimhir', little would come of the
resolve expressed here. Tree imagery recurs notably at the
end of XLIII, and again in LVI. MacLean's words in a letter
to Young of February 22nd 1941, following on from criticism
of Eliot, and of Auden and associated poets, are illuminating
in this respect:

> All this contemporaneity I think just nonsense. Con-
> temporary likenesses can be only in very superficial
> things, just as all sophistication is merely superficial. Why
> should you or I talk of mechanisms, tractors or anything
> of the kind if we are not at all moved by them? A poet's
> imagery can in the main come only from what moves
> him, unless of course he files images.

1–2   Her influence is to be excised from his poetry, as if it
were merely decorative, an excrescence (an attitude at the
opposite pole from the explicit Platonism of so many lyrics in
the sequence).
3   Contrast the characterisation of MacLean's poetry by an
unnamed critic in XXVII: 2–3.
4   Karl Liebknecht (1871–1919) was assassinated along with
Rosa Luxemburg in Berlin on January 15th 1919, in the
course of a revolutionary uprising which it was hoped would
spearhead a Communist takeover on the model of what had
happened in Russia. He had been one of the founders of a
clandestine organisation in Berlin known as the Spartacus
League, which came to form the nucleus of the Communist
Party of Germany. His killers were counterrevolutionary
volunteers who claimed he and Luxemburg had tried to
escape while under arrest. See further 'An Cuilithionn' Parts
II ('fuil Liebknecht'), V ('Liebknecht sa Ghearmailt, / marbh
ach neo-bhàsmhor'), VI ('Liebknecht, Thaelmann is daorsa')
and VII.[188]

---

[188] 'Liebknecht's blood', 'Liebknecht in Germany / dead but undying',
'Liebknecht, Thaelmann and slavery' MacLean 1999: 80–81, 104–105,
114–115, 124–125.

8 It is as if the poet's task could be compared to that of an iron founder. The foundries of a Communist society would hopefully be means of liberating the masses rather than enslaving them, as under Capitalism.

Predominantly three stresses, rhyming *aabbbcdd.* Note the *aicill* in lines 5 and 6.

XXXIII

The speaker's suffering cannot be laid to the account of his being a poet, since they experience good and bad fortune just like ordinary people. There can be no doubt about the speaker's identification with Ross rather than Macintyre at this juncture. An early version of this item[189] fails to contrast good and ill fortune and sets the two Williams, Ross and Yeats, side by side:

> Carson a bhiodh càs nam bàrd
> atharraichte air mo sgàth?
> Cha d' fhuair Uilleam Yeats a ghràdh
> 's fhuair Uilleam Ros a shàth
> den àmhghar, [den] chaitheamh 's den bhàs.

3 Duncan Bàn Macintyre (Donnchadh Bàn Mac an t-Saoir) (1724–1812) was born in Glen Orchy, fought on the Hanoverian side at the Battle of Falkirk in 1746 and, after spending 20 years as a forester in Glen Lochay, Ben Dorain and Glen Etive, was a member of the Edinburgh City Guard from 1766–1793. He was neither a renegade because of his political and religious affiliations (like Mac Mhaighstir Alasdair) nor a poet of unrequited love (like William Ross) but rather the author of songs written both for the established monarch and for the London Highland Society's competitions and, most importantly, of

---

[189] See note to V for the survival of this variant. The original has a full stop rather than a question mark after 'sgàth' and 'gràidh' rather than 'gràdh'. Editor's translation: 'Why should the predicament of poets / be altered on my behalf? / William Yeats did not get his love / and William Ross got his fill / of anguish, [of] consumption and of death.'

'Moladh Beinn Dòbhrain' and 'Òran Coire a' Cheathaich',[190] splendid descriptions of the landscape and wildlife of the area where he grew up. MacLean chooses him as a Gaelic example of a poet living in comparative peace with contemporary society, apparently alien to deeper currents of anguish or uncertainty. In a later essay he describes Duncan Bàn as 'not a contentious man', one who lacked 'any very strong political, social or religious convictions... a naive conservative, accepting the dictates of his social and political superiors... until it came to the Clearances'.[191]

Predominantly three stresses per line, end-rhyme throughout on 'à'.

XXXIV

The speaker insists that his understanding of the catastrophic political situation is sufficiently acute for his praise of Eimhir not to be invalidated as a consequence.

1–2 'Aodann' and 'spiorad' are paired, here as elsewhere (see note to IX).
5 Here, and in line 10, MacLean is thinking of the marsh of Maraulin, at the top of Glen Brittle north of the Cuillin hills, as the physical equivalent of the degradation of the bourgeoisie.[192] This marsh appears in the closing section of Part II of 'An Cuilithionn' and functions as the dominant image of Parts III and IV, in lines such as these:

> Och, a bhoglaichean sanntach,
> shluig sibh an t-Ar-a-mach mór Frangach,
> shluig sibh a' Ghearmailt is an Eadailt,
> is fhad' on shluig Alba 's Breatainn;
> shluig sibh Aimeireaga 's na h-Innsean,
> an Aifric is magh mór na Sine,

---

[190] 'Praise of Ben Dorain' and 'Song of the Misty Corrie'.
[191] MacLean 1985: 131.
[192] Ross and Hendry 1986: 54.

's a Thì mhóir, b' e siod an t-àmhghar,
gun d' shluig sibh gaisge na Spàinne.[193]

Writing to Douglas Young on September 7th 1941, MacLean,
'billeted in a very comfortable pub where I enjoy all
civilian comforts', was amused to find Stalin and Lenin
'occupying wall space with Clavers and Montrose', given
that 'my place for the latter would be fairly low in
Maraulin'.

7   The first mention in the sequence of MacLean's beloved
mountains on Skye, which were to play such an important
role in his poetry. Usually referred to in the plural, and
known also as the 'Coolins' or even 'Cuchullins'. There is a
fine description of them in the 1894 *Ordnance Gazetteer of
Scotland*:

> Rising from the sea-shore to the E of Loch Brittle and
> N of Loch Scavaig, and extending north-eastward to
> Glen Sligachan... they occupy an area of about 35
> square miles, and are a confused assemblage of barren
> heights, from 2000 to 3000 feet high, distinguishable, by
> striking differences in outline, feature, and colouring,
> into two great sections. The southern and larger...
> consists of smooth, conoidal masses, that rise from a
> labyrinth of low ground... nearly all streaked from
> summit to base with broad reddish sheets of *débris*, and
> many of them abrupt, acclivitous, and rounded like vast
> bare cones. The northern section, on the other hand,
> consists of singularly rugged and serrated ranges and
> masses of mountains, intersected by wild ravines, and
> shooting up in sharp and jagged peaks... whose dark
> metallic aspect is relieved by scarce one blade of
> vegetation... strongly attracting rain-clouds from the
> ocean, it often is lashed with storms. Always, even amid
> the blaze of summer sunshine, a region of desolation,
> without any play of colours, it looks under a wreathing
> of clouds to be little else than an assemblage of deep

---

[193] 'O greedy morasses, / you swallowed the great French Revolution, /
you swallowed Germany and Italy, / long ago you swallowed Scotland
and Britain, / you swallowed America and India, / Africa and the great
plain of China, / and, great One, that is the anguish, / that you swallowed
the heroism of Spain.' MacLean 1999: 86–87.

and horrible abysses, which the eye vainly endeavours to penetrate...[194]

In conversation with Donald Archie MacDonald, MacLean describes these mountains as

a very, very spectacular landscape... the kind of landscape that easily resolves itself into what you might call heroic symbols... in my early twenties, I went to teach in Portree School and started going to the Cuillins. In those days I could get very few people to go with me, practically nobody in those days, and I used to wander about alone on them, ridge-wandering and doing some rock-climbing to avoid detours and being there in all kinds of conditions. To me the whole thing was bound up with the history of Skye and Raasay... my symbols came mostly from my immediate environment, because in many ways my immediate physical environment was very varied. The Cuillins naturally became a symbol of difficulty, hardship and heroic qualities as against, as it were, the softness and relative luxury of the woods of Raasay with all their own contradictions. I grew up at that time, when symbolism was such a thing in European poetry... and my symbols almost automatically became the landscape of my physical environment.[195]

His comments are, of course, equally relevant to 'An Cuilithionn' and 'Coilltean Ratharsair' ('The Woods of Raasay').[196]
11–12 Spirit and heart are contrasted, rather than being in harmony.

Lines of three or four stresses with end-rhymes in couplets (stretched over four lines at 3–6).

XXXV

Another nocturne, calling on night to descend, dreamier and more restful than XXVIII.

---

[194] II, 315.
[195] Ross and Hendry 1986: 218–220.
[196] See MacLean 1999: 170–183.

3–4   In XVIII, purification and flaying were seen as moral imperatives, and in the previous poem the bourgeoisie was viewed as drowning in a black morass. Here cleansing is not feasible, yet peace and harmony can be invoked. For 'gaoir na Spàinn', see IV and XVIII.

5   For Maol Donn, see note to XXIII: 23. The notion of the pibroch itself as 'singing' ('a' seinn') is unusual. Ronald Black points out that the word can mean 'playing' as well as 'singing' in many dialects, while finding that 'a' seirm' would sound more normal in this context.

8–10   Doubling and splitting recur throughout the sequence. But here the speaker is unable, thanks to the darkness, to see his own shadow and can, temporarily, be at one with himself.

12   MacLean translates 'comprehend', though at XIII: 20 and at XXVI: 3 the same words are used in the sense of 'fashion, compose'.

13   Cf. 'fonn / Maoil Duinn nan gath' in Part V of 'An Cuilithionn'.[197]

Lines with predominantly four stresses and end-rhyme for each pair, extended to three lines at the close.

XXXVI

Young sent his transcript of this poem to MacLean in April 1968 (see note to V). An English prose translation, in pencil and in MacLean's hand, is among the Caird papers in the National Library of Scotland.[198] Along with XIV and XXXVIII, XXXVI forms a group concerned with the motif of selling one's soul which, for the purposes of the sequence, can be considered as having a single addressee. It is worth noting that the refusal spoken of here does not correspond to the biographical situation as far as we know it (see note to XXVIII).

Four lines with three or four stresses, rhyming *abab*.

---

[197] 'the melody / of the piercing Maol Donn'. MacLean 1999: 98–99.
[198] MS 14978.

XXXVII

This and the lyrics that follow, as far as LV, were 'written in Hawick about March 1940, possibly some in February and some in April, I am not sure' (letter to Douglas Young, March 30th 1942). A notion of MacLean's faithfulness to the Platonism characteristic of the Petrarchan tradition may be gained by comparing the present poem with sonnet XLVIII of Ronsard's 'Amours de Cassandre'.[199] Though there may be no direct textual connection, MacLean's poem reads like a compression and paraphrase of the French sonnet.

3 The speaker wishes to make clear the nature of the beauty which affects him like a blindfold. MacLean glosses 'dallabhrat' as 'blinding mantle', 'veil' or 'covering' in a letter to Douglas Young dated May 26th 1940.
4 This phrase is used to generate a whole poem in XLI.
6 Notice the delicate semantics of 'dealbh' in line 1 ('picture, image, physical form') and 'dealbhach' here ('made manifest, revealed, given physical form').

Two or three stresses per line, even lines rhyming in 'ao' while the end-rhyme of 1, 3 and 5 is echoed internally by 'dh'fhalbh' and 'dealbhach'. Further *aicill* in the last two lines.

XXXVIII

For the motif of selling one's soul, see XIV and XXXVI. These three poems are an instance of how successive items in the sequence can interact with, comment on or rectify one another (even when the addressee, in terms of the poet's biography, would appear to differ). Here the speaker's readiness to betray himself in the earlier lyrics is vigorously rejected. Editor's translation.

8 For 'daorsa' in the sense of enslavement see IV: 24, XIV: 2, XXIII: 52 and XXXII: 4. But is there not an underlying

[199] Ronsard 1974: 47.

resonance of the other possible meaning of the adjective 'daor', that is, 'dear', 'precious'?

An alternation of longer (8 or 10 syllables) and shorter (5 or 6 syllables) lines. Even lines rhyme in 'ao', while there is consistent *aicill* with the 'à' end-rhyme of odd lines (note the anomalous half-rhyme with 'anama').

XXXIX

For the fire imagery in this poem, cf. MacLean's 'Prometheus poem', XXV, as well as XLV: 9–10. Also the following passage from 'An Cuilithionn' Part III:

> Bha deuchainn na mo spiorad aognaidh
> nuair a smaoinich mi gum b' e t' aodann
> a chunnaic mi sa mhòintich bhaoith ud.
> A luaidh, m' annsachd is mo ghaol geal,
> tha fhios nach diù leatsa 'n taobh ud.
> Lìon mo chridhe 'na lasair caoire
> ri t' fhaicinn air a' mhullach fhaoilidh.[200]

4 White heat is, of course, the hottest and most extreme.

The metre here resembles ballad metre. There is end rhyme in lines 2 and 4, and internally 'caoir' is echoed in 'gaol' and 'adhradh'.

XL

This poem, like XLV and XLVI, was first published in 1970 in *Lines Review* 34, with accompanying English translation. The poems are here restored to their place within the sequence. There can be little doubt that MacLean hesitated to

---

[200] 'My chill heart was anguished / when I thought that it was your face / that I saw in that foolish bog. / My dear, my delight and my white love, / surely you did not think that side worthy. / My heart filled with bursting flames / to see you on the generous mountain.' MacLean 1999: 90–93.

publish them because of the graphic manner in which they describe the mutilation he believed the Scottish woman to have suffered. In the list appended to his letter to Young of April 27th 1941, XL came second among the items 'of which I myself disapprove but concerning which I am indifferent to publication', being subsequently scored out vigorously in pencil, whether by MacLean or Young is not clear. The three lyrics from the sequence are followed in *Lines Review* by four other poems on the 'wounded Eimhir': 'Uilleam Ros is mi fhìn', 'An Cogadh Ceart', 'Am Mac Stròidheil' and 'A' Mhalairt Bhreugach' ('William Ross and I', 'The Proper War', 'The Prodigal Son' and 'The False Exchange').[201] XL gave the title to MacLean's 1977 selected volume, *Reothairt is Contraigh* or *Spring tide and Neap tide*.

1ff.   The opening quatrain is a bitter reworking of the sixth verse of the old song 'Mo rùn geal, dìleas' as given in Archibald Sinclair's *An t-Òranaiche*:

Cha bhi mi 'strìth ris a' chraoibh nach lùb leam,
   Ged chinneadh ùbhlan air bhàrr gach géig;
Mo shoraidh slàn leat ma rinn thu m' fhàgail,
   Cha d' thàinig tràigh gun mhuir-làn 'n a déigh.[202]

Note how carefully MacLean alters the wording while respecting metre and rhyme. Later he would cite this instance of 'John MacLean holding off his passion for the Campbell woman, with his unbending tree and ebb followed by flood' as one of the high points of Gaelic song before 1800.[203]

3–4   The rich vowel music of this couplet, where 'slàn', 'fhàgail', 'tràigh' and 'bhàin' are followed by 'dèidh' (rhyming with 'geug' in line 2), is not uncommon among traditional songs. MacLean's stanza simplifies and standardises, restricting itself to two rhymes rather than three.

---

[201] Subsequently included, in a slightly different order, in the section entitled 'An Ìomhaigh Bhriste' ('The Broken Image') in MacLean's 1977 and 1989 volumes (now 1999: 188–190, 192–195, 198–199).

[202] Sinclair 1879: 294, cited in Ross and Hendry 1986: 67. ('I am not striving with the tree that will not bend for me, / Although apples should grow on top of each branch; / Farewell to you if you have left me, / No ebb came without a floodtide after it.' Editor's modification of MacLean's translation.)

[203] MacLean 1985: 112.

5ff. The last line of the borrowed stanza may have prompted the tidal imagery of MacLean's second, which also evokes the menstrual cycle with its traditional links to the moon, especially poignant when the poem concerns a woman for whom intercourse and childbirth seemed now to be precluded.

Two quatrains with four stresses per line. Even lines have end-rhyme in pairs, and there is consistent *aicill*, in all but one case on 'ù'. There is a shift from the song metre of the first stanza to more natural speech rhythms in the second.

XLI

Published here for the first time. Included, along with an English translation, in a letter to Douglas Young of April 15th 1942. On May 3rd 1941 MacLean instructed Young to 'use your discretion' regarding the inclusion of this poem, though 'I myself think it turgid', repeating on November 19th of the same year that 'I told you already to include "E[imhir]" XLI "Chaidh mo ghaol ort thar bàrdachd" if you like...' The lyric modifies a line from XXXVII and expands it to form an entire poem.

8 Cf. XXIII: 12 'bhàrc an taigh mòr lem ghràdh-sa' ('the big hall surged with my love'). The concluding adjective epitomises the exultant energy of this short poem.

Eight lines with two (occasionally three) stresses and end-rhyme throughout on 'à'.

XLII

XLII to XLIV, XLVIII and XLIX constitute moments of reflection in the progress of the sequence. The landscape of Gaelic Scotland acts as a backdrop to the speaker's relationship with Eimhir, which is anything but uniformly tragic in nature. One wonders if MacLean viewed the Highland landscape with particular intensity or tenderness due to his distance from it in Hawick. Here the poet and his beloved appear on five different beaches. The speaker's protective

tone indicates a wish to defend their love from the onward
march of time, which will become the focus of anguished
questioning in several lyrics from L to LVII. See the final
verse of 'An Mhaighdean Óg', the song which immediately
precedes the section on Thomas Costello (see note on XIII: 7)
in Hyde's *Love Songs of Connacht*:

> Dá mbéidhinn-se 's mo ghrádh
> Cois taoide no tráigh
>   'S gan aon neach beó 'nn ár dtimchioll
> An oidhche fhada, 's lá;
> Do bhéidhinn-se ag chómradh
> Le Neilidh an chúil bháin
>   Is liom-sa 'budh h-aoibhinn
> Bheith ag coímhdeacht mo ghrádh.[204]

1   Talisker Bay is on the western shore of Minginish in Skye,
at the foot of the hill known as Preshal More (which, at
317m, is slightly lower than Preshal Beg 347m to the south)
and reached by a road through Gleann Oraid.
2   Although MacLean speaks of the beach as being pale or
white, it is in reality composed of black boulders rounded by
the sea and of fine, almost black sand.
4   Two points on the coast to the north and south respectively of Talisker, far beyond the extent of the beach itself.
The Bioda Ruadh lies beneath Preshal Beg, while at the
promontory of Rubha nan Clach the coast swerves east-
wards.
6   See 'Copytexts and Variant Readings' for an inferior
early version of this line, preserved in George Campbell
Hay's transcription of the poem.
9–10   The trope here is related to the classical figure of the
adynaton where an event linked to impossible circumstances
will, by implication, never take place. The poet and his love
will remain on the beach for ever. For Preshal, see note
to 1.
11   Douglas Sealy quotes a passage from 'Là a' Bhreith-

---

[204] 'If I and my love were / Beside the tide or the shore / Without
anyone alive around us, / And the long night and the day / I would be
conversing / With Nelly of the fair cool [i.e. hair], / It's I who would
think it pleasant / To be accompanying my love.' Hyde 1969: 46–47.

eanais' ('The Day of Judgement') by Dugald Buchanan (1716–1768) as a possible inspiration for this stanza:

> Ged àir'mhinn uile reulta néimh,
> Gach feur is duilleach riamh a dh'fhàs,
> Mar ris gach braon ata sa' chuan
> 'S gach gaineamh chuairticheas an tràigh;
> Ged chuirinn mìle bliadhna seach,
> As leth gach aon diubh sud go léir,
> Cha d' imich seach de'n t-sìorruidheachd mhóir
> Ach mar gun tòisicheadh i 'n dé.[205]

MacLean once heard 'a humanist agnostic call Buchanan the greatest of all Gaelic poets' on the basis of these very lines.[206] In a letter to Young dated September 7th 1941, he speaks of 'Là a' Bhreitheanais' as giving 'a good idea of Seceder cosmic imagery. It is a very great poem'.

12 Calgary Bay is on the north west coast of Mull. Though Coll is in fact closer, the bay points westwards and slightly to the south, in the direction of the more distant Tiree, beyond which lies the expanse of the Atlantic Ocean.

13–14 Mainland Scotland and Tiree are redefined in symbolic terms. The beach is a liminal location, where two different elements (land and water) and two different kinds of time (human time and eternity) meet.

16 Another of MacLean's word clusters, connecting 'bruan' and 'braon', powder and liquid. Though not present at this point, the word 'bròn' or sorrow is not far away. Cp. XLV: 18, 22, L: 1–2 ('bròn', 'bruan') and the line from 'Reothairt': ' 's i tràghadh *boinn'* air *bhoinne bròin*'[207] (my italics).

17 Hosta is on the north west coast of North Uist, close to Tigharry. The beaches on the stretch of coast between Tigharry and Griminish to the north east are in fact less extensive than those east of Griminish or around Kirkibost Island and Baleshare to the south.

---

[205] 'Though I counted all the stars of heaven, / each grassblade and leaf that ever grew, / along with every drop that is in the sea / and each grain of sand the shore collects; / though I lived a thousand years / for each one of them all, / no more of vast eternity would have passed / than if it had begun yesterday.' Cited with translation in Ross and Hendry 1986: 62.
[206] MacLean 1985: 131.
[207] MacLean 1999: 192 ('ebbing drop by drop of grief').

19–20 See note on 9–10 above. Conceiving of the sea as drops brings close the paradoxical juxtaposition of fragments and hugeness in XLV.

21 Moidart, south of Mallaig, between Morar and Ardnamurchan.

23–24 A reminiscence of the 'concert poem', XXIII. The synthesis attempted here is of irreconcilable physical particles.

25 The fifth and last beach mentioned is again in Skye. Staffin Bay lies on the north-east coast of the island, protected to the west by Staffin Island and with the rivers Brogaig and Stenscholl flowing into it. Stenscholl village is situated between Staffin township and the Bay. 'Mol' indicates a beach composed of pebbles or shingle. According to one tradition, the Raasay hero Iain Garbh was shipwrecked and drowned off this beach around 1671. The event was marked with a pibroch by Pàdraig Mòr MacCrimmon and an elegy by the poet Màiri Nighean Alasdair Ruaidh.[208] In conversation with Donald Archie MacDonald, MacLean refers to 'an old story that the boulders of Mol Stamhain were thrown up on dry land the day that Iain Garbh Mac Gille Chaluim was drowned'.[209]

26–27 The ocean takes on personal qualities in the hostility which leads it to hurl pebbles at the lovers.

Three stanzas, of 10, 10 and 9 lines respectively, rhyming in couplets. The missing line in the last stanza is resolved in a rhyme on three lines. Three or four stresses in each line.

XLIII

The first four stanzas present a series of desirable states, of containment, free range, mental exertion and rationality, all of them transcended by Eimhir's 'edict'.

1 The second mention of the mountain range in the sequence. See note on XXXIV: 7.

5–6 A clear reminiscence of the preceding poem. For the colour of the sand in Talisker Bay, see note to XLII: 2.

---

[208] Sharpe 1982: 42.
[209] Ross and Hendry 1986: 219.

9 MacLean may be thinking of the different seas visible from the beaches enumerated in XLII.

18 The name of a famous pibroch, or classical pipe tune, also rendered in English as 'Lament for the Harp Tree', not capitalised in the 1943 edition, which made its interpretation as an actual tree in this context more natural. MacLean took it as the point of departure for a long poem included in the 1943 volume and reprinted, in modified form, in the 1999 collection.[210] This stanza reads like a citation from that poem, which had either been completed or was in the process of writing at this time: 'I forget whether "Craobh nan Teud" was in November or December 1939 or in the early months of 1940...' (letter to Douglas Young of March 30th 1942). See in particular the lines from section III: 'Eibhneach anns a' mheangach bhlàthmhor / suaimhneas geal an aodainn àlainn'.[211]

In the note 'Airs and Metres' to his edition of the songs of Roderick Morison, 'An Clàrsair Dall' (c.1656–1713/4), William Matheson suggests that the harper's poem about a lost harp-key could appropriately be entitled 'Cumha Crann nan Teud', and refers to the bagpipe lament cited at line 18 of MacLean's poem, whose first part or 'ùrlar' fits the Harper's words. 'Craobh nan Teud' is included in Angus Fraser's manuscript collection of Gaelic music (now in Edinburgh University Library) in a version for the harp. Matheson believes that the word 'craobh' had been substituted at some stage for 'crann', which originally carried the meaning of 'tree' alongside that of 'harp key', 'thus opening the way for such fanciful explanations as "the tree of strings", supposed to denote the harp'. MacLean's interpretation of the title would thus be a fruit of earlier misunderstandings.[212]

19 The image of the leafy branch contradicts the aims of the 'lopping' poem, XXXII, which viewed from this point proves to have led nowhere.

20 Stars will play in important role in the poems from L onwards. Eimhir is herself recognised as one in LII.

---

[210] MacLean 1943: 62–68, 1999: 48–57.

[211] MacLean 1999: 52 ('Joyful in among the thick branches / the fair serenity of the beautiful face').

[212] See Matheson 1970: 154–155.

Four stanzas with end-rhyme in the even lines and consistent *aicill* or internal rhyme in each couplet. Mainly three stresses per line.

XLIV

For Ronald Black this poem is 'a jewel that must be held up to the light, a perfect example of MacLean's mischievous, probing subtlety'.[213] As such it is well-nigh untranslatable, and the editor is fully aware of the unsatisfactory nature of the solutions proposed, especially where line 6 is concerned (see below).

1 The poem envisages a different kind of 'stripping' from that of **XXXII**. Though it mentions clothing, the speaker's transformation into a 'firebrand' suggests a move beyond the fleshly or physical, and the notion of delivering this firebrand to the loved one is emblematic of the transcending or denial of sensuality which characterises MacLean's passion (see following poem). The firebrand may be Promethean in origin (see **XXV**).
6 As the Gaelic terms 'gaol', 'ciall' (with genitive 'cèille') and 'luaidh' can all mean 'love', it would be possible in theory (though unhelpful) to render this and the preceding line as 'I would reach the love-core [literally 'clay-love'] / of my love of love'. Here 'luaidh' is translated as 'devotion', while the alternative meaning of 'ciall', 'reason' (see **II**), has been preferred. MacLean is of course playing on the semantic richness of the Gaelic terms in a manner impossible to reconstruct in English.

Mainly three stresses per line. The rhyme scheme is *ababababab*, with *aicill* on the *a* rhyme in lines 4, 6 and 8.

XLV

It is helpful to discern in this poem a series of 'movements'. Stanzas 1 to 4 are concerned with incision, fragmentation

---

[213] Black 1999: 768. For his translation, see 299.

and paradoxical wholeness. The first two describe the analysis, the second two the state of the stone after it. Stanzas 5 to 9 are concerned with expansion and contraction, with dimensions that oscillate between the huge and the tiny, stanzas 7 to 9 also discussing the origin of the stone. Stanzas 10 and 11 draw conclusions about love and about the stone respectively, while stanza 12 closes the poem by once more addressing Eimhir, as at the beginning. The exasperated cerebrality of this item owes much to MacLean's reading of the Metaphysicals, as does his 'inappropriate' deployment of scientific imagery in the context of a love sequence. XLV is indeed one of the poems where MacLean acknowledged the influence of Donne (letter to Douglas Young of September 11th 1941). It is also characteristic of the curiously antisensual nature of MacLean's love lyrics, which it is tempting to ascribe to his Free Presbyterian background, though these are of course poems of love unrequited rather than fulfilled. The cutting imagery recalls XXXII 'Sgatham...',[214] while also anticipating the tearing and wounding in the next poem, XLVI ('do chreuchdan', 'colainn reubte', 'do cholainn chreuchdaich').[215] In XXXII the urge was towards amputation or removal. Here cutting is intended to take the speaker to the heart of the object being examined. Emotion is dissected but proves ultimately resistant to analysis.

2   Initially, his love is just a stone. At 5, its fragments are jewels while at 13 it is a kind of talisman with magical properties.

6–7   There is no hiding the aggressive, potentially destructive nature of the intellect's examination of love. The stone is seared and cut (see 11), and the lens through which he scrutinises it is cold and sharp.

13   The spelling 'seun-chlach' would make the word's implied relationship to 'seun' ('charm, spell, amulet') more explicit.

14   The lyric's chain of bewildering paradoxes begins here with a key word for the sequence as a whole, 'slàn' ('whole, entire' but also 'healthy, integral'), already highlighted at

---

[214] 'Let me lop...'
[215] 'your wounds', 'a torn body', 'of your wounded body'.

the conclusions of two important poems (XVIII: 85 and XXII: 28).

18 For the cluster 'bruan, braon' see note to XLII: 16.

19 The word 'aonachd' can be related to 'slàn' (line 16), but is here inaccessible (' 'na h-aonar') and has taken on un-attractive attributes ('cruaidh teann', line 20).

23–24 Paradox reaches its acme here, with 'hard' water and an expansion which is at the same time compression. The operation of love is indeed impermeable to the intellect.

25ff. Three origins for the stone of love are proposed in the next three stanzas. 'Aigne', rendered 'spirit' by MacLean, is also 'mind, temper, disposition',[216] while 'eanchainn' stands for the brain in a more anatomical sense.

30 While redefining the stone's origin with respect to the preceding stanza, this one develops further the idea of its paradoxical dimensions. Though it had been confined within his 'aigne', and within the less restricted space of his body ('com', however, more precisely indicates 'the cavity of the chest, the region of the viscera',[217] deriving his love from an act of aggression on himself), its progenitor had once formed part of a distant constellation.

32 Betelgeuse is the brightest star in the constellation of Orion, among the largest stars known and easily visible to the naked eye thanks to its deep red colour. Its name derives from the Arabic for 'giant's shoulder'.

33ff. The meaning is hard to elucidate, and it does not help that MacLean translates 'meanmna' as both 'mettle' and 'spirit', thereby encouraging confusion with 'aigne' (above) and with 'spiorad' (see line 39). A possible interpretation would be that his love took courage from the fact that any courage it might feel or generate would then be transmitted back to the brain where it had originated.

37ff. First of two stanzas which summarise the conclusions drawn from the experiment the speaker has undertaken. The source of his love is redefined as his heart, thus gaining a sense of freedom in the midst of servitude and laying the bases of an intellectual apprehension of love's value.

41ff. The effect of the brain's aggression is to render love

---

[216] Dwelly s.v. 'aigne'.

[217] Dwelly s.v. 'com'.

even more impregnable to all assaults. Note the recurrence of 'shlàn' in line 42.

47 Though not evident in the translation, the effect of 'tha fhios gun...' is to suggest that the experiment has merely served to bear out a truth which was generally accessible even without it.

48 For exigencies of rhyme, MacLean uses both pronunciations of 'geur / giar' in one poem (cf. lines 10 and 16).

Lines predominantly with three stresses. Twelve quatrains with consistent end-rhyme between even lines and sporadic *aicill*. Odd lines also rhyme in stanzas 1, 2, 6, 9 and 10.

XLVI

MacLean withheld this poem from publication until 1970, when it appeared along with XL and XLVII in *Lines Review* (see note on XL above).

1–2 A sad echoing of poem XI.

3–4 What the face of the 'wounded Eimhir' hides here may be contrasted with what it manifests in a poem such as XXXVII.

10 For love as a firebrand, cf. XLIV.

13–15 The only explicit, rather than implied, acknowledgement within the sequence that the figure of Eimhir encompasses more than one woman. Could this have been a factor in MacLean's original decision to withhold the poem?

End-rhyme in all even lines on 'è', with *aicill* in a majority of the couplets. Predominantly three stresses per line.

XLVII

For publication history, see previous poem and XL.

1ff. The lines evoke an image of the speaker's body lying next to his beloved's, filled with shame and remorse at his

own eagerness and readiness for sex, which contrasts so
strongly with her mutilated condition.

9–10   Presumably the chance to love her in a physical sense.
The only indication within the sequence that the wounded
Eimhir's plight is due to a previous lover who was, further, a
Lowlander, and therefore to some extent an alien and even
hostile figure for the speaker. It is these lines, along with the
mention of an 'operation' in Hendry's essay[218] that prompt
the hypothesis that an abortion, carried out inexpertly at a
time when such things were illegal, was the pretext the
Scottish woman offered for being physically unavailable to
MacLean. His subsequent disillusionment is evident from the
bitter lines entitled 'Knightsbridge, Libya, an t-Òg-mhios
1942'.[219] In a letter to Douglas Young from Raigmore
Hospital, dated May 27th 1943, he mentions 'certain bitter
poems I had written in the desert... they are about 25 in
number but I am very doubtful if they can ever be published,
or if I want ever to publish, or even preserve them. They hint
pretty clearly at the real truth behind others, but I should
have appreciated that truth much earlier than I did. Even
now I am not altogether sure of it.' In a much later interview
with Colin Nicholson,[220] MacLean said that 'References in
several of the poems about this time to a woman's wounded
and mutilated body are to be taken literally. I was wrong
about this, too, but I had no way at all, as far as I can see, of
finding out, because between one thing and another, I saw
her only once between December 1939 and late July or early
August 1941... the point is, after such an experience, and the
fact that the business was not really properly resolved, it
wasn't so much a tragedy now, but a kind of perplexity; not
knowing what was what. It was the business of having to go
away to the desert on top of all this; of having made a fool of
myself, through what I can only describe as a kind of quixotic
rashness.'

13ff.   There may be a reminiscence of Blake's 'The Sick
Rose', where an 'invisible worm' has 'found out thy bed / Of

---

[218] Ross and Hendry 1986: 25.
[219] Quoted in the 'Introduction' p. 9 and first published in *Poetry Scotland*
2 in 1945.
[220] Nicholson 1986.

crimson joy: / And his dark secret love / Does thy life destroy'.[221]

An octave and two quatrains, with even lines rhyming in pairs and occasional *aicill* ('pòg' / 'leòn', 'manadh' / 'rathad', 'bhòidhche' / 'òir'). Three stresses per line in the octave, three or four in the quatrains.

XLVIII

A series of paradoxes celebrating the manner in which Eimhir's proximity makes the inconceivable actual. It is hardly surprising that a love sequence which laments the impossibility of synthesis, and emphasises division and polarisation, should show such fondness for grouping paradoxes together, as in this poem and in XLV.

13 Cp. '...Dimitrov 'na aonar / a' toirt air an spiorad dhaonda / leum as a chochull le faoisgneadh...' ('An Cuilithionn' Part VII).[222]
14 'Rèis' here in the sense of 'span', 'measurement', more precisely 'allotted span (of years)'.
15–16 Is MacLean's rendering of 'allaban' as 'suffering' influenced by the word here ('arraban')? See III: 3 and XXIII: 26. The English 'adamant' suggests that it is the hardness of the resultant jewel that matters to MacLean, though such an emphasis is not clear in the Gaelic. The 1943 translation has 'jewel-hard' here. Cf. XLV: 47–48: 'mur biodh gaol mo chridhe / ort mar chruas na lèig...'.[223] Note how contradictory is the notion of a blossom turning into a jewel.

Quatrains alternating longer and shorter lines. Mainly three stresses throughout. Even lines rhyme in pairs and there is *aicill* in all couplets except one. Note the use, for purposes of rhyme, of 'rium fhèin' instead of the more standard 'rium fhìn' in line 10.

---

[221] Blake 1972: 213.
[222] '...Dimitrov alone / making the human spirit / leap out of his shell, unhusked...' MacLean 1999: 120–121.
[223] 'if my heart love / of you were not like the hardness of the jewel...'.

XLIX

This lyric brings to mind the other 'boat poem', I, lines 1 and 3 in particular recalling lines 5 and 6 of the earlier lyric. Its energetic forward movement (the sea water laughing against the prow) contrasts with the stagnation evident in I, as does the fact that here the beloved is (imagined as being?) present, whereas in the opening poem she is absent and presumably indifferent. Utopistic and gently boastful, XLIX strikes a hopeful note, while also recalling elements of earlier poems, before the onset of a new problematic in L and the following lyrics.

1 'A' Chlàrach' is that part of the Sound of Raasay which lies between Caol na h-Àirde to the north and An Caol Mòr to the south, between the Braes promontory and Scalpay on the Skye side.
7 The mention of Eimhir's hair with the key word 'cuailean' evokes its importance at the beginning of the sequence (see I and IV), here with overtones of entrapment and entanglement.
8 The reference to gold comes as something of a surprise, since the colour is associated with the Irishwoman rather than the Scotswoman (see note to I: 1). The parallelism with line 4 leaves hovering in the reader's mind the notion that the speaker's left hand could be entangled in Eimhir's hair, even though she is sitting opposite him. Cf. Yeats's 'Brown Penny' ('I am looped in the loops of her hair')[224] but also Petrarch cxcvii, 9–11 ('dico le chiome bionde e 'l crespo laccio / che sì soavemente lega e stringe / l'alma').[225]
11 The Butt of Lewis is the northernmost tip of the Isle of Lewis in the Outer Hebrides. The implication is that MacLean's projected voyage would be unending.

Three quatrains with all even lines rhyming in 'ò' and *aicill* in most couplets. The second stanza has additional rhyme on 'fhuaraidh', 'cuailein' and 'shuaineadh'.

---

[224] Yeats 1983: 98.
[225] 'I mean her golden hair, the curly snare / that with such softness binds and tightens round / my soul...' Petrarch 1996: 288–289.

L

This poem sets human issues of love, remembering and forgetfulness against the inhuman background of the universe, and a human scale of time against the barely conceivable scale of the universe's coming into being and persistence. The issue is no longer the possibility of gaining Eimhir's love, but whether or not poetry can confer permanence on what has taken place. It will acquire an almost obsessive intensity in LVII. In XVII the speaker managed to dismiss the apparent indifference of planets and stars. Here he challenges both time and the Earth because they will not give him what he seeks.

1–2   For the cluster 'bròn', 'bruan', 'braon' see notes to XLII: 16 and XLV: 18.
7–8   The galactic imagery that marks the final group of poems in the sequence recalls the closing section of MacDiarmid's *A Drunk Man Looks at the Thistle*, couched in tercets each with a single rhyme, which sets human activity and aspirations in a deterministic perspective against a background of astronomical cycles.[226] MacLean's poem similarly questions what human initiative, and more specifically poetry, can achieve when confronted with the large-scale indifference of the planetary cycles.
11–12   What concerns the speaker is not the happiness he might derive from his love, but how the latter can be given permanence. His interlocutor is no longer Eimhir, but history in its human and inhuman manifestations.
15–20   The Earth resists the poet's aspiration, motivated by love, to fashion an image of it which will accord with his reason. He therefore dismisses it contemptuously, along with the multitude of love stories it has accumulated in its gyrations. The words 'dom chèill' could also be interpreted as 'for my beloved'.
21–22   Here, as in LVII, Eimhir is reduced, compressed to her face, of fundamental importance throughout the sequence, given MacLean's persistent Platonism. At this stage it has

---

[226] See MacDiarmid 1978: I 157–166, a section later entitled 'The Great Wheel'. For a detailed commentary, Buthlay 1987: 173ff.

practically become an icon, a shorthand for what has been and demands eternal form.

23   Time, rather than Eimhir's wounds, her indifference, or the way she distracts him from his political affiliations, has become the speaker's adversary.

Six quatrains of lines with three stresses, rhyming *abab* (except for lines 1 and 3) and alternating feminine and masculine rhymes. Identical rhymes in stanzas 2 and 3. The fact that all couplets except the first have *aicill* means the feminine rhyme occurs no fewer than four times in each stanza, giving an obsessive energy to the poem which matches the belligerent indignation of its sentiments. Note also the persistence of 'ia' and 'ua' rhyming.

LI

MacLean was delighted when Douglas Young found this poem to be 'in the later style of Yeats' (letter of August 19th 1940). Another interior dialogue in the manner of XXII, in which the speaker warns himself against the dangers of deifying Eimhir and his love for her.

2   Here 'reul', and in line 6 'speur', connect to the overall galactic imagery in this concluding section of the sequence.
5–6   The prediction of catastrophe, at this point and in lines 10–11, recalls the apocalyptic vision of XVIII (see stanzas 5 and 6).
17–18   For Eimhir's ability to make him forget all other considerations, and the sovereign power of her face, cf. XLIII: 13ff. MacLean's English foregrounds the notion of death, which is only one possible resonance of Gaelic 'caochladh', literally 'change'. Note the alliteration on 't-' in line 17 and on 'c-' in line 18.

Three stanzas of six lines having mainly three stresses (but see lines 15–16). End-rhyme in even lines and *aicill* within each couplet. The first two stanzas share the same end-rhyme.

LII

The mention of ten years in this poem (lines 12, 16, 22) is

not quite exact, given that it dates from March (or possibly
April) 1940, while poem I was written in August or
September 1931. What is significant is that it dissuades us
from interpreting the sequence primarily in terms of the
individual women who fired the poet's imagination, prompting us instead to view it as a whole, with a single addressee
in mind. Such a perspective accompanies the introduction of
the 'faodail', or treasured object found by chance which, with
LVI and LIX, will increasingly come to denote the sequence
itself, and the realisation of MacLean's poetic ambitions
which it entails. The trajectory of the 'Dàin do Eimhir' is thus
subtly redefined, the port of arrival being no longer an achieved
relationship with the desired partner, or the championing of a
political cause, but the completion of a literary artefact. In
terms of this third objective, the sequence is emphatically not
a narrative of frustration or failed achievement.

6   The words 'trì-an-aon' and 'trianaid' evoke the threefold
Godhead of Father, Son and Holy Ghost. Becoming a star
was a means of attaining divine status for classical heroes
and heroines. In celebrating Eimhir's elevation to the status
of a star, MacLean carries out an analogous operation. It
also has implications for her persistence through time, as the
timescale associated with stars goes far beyond human
measurement.

12   Time and its effects continue to be a preoccupation,
notwithstanding the poem's tone of celebration. Eimhir has
withstood the test of time, and the rays which the poet
identified with elements in himself (lines 3–4) are now acknowledged as hers by right (see also the following stanza).
There are many precedents for a poet's calculating the
number of years a fruitless devotion has lasted. See Petrarch
cxxii, 1–2 ('Dicesette anni à già rivolto il cielo / poi che
'mprima arsi'), and ccclxiv 1, 4 ('Tennemi Amor anni ven-
tuno ardendo / ...dieci altri anni piangendo'),[227] and also
the Catalan poet Ausiàs March (1400/01–1459): 'He fet
senyor del seny a mon voler, / veent amor de mon seny mal

---

[227] 'Seventeen years the heavens have revolved / since I first burned...'
'Twenty-one years Love kept me burning... another ten years weeping.'
Petrarch 1996: 186–187, 508–509.

servit; / rapaç l'he fet, e Déu a part jaquit. / E són setze anys que lo guardó esper!'[228]

17, 19   Addressing abstract concepts in this fashion is indicative of the increasing rarefaction of MacLean's thinking as the sequence approaches its close. Thus in LVII the speaker will address, not just Eimhir's face, but also the period of time during which they knew one another (69, 73ff.), as if it were personified, could hear him and could offer an answer.

18   As so often before, Eimhir's inner qualities are made manifest in her face.

23   The 'faodail' proves to be the object of the 'tòir' or hunt which was announced at the very start of the sequence (I: 2, 19).

24   Towards the close of MacDiarmid's *A Drunk Man Looks at the Thistle*, the notion of a sufficiency takes over[229] (surprisingly, given the predilection for extremes which characterises the main body of the poem). Here, too, the poet is concerned with 'na dh'fhòghnadh', what can be enough (see also LIII: 2).

Six quatrains of lines alternating four and three stresses in a manner reminiscent of ballad metre. End-rhyme as in L, where the alternation is masculine / feminine rather than feminine / masculine as here. *Aicill* is used consistently (in stanza 5 it replaces the masculine end-rhyme) and is twofold in stanza 4 ('leòis... fhìn / bheothaich... lì', 'cailleadh... brìgh / glasadh... tìm').

LIII

Reminiscent of IX or XI, MacLean chose never to reprint this epigrammatic quatrain. It marks the resounding victory of love over the speaker's Communist affiliation (see XXX)

---

[228] 'Since my reason refused to do love's bidding, I have appointed my desire as its master. I have turned reason into a lowly thrall, and have given no thought to God. Sixteen years of this, and I am still waiting for my reward!' March 1992: 68–69.

[229] 'And we may aiblins swing content / Upon the wheel in which we're pent / In *adequate* enlightenment' (my italics). MacDiarmid 1993: I, 161.

while reiterating the pervasive Platonism of earlier lyrics.
The translation is reproduced from NLS MS 14978.

2   Though the great revolution might resolve satisfactorily
the plight of humankind, it no longer embodies the speaker's
aspirations.
3–4   Eimhir's face manifested the just and the good (cf.
XXXVII: 5–6).

This quatrain has the same structure as those in L and LII.

LIV

This and the following poem were published in Scott-
Moncrieff's journal *New Alliance* in May 1940. Rather than
being viewed against the background of the Hebrides and the
western seaboard, as in XLII and XLIX, Eimhir is here
identified with that landscape. For Black the poem 'has a
sting in the tail worthy of Heine himself',[230] though it has to
be said that Heine's pervasive and ludic self-irony is alien to
MacLean.

1   See note on XXXIV: 7.
2   For the Clàrach, see note to XLIX: 1.
7   For the reference to Eimhir's hair, see note to XLIX: 7.
9   Addressing Eimhir as a jewel evokes the imagery of
XLV.
12   MacLean wrote to Douglas Young (August 28th 1940)
that 'I want to make a slight alteration in the last two lines...
I have realised that those lines are capable of a reading which
I did not intend them to have and do not wish them to have.
It is a point of a possible vagueness which for personal
reasons I do not wish to arise.' As first printed in *The New
Alliance*, the line read 'troimh chliabh m'ògalachd sàthte'.[231]
On October 4th, MacLean told Young that 'ògalachd'
['youthfulness'] was 'a genuine word in spite of your three
lexica', even though ' "òg-mhaidne" is better'. He had already

---

[230] Black 1999: xxxiv.
[231] *The New Alliance* Vol. 1 No. 5 New Series (Aug–Sept 1940) p. 6.

deployed the latter term in the first quatrain of XXIII ('òg-mhadainn ceòl Bheethoven').

Four quatrains of lines with three or four stresses, with end-rhyme on pairs of even lines and consistent use of *aicill* within each couplet.

LV

Another poem indicating how the speaker looks back over what he has written to evaluate it in retrospect. Concern for the future of his language is also, by implication, concern for the future of his poetry and for the permanence it can confer on Eimhir and his love for her. This poem marks the end of MacLean's second great outpouring in Hawick, comprising 19 poems written mainly in March but possibly also in February and April 1940. When first published in *The New Alliance* the poem was divided into two quatrains.

1 The toil referred to here is the poet's rather than the lover's.
2 MacLean wrote to Douglas Young from Raigmore Hospital on June 15th 1943 that 'The whole prospect of Gaelic appals me, the more I think of the difficulties and the likelihood of its extinction in a generation or two. A highly inflected language, with a ridiculous (because etymological) spelling, no modern prose of any account, no philosophical or technical vocabulary to speak of, no correct usage except among old people and a few university students, colloquially full of gross English idiom lately taken over, exact shades of meanings of most words not to be found in any of its dictionaries and dialectally varying enormously (what chance of the appreciation of the overtones of poetry, except among a handful?) Above all, all economic, social and political factors working against it, and, with that, the notorious moral cowardice of the Highlanders themselves. What chance has any Gaelic poetry when "Cumha na Cloinne", probably one of the greatest pieces of music in the world, and not hampered by language difficulties, is all but unknown in Scotland, even among Highlanders?'
3-4 At the time of writing (March, or just possibly April

1940) more than a year had passed since Franco's nationalists secured complete control of Spain, while effective opposition had yet to be offered to Hitler's expansionist policies on mainland Europe. Polish resistance to the combined German and Russian invasion of September 1939 had collapsed within little more than a month and the country was partitioned. German troops were to occupy the principal Norwegian ports on April 9th. The invasion of the Low Countries and France began on May 10th.

5 In this grimmer poem, as in LIII, love offers a kind of transcendence. The reference to 'am millean bliadhna' recalls the language of L in a context of greater acceptance. However incommensurable for the human mind, the million years are themselves only a 'mìr' or fragment of something infinitely larger. And the seven-figure numeral makes the heroism of some few hundreds (line 7) all the more poignant and deserving of celebration.

8 The miraculous quality of Eimhir's face has withstood all the vicissitudes of the sequence. Cf. XVII: 11–12.

Two quatrains are run together as a single unit, with consistent *aicill* and end-rhyme pattern *abab* (missing between lines 1 and 3).

LVI

Not reprinted after 1943, this poem was written in Catterick Camp, Yorkshire, where MacLean arrived towards the end of September 1940. The headings of his letters from Catterick indicate that he formed part of Squad 407 of A Company in the Royal Signals. The poem is dated early 1941 in his letter to Douglas Young of March 30th 1942. Editor's translation.

1 The opening line echoes LV, and the ten-year span identified in LII (see lines 12, 16, 22). As in LV, the poet's rather than the lover's travail is intended in 'saothrach'.

2 A crucial line, with its suggestion that the 'faodail' offering compensation to both poet and lover can be interpreted in a literary sense.

3 MacLean comments that 'suaimhneach' is 'very difficult to render', and glosses it as ' "felix", "serene", suggesting the

meanings of "felix" and "repose" and almost of "triumph"
or rather "triumphant", while "craobhach" suggests a "flowing growth"' (letter to Douglas Young, February 22nd
1941). The adjective 'craobhach' (literally 'tree-like') should
also be read in the light of XXXII: 5–6 ('loisgeam gach
meanglan craoibhe / a dh'fhàs aoibhneach thar duilghe')[232]
and XLIII: 18–19 ('Craobh nan Teud, / 'na meangach
duillich t' aodann').[233] The latter poem links the idea of a tree
with Eimhir's face, an association which also occurs here.
For Eimhir's 'cuailean' see III: 8, XLIX: 7 and LIV: 7.

Four lines of three or four stresses, with end-rhyme on -ao-.
Note the rich internal rhyming across a short space: 'bliadhna
/ riamh', 'd'fhuair / suaimhneach / chuailean' and 'dàn /
àlainn'.

LVII

A precise dating of this and the two following poems is
possible thanks to a letter to Young dated Sunday August
3rd 1941: 'This weekend I have written three poems (all to
Eimhir), one 120 lines long. I shall send them to you when I
get time to write versions.' In his next letter, MacLean adds:
'I enclose three pieces but I have quite a lot of other stuff in
the making. My poetry is rapidly recovering from a year's
blight.' By the end of August he had received Young's Scots
version of the poem,[234] and on September 9th he wrote:

> The version of LVII is remarkably good, I think the best
> of your versions of my stuff which I have seen. I
> showed it and the original to Deòrsa[235] who liked it
> immensely... [we] had two splendid afternoons and
> evenings when we talked of Gaelic poetry the whole
> time. He has my obsessing [sic] admiration for the
> anonymous ballad-like stuff which we both regard as the
> greatest thing in all Gaelic poetry...

---

[232] 'let me burn every tree branch / that grew joyous above grief'.

[233] 'the Tree of Strings, / among its leafy branches your face'.

[234] See Young 1947: 34–37.

[235] George Campbell Hay (1915–1984).

On September 11th 1941, MacLean told Young that 'I now
see the germ of LVII was Yeats' "Where had her sweetness
gone?" '[236] The second stanza of this poem reads as follows:

> All lives that has lived;
> So much is certain;
> Old sages were not deceived:
> Somewhere beyond the curtain
> Of distorting days
> Lives that lonely thing
> That shone before these eyes
> Targeted, trod like Spring.[237]

MacLean, however, distances himself notably in this poem
from Yeats' unalloyed Platonism. For an extended discussion
of Platonic elements in the sequence, see note to IX.

As with XLV, it will be helpful to divide the 120 lines of
LVII into sections of varying lengths (partly guided by the
recurrent invocations of Eimhir's face at lines 33, 49 and
105). While the 1999 text resolves the whole poem into
quatrains, the 1943 text runs together lines 5–32, 37–48 and
57–64.

The first quatrain (1–4) presents the situation: the speaker
is haunted by Eimhir's pleading face. The next seven (5–32)
tell us what she claims to be the case: that her beauty and the
period during which they knew each other are immune to
the ravages of time and change, even though music, sculpture
and painting cannot capture them. The speaker, however, is
not convinced by what she says, and fears that the wonder of
her beauty may be lost (33–36), especially if her image resists
embodiment in art, and if there is no way of immobilising
the onward drift of time (37–48). Her pleading may therefore
prove pointless, especially once everyone who has known
her is dead (49–56). If she is to have immortality, it must be
absolutely faithful, and in this respect he is sceptical about
the powers of music or painting (57–68). She therefore cannot
be separated from the period of time in which he knew her
(69–72). Time of its nature cannot be stopped, though we
have no way of knowing where its indefatigable journeying

---

[236] See 'Quarrel in Old Age' in Yeats 1983: 253.
[237] Yeats 1983: 253.

will lead. It cannot exist unless it is perceived, just like Eimhir's beauty. And who or what will do the perceiving when that is lost to living memory? (73–104). Two anguished quatrains sum up what has so far been said. Is there any fixed point of arrival for her face other than the grave? Is there any better way of conserving her memory than music, painting or poetry? (105–112) The last two quatrains are a kind of tailpiece, restating more savagely the content of poem LIII. The speaker's concern for the Red Army, engaged in a desperate defence of their Russian homeland now that Hitler has turned upon Stalin, is as nothing to the turmoil provoked in him by the vision of Eimhir's face and its plea (113–120).

1   The chase or 'tòir' which during much of the sequence saw the poet pursuing Eimhir's love has been reversed. Now it is her all-important face which pursues him with a plea.

5–8   The concept of unrequited love is negated, for desire and its object are, she claims, indistinguishable. Eimhir's ghost is here upholding the value of the 'susbaint' or 'substance' of which her physical attractiveness had been merely the manifestation. The speaker comes roundly to reject her position in the course of the poem.

9ff.   Eimhir claims that her beauty is not limited to its physical manifestation, but exists on a level where decay and destruction are unthinkable. See also 17ff. for the continuation of this argument.

16   The word 'rèim' has already been used (LII: 10) to denote Eimhir's 'sway', her authority and dominion, in the context of a possible threat to it.

22–24   The lines offer a formulation of what the poems in the sequence constitute. They are innovative ('briathran ùra'), and give a form which is permanent ('sìorraidh') to the poet's secret thoughts and inclinations ('rùintean').

26   For the MacCrimmon pipers, see note to XXIII: 39–40, where art's ability to deal with suffering and resist forgetfulness is also questioned.

31   The preoccupations of lines 73–100 are anticipated. How are those who will never have the chance of meeting Eimhir to be made aware of her beauty and its significance?

33–36   The poet responds in a very different tone to Eimhir's proud assertions and gives open expression to his fears.

39ff.   MacLean's image for the unarrestable movement of calendar time, and for the impossibility of fixing an expanse of it, is a ship whose departure cannot be prevented, because its anchor cannot get a grip on sand. (Gaelic 'seòl' also means 'sail', used in the plural at line 45.)

49–56 Never before in the sequence has the speaker so directly questioned Eimhir's power. She risks being swept off in the flow of time despite her pleading, and her power may be limited to the life span of those who knew her.[238] The 'aonachd' or unity which is such an attractive quality risks being lost once she has become forgotten and 'faoin' or vain. The speaker's divergence from Yeats is obvious. Eimhir's beauty exists only as long as it is perceived. It cannot therefore be divorced from the act of perception's placing in time. It would, of course, be possible to relate the speaker's distancing from Platonism to the teachings of the 18th century Scottish Common Sense school of philosophers with their emphasis on the inherent reliability of sense perceptions.

57–68 The speaker sets a series of conditions which artistic reproduction, whether in music or in painting, cannot meet.

64 Note the renewed emphasis on the act of perceiving.

69–72 He draws, in the quatrain that follows, the inevitable conclusion that she cannot be divorced from her manifestation in the present, or carried over into a different time.

73ff. As a logical consequence of what has gone before, the speaker now addresses, not Eimhir, but the period of time during which she was part of his present. Its 'rèim', rather than Eimhir's (see note to line 16) risks dissolving like mist. The abstraction of MacLean's thought at this point requires a considerable effort from the reader in order to accompany him further.

75 The importance of perception is again underlined by the notion of a new consciousness which could hypothetically register Eimhir's existence.

78 It is not clear whether the 1st person plural here (and at lines 80 and 82) is general, or confined to the speaker and Eimhir.

---

[238] There is a similarity of argument here to the closing lines of 'Hallaig' (MacLean 1999: 230), whose juxtaposition of 'bullet' and 'love' ('peileir' and 'gaol') recurs in 'The Cuillin' Part I (MacLean 1999: 68–69).

85ff.   These five stanzas, which represent the culmination of the poem before its tailpiece, repeat the speaker's conviction that some form of perception is necessary if Eimhir's beauty, or the period of time corresponding to the sequence, is to continue to exist. Note 'sùil' (85, 91), 'cluas' (86, 95), 'reusain' (91), the repetition of 'càileachd', 'càil', 'càiltean' (91, 93, 102), 'a mhothaicheas' (94), 'blas, suathadh no fàileadh' (96), 'cuimhne bheò' (98), 'smuainteannan siùbhlach' (99) and 'air chor 's gum mothaich' (101).

105   This quatrain makes explicit that the preoccupations of this poem are elegiac, concerned with the ability of language (or any other artistic medium) to withstand the passage of time and thus gain victory over death.

111   The crucial term 'slàn' returns, in a slightly different context. Cf. XVIII: 85, XXII: 28, XL: 4, XLV: 16.

113–114   Originally planned for the middle of May, the German offensive on the Soviet Union, in breach of the non-aggression pact concluded between the two countries in 1939, was delayed until June 22nd 1941. German tanks crossed the River Dnieper on July 10th and by the middle of the month the German forces were only 200 miles from Moscow. MacLean told Young (August 3rd 1941): 'For myself, if Russia goes down, my single aim will be vengeance at any price. If Russia wins, the day of reckoning will be near in Scotland as well as in Spain, Italy etc....' A measure of the transformation that has overtaken MacLean can be got by comparing those lines from 'An Cuilithionn' which envisage a triumphant disembarking of the Soviet army on British shores: ''S gus an tig an t-Arm Dearg còmhla / le caismeachd tormaim na Roinn Eòrpa, / drùidhidh iorram na truaighe / air mo chridhe 's mo bhuadhan', and again 'Co bheir faochadh dhan àmhghair / mur tig an t-Arm Dearg sa chàs seo?'[239]

117–120   Repetition of the opening stanza gives a circular form to the lyric, indicative of the speaker's failure to reach a satisfactory answer to any of the interrogatives he has posed.

---

[239] '...and until the Red Army comes / battle-marching across Europe, / that song of wretchedness will seep / into my heart and my senses' and 'Who will give respite to the agony / unless the Red Army comes in this extremity?'. MacLean 1999: 74–75, 84–85.

At thirty quatrains, this is the longest poem in the sequence. With very few exceptions, the quatrains have end rhyme following an *aaba* pattern, with the *b* vowel echoed internally (*aicill*) in the fourth line. Where the rhyme is *aaaa* (as at 57ff., 61ff.) there is no *aicill* in the second couplet. Lines have three or two stresses, with a tendency for shorter lines to appear at the end of a quatrain.

LVIII

For dating, see previous poem. The lyric gives further expression to the main preoccupation of LVII, namely how permanence can be conferred on Eimhir's beauty and on the stretch of time corresponding to the poetic sequence. Stylistically it is a most striking poem (see comments on the metre below), with further instances of MacLean's idiosyncratic fondness for apostrophising abstract concepts. Editor's translation.

1ff. Continuing the thought of LVII: 37ff. There is an increased urgency now that the 'tràth' or extended period of the previous poem has shrunk to 'tacan', a moment. The words 'bhacar' (1), 'ghlacar' (5, 27) and 'thasgar' (7, 29) are all echoes of LVII. Note how the parallelisms in 3–8 create an impression of speed. Something has to be done *very* quickly!

8 Cf. XXII: 14–16 ('an rionnag leugach òir, / gum beirinn oirre 's gun cuirinn i / gu ciallach 'na mo phoc?').[240]

11–12 Cf. LIV: 1–2 ('Bu tu camhanaich air a' Chuilithionn').[241]

14 Note the change to the singular, echoed at 19 ('a chosgar *leam*'). The first person plural returns at 27 and 29. Preserving Eimhir's beauty is both a personal and a general concern.

15–16 Cf. the image of MacLean's poems as horses at XXXI: 6.

---

[240] 'the radiant golden star, / that I would catch it and put it / prudently in my pocket?'.

[241] 'You were dawn on the Cuillin...'

25 Despite the scepticism of LVII, the recurrence of 'aodann' (here, in line 33 and at LIX: 11) suggests that something of MacLean's Platonism has nonetheless survived. See also 18, where Eimhir's gaze is an incitement to probity and fair dealing.

31–32 Cf. LVII: 83–84 ('ciamar thigeadh sgeul... / bho chèin-thràighean?')[242]

37–40 A narrowing of focus with respect to the previous poem, where considerable reservations are voiced as to the efficacy of artistic representations. Here the poet's aspiration is for the Muses to provide a valid refuge for Eimhir's beauty. For 'faodail', see LII: 23, LVI: 2 and LIX: 2.

There is a persistent dactylic rhythm, with the alternation of six and five syllables dictated by the pattern of rhyming (three syllables from the end in odd-numbered lines, two in even). All stanzas rhyme *abababab*, with sharing of rhyme between stanzas (the *a* rhyme of stanzas 1, 2 and 4, and the *b* rhyme of stanzas 1 and 4, then 2, 3 and 5). In addition there is *aicill* on a single vowel throughout each stanza, so that the *a* rhyme occurs, internally and in final position, 8 times per stanza, and, in its realisation as 'beairteachadh / tacan / bhacar leinn' etc., 24 times in the course of the poem.

LIX

A lessening of tension can be detected once the sequence has reached its climax in LVII. It is fitting, given MacLean's often stated predilection for the anonymous Gaelic song poetry preserved in oral tradition, that in summing up his own achievement as a lyricist he should seek comparison, not with William Ross or Blok or Yeats, but with one of the most celebrated findings (a 'faodail') of the Scottish collector Alexander Carmichael (see note to line 1 below).

1 Alexander Carmichael was born on the island of Lismore, off the coast of Argyllshire, in 1832. His father was a farmer who would also appear to have kept a public house. After attending the parish school, Carmichael is said to have

---

[242] 'how would a tale... come / from distant shores?'

continued his education in Greenock and Edinburgh, though Ronald Black points to the lack of concrete evidence for this. He then began a career as an officer of Her Majesty's Customs and Excise. From 1865 to 1882 his family resided permanently in the Hebrides. The material which went to form the *Carmina Gadelica*, for which he is principally remembered, was gathered mainly between 1855 and 1899, though he undertook a further expedition in search of oral lore as late as 1910. The first two volumes were published in 1900, earning widespread praise. Four more would follow, between 1940 and 1971. Carmichael was awarded a Civil List pension in 1906 and an honorary degree by Edinburgh University in 1909. Again according to Black, he was 'For the last thirty years of his life the doyen of Edinburgh's Gaelic intellectual community'.[243] He died in 1912.

The controversy about the degree to which Carmichael intervened in his published texts postdates the writing of the 'Dàin do Eimhir'. For John MacInnes

> it is now clear that *Carmina Gadelica* is not a monumental exercise in literary fabrication nor, on the other hand, is it a transcript of ancient poems and spells reproduced exactly in the form in which they survived in oral tradition. There are elements of fabrication undoubtedly... few texts in *Carmina* are totally free of some editorial repair-work and some, including the "Invocation of the Graces", may have it to a very high degree. But throughout the collection, the core of the material is the treasure-trove of oral literature that Carmichael discovered in Gaelic Scotland.[244]

Black, 'an unrepentant admirer of Alexander Carmichael's achievement as an ethnologist', considers that between 1976 and 1992 'the authenticity of *Carmina Gadelica* provided Scottish Gaelic studies with its liveliest debate of the century, a debate akin in some ways to the Ossianic controversy 200 years before'.[245] For the 'Invocation of the Graces', see line 16 below.

---

[243] Black 1999: 710. 'Ora nam Buadh' appears on the first page of Black's anthology.

[244] 'Preface' to Carmichael 1992: 17.

[245] Black 1999: 711.

2   The speaker is perhaps distancing himself from authorship, with an insinuation that his poems, like those printed in the *Carmina Gadelica*, have been 'found' rather than 'made'.

7–8   Lines perhaps inspired by MacLean's gloomy prognostications about the future of Gaelic (see note to LV: 2).

15–16   A further Platonic touch. The comparison with Carmichael suggests that MacLean's poem already existed on a subliminal level (perhaps in Eimhir's face?), needing only to be discovered. The Gaelic text whose title Carmichael gives as 'Ora nam Buadh' can be found, with facing English translation, in the *Carmina Gadelica* I: 6–11. Interestingly, the fourth section mentions 'sgeimh na h-Eimir aluinn'.[246] Carmichael's source for this poem was Duncan Maclellan, a crofter from Carnan in South Uist, who heard it in his turn from a homeless old woman with a rich store of tradition, Catherine Macaulay, in the early years of the 19th century. Carmichael was also in possession of a fragment taken down in Tiree, and concluded that the poem must have been widely known in the past.[247]

Two octaves, with lines alternating four and three stresses. Even-numbered lines have an identical rhyme throughout the poem. There is consistent *aicill*, extending through four lines in the first half of the second stanza.

LX

Not reprinted after 1943. Dated early September 1941 in MacLean's letter of March 30th 1942. Whether the incident said to have prompted this poem was real or imagined we cannot know. Editor's translation.

1   A direct and presumably deliberate link with the opening line of the sequence (I: 1, 'A nighean a' chùil ruaidh òir').

4   Cf. XXII: 9 ('Bhac mi 'n cridhe bha 'g èirigh...').[248]

---

[246] 'the beauty of Emir the lovely'.

[247] Carmichael 1992: 575–576.

[248] 'I checked the heart that was rising.'

5 The shock of seeing her again resolves in measured, patterned praise of her qualities, in its way a vindication of the speaker's love.
12 An abrupt change of emphasis in the third recurrence of the syntactical pattern set up by 5–6. 'M' fheòla' anticipates the poem's conclusion.
13ff. A clear impression of closure, of this lyric and of the sequence as a whole, derives from the double repetition of 'chunna mi 'n cùl ruadh' and the echoing of line 2 in line 14.
15 The opening poem narrated a failed awakening (I: 13, 17 'dùiseal tharam' and 'ri cath a dhùisgeas'). Here the internal dividedness which has been such a crucial part of the speaker's experience reawakens in a fashion that would appear to negate any possibility of healing. Note the oxymoron of 'seann roinneadh ùr'.

8 couplets of lines alternating four and three stresses. End-rhyme on 'o' in even-numbered lines, and *aicill* within each couplet.

Dimitto

MacLean wrote to Douglas Young concerning this poem (November 9th 1941): 'Leave it out. It sounds damnably silly to me now. I don't suppose you would think of putting it in at any rate.' Among the long and venerable tradition of addresses to a book on the part of a poet, more often than not viewing it as an ambassador to an indifferent or hostile beloved, the most recent and closest to MacLean was probably the 1921 'Envoi' appended to Pound's 'Hugh Selwyn Mauberley' sequence.[249] This poem is in its way a pastiche, a conscious link to the literary tradition within which MacLean was writing, combining a modesty demanded by convention ('neo-euchdaich', line 1 and 'bacach', line 3) with a quietly confident, but coded prediction of fame and immortality (line 4). MacLean's translation is reproduced from a letter to Young dated April 15th 1942, where it appears as prose.

Four lines of four stresses each with end-rhyme in 'è'.

[249] Pound 1975: 105.

BIBLIOGRAPHY

Unpublished sources

National Library of Scotland

MS 14978 Caird papers: manuscript and collected typescript translations, [ca.] 1943, of parts of 'Dàin do Eimhir', and typescript of English version of 'The Cuillin' by Douglas Young

MS 26153 f8 Letter of Sorley MacLean to Sydney Goodsir Smith

MS 26630 First edition of *17 Poems for 6d* [see below] with manuscript corrections by MacLean

MS 26722 Manuscript notebook of George Campbell Hay (dating from the late 1930s)

Acc. 6419 Boxes 5 and 6 General Correspondence of Douglas Young; Box 38b Letters of Sorley MacLean to Douglas Young; Box 101 Incomplete English version of 'The Cuillin'

Acc. 10090/208 Robert McIntyre papers

Acc. 10397/3 Scots translation of LVII by Sydney Goodsir Smith

Acc. 11572/6 Letters of Douglas Young to Sorley MacLean

Acc. 12022 Sorley MacLean papers

Edinburgh University Library

MS 2954.13 Letters of Sorley MacLean to Hugh MacDiarmid

Published sources

1: By Sorley MacLean

MacLean [and Robert Garioch] 1939 *17 Poems for 6d* (Edinburgh, the Chalmers Press)

MacLean [and Robert Garioch] 1940 *17 Poems for 6d* (Edinburgh, the Chalmers Press), second edition with some alterations

MacLean 1943 *Dàin do Eimhir agus Dàin eile* (Glasgow, William Maclellan)

MacLean 1946 'Do Bhoirionnach Briagach Coirbte' in *Poetry Scotland* 3 (Glasgow, William Maclellan): 32–33 (with English translation)

MacLean 1971 *Poems to Eimhir translated from the Gaelic* by Iain Crichton Smith (Newcastle on Tyne, Northern House)

MacLean 1977a *Reothairt is Contraigh* [sic]: *Taghadh de Dhàin 1932–72 / Spring tide and Neap tide: Selected Poems 1932–72* (Edinburgh, Canongate)

MacLean 1977b 'Some Raasay Traditions' *TGSI* XLIX (1974–1976): 377–97

MacLean 1981 'Some Gaelic and non-Gaelic influences on myself' in Robert O' Driscoll ed. *The Celtic Consciousness* (Portlaoise, the Dolmen Press and Edinburgh, Canongate): 499–501

MacLean 1985 *Ris a' Bhruthaich: The Criticism and Prose Writings of Sorley MacLean* ed. William Gillies (Stornoway, Acair)

MacLean 1999 *O Choille gu Bearradh: Dàin Chruinnichte / From Wood to Ridge: Collected Poems* (Manchester, Carcanet and Edinburgh, Birlinn)

2: Concerning Sorley MacLean

Ní Annracháin, Máire 1992 *Aisling agus tóir: an slánú i bhfilíocht Shomhairle MhicGill-Eain* (Maynooth, An Sagart) 220 pp

—— 1997 'Vision and Quest in Somhairle MacGill-Eain's "An Cuilithionn"' *Lines Review* 141: 5–11

Burnett, Ray 1985 'Sorley MacLean's *Hallaig*' *Lines Review* 92: 13–22

Caird James B. 1986 'Sorley MacLean; Fionn MacColla' *Edinburgh Review* 74 (August 1986): 50–62

—— 1995 'Sorley MacLean' in Murdo Macdonald ed. *Nothing is Altogether Trivial* (Edinburgh, Edinburgh University Press): 196–202

Campbell, Angus Peter ed. 1991 *Somhairle: Dàin is Deilbh: a Celebration on the 80th birthday of Sorley MacLean* (Stornoway, Acair)

Crawford, Robert 1987 'Recent Scottish Poetry and the Scottish Tradition' *Verse* 4 No. 2: 36–46

—— 1993 'Somhairle MacGill-Eain / Sorley Maclean' in his *Identifying Poets* (Edinburgh, Edinburgh University Press): 64–7

Gibault, Henri 1997 'Sorley MacLean (1911–1996)' *Études écossaises* 4: 11–17

Gifford, Terry 1995 'A culture of kinship and place: the poetry of Sorley MacLean' in his *Green Voices* (Manchester, Manchester University Press): 72–93

Heaney, Seamus 1988 'The voice of a bard' *Antaeus* 60 (Spring 1988): 297–306

Hendry, Joy 1991 'An Interview with Sorley MacLean' *Chapman* 66 (Autumn 1991): 1–8

Herdman, John 1977 'The Poetry of Sorley Maclean: a Non-Gael's View' *Lines Review* 61: 25–36

—— 1983 'Sorley MacLean's "Calbharaigh"' *Akros* Vol. 17 No. 51: 26–8

McCaughey, Terence 1987 'Somhairle MacGill-eain' in Cairns Craig ed. *The History of Scottish Literature Vol. 4: the Twentieth* Century (Aberdeen, Aberdeen University Press) 147–62

McClure, J. Derrick 1988 'Douglas Young and Sorley MacLean' in Derick Thomson ed. *Gaelic and Scots in Harmony* (Glasgow, Glasgow University): 136–48

MacInnes, John 1975 'Sorley MacLean's "Hallaig": a Note' in *Calgacus* No. 2. 29 32

—— 1981 'A radically traditional voice: Sorley MacLean and the evangelical background' *Cencrastus* 7 (Winter 1981–82): 14–17

Somhairle MacGill-Eain / Sorley MacLean exhibition catalogue (Edinburgh, National Library of Scotland 1981)

Macrae, Alasdair 1997 'Sorley MacLean in a context beyond Gaeldom' *Etudes écossaises* 4: 19–30

Montague, John 1982 'A Northern Vision' in Seán Mac Réamoinn ed. *The Pleasures of Gaelic Poetry* (London, Allen Lane): 161–74

Nicolson, Angus 1979 'An Interview with Sorley MacLean' *Studies in Scottish Literature* XIV: 23–36

Nicholson, Colin 1986 'To Sing a People's Fate' *The Scotsman* October 25
—— 1988 'Sorley MacLean at 75' *Clan Maclean* II (2): 7–10
Ross, Raymond and Hendry, Joy 1986 *Sorley MacLean: Critical Essays* (Edinburgh, Scottish Academic Press)
Sassi, Carla 1991 'Sorley Maclean: l'incanto della parola' *Diverse Lingue* 10 (1991): 105–15
—— 1992 'Risposte di Sorley Maclean' *Diverse Lingue* 11: 17–22
Smith, Iain Crichton 1958a 'The Poetry of Sorley Maclean' *An Gaidheal* 53: 99–100, 109–10
—— 1958b 'Homage to Sorley Maclean' *Saltire Review* 5 No. 15: 37–40
—— 1971 'A Note on Sorley Maclean's *Dàin do Eimhir*' *Stand* 12 No. 2: 8
—— 1973 'The Poetry of Sorley Maclean' *The Glasgow Review* 4 No. 3: 38–41
—— 1986 'Gaelic Master: Sorley MacLean' in *Towards the Human* (Edinburgh, Macdonald): 123–31
Thomson, Derick 1988 'At the Starting Line' (review of Ross and Hendry 1986) in *Lines Review* 105: 39–40
Whyte, Christopher 1990 'The Cohesion of *Dàin do Eimhir*' *Scottish Literary Journal* Vol. 17 No. 1 (May) pp. 46–70
—— 1996 'A Note on *Dàin do Eimhir* XIII' in *Scottish Gaelic Studies* XVII: 383–92
—— 1997 'The Gaelic Renaissance: Sorley MacLean and Derick Thomson' in Gary Day and Brian Docherty eds. *British Poetry from the 1950s to the 1990s* (Macmillan, London): 143–69

3: Other Works

Baldwin, Anna and Hutton, Sarah eds 1994 *Platonism and the English Imagination* (Cambridge, Cambridge University Press)
Baudelaire, Charles 1997 *Complete Poems* translated by Walter Martin (Manchester, Carcanet)
Bethea, David M. 1994 *Joseph Brodsky and the Creation of Exile* (Princeton, New Jersey, Princeton University Press)
Black, Ronald 1999 *An Tuil: Anthology of 20th Century Scottish Gaelic Verse* (Edinburgh, Polygon)

Blake, William 1972 *Complete Writings* ed. Geoffrey Keynes (London, Oxford University Press)

Bold, Alan 1988 *MacDiarmid: a Critical Biography* (London, John Murray)

Buthlay, Kenneth 1987 *A Drunk Man Looks at the Thistle* by Hugh MacDiarmid: annotated edition (Edinburgh, Scottish Academic Press)

Byrne, Michel ed. 2000 *Collected Poems and Songs of George Campbell Hay (Deòrsa Mac Iain Dheòrsa)* 2 vols. (Edinburgh, Edinburgh University Press)

Caerwyn Williams, J. E. and Ford, Patrick 1992 *The Irish Literary Tradition* (Cardiff, University of Wales Press; Belmont, Massachusetts, Ford and Bailie)

Calder, George ed. 1937 *Gaelic Songs by William Ross* (Edinburgh, Oliver & Boyd)

Cameron, Alexander 1894 *Reliquiae Celticae* (Inverness, Northern Chronicle)

Carmichael, Alexander 1914 *Deirdire and the Lay of the Children of Uisne* 2nd ed. (Paisley, Alexander Gardner; London, Kenneth Mackenzie and Dublin, Hodges, Figgis and Co.)

—— 1928 *Carmina Gadelica: Ortha nan Gaidheal* 2nd ed. 2 vols (Edinburgh and London, Oliver & Boyd) (originally 1900)

—— 1992 *Carmina Gadelica: Hymns and Incantations* (Edinburgh, Floris Books)

Cornford, John 1986 *Collected Writings* ed. Jonathan Galassi (Manchester, Carcanet)

Craig, K. C. 1949 *Orain Luaidh* (Glasgow, Alasdair Matheson)

Cross, Tom Peete and Slover, Clark Harris 1936 *Ancient Irish Tales* (London, Harrap)

Cuddon, J. A. 1998 *A Dictionary of Literary Terms and Literary Theory* 4th edition (Blackwell, Oxford)

Domhnullach, Eoin 1903 *Leabhar Aithghearr nan Ceist* (Edinburgh, John Grant)

Dwelly, Edward 2001 *The Illustrated Gaelic-English Dictionary* (Glasgow, Gairm) (originally 1911)

Gantz, Jeffrey 1981 *Early Irish Myths and Sagas* translated with an introduction and notes (Penguin, Harmondsworth)

Garioch, Robert *Complete Poetical Works* ed. Robin Fulton (Edinburgh, Macdonald)

Gide, André 1937 'Journal des *Faux Monnayeurs*' in *Oeuvres complètes* XIII (Paris, NRF)

Gregory, Lady Augusta 1970a *Cuchulain of Muirthemne: the Story of the Men of the Red Branch of Ulster* arranged and put into English by Lady Gregory, with a preface by W. B. Yeats (Gerrards Cross, Colin Smythe) (originally 1902)

—— 1970b *Gods and Fighting Men: the Story of the Tuatha de Danaan and of the Fianna of Ireland* arranged and put into English by Lady Gregory, with a preface by W. B. Yeats (Gerrards Cross, Colin Smythe) (originally 1902)

Haddow, M. R. S. 1982 *The History and Structure of Ceòl Mòr* (Glasgow? s.n.)

Harrison, John Smith 1903 *Platonism in English Poetry* (New York, Columbia UP and London, Macmillan)

Hecht, Anthony 1993 *The Hidden Law: the Poetry of W. H. Auden* (Cambridge Massachusetts and London, Harvard University Press)

Horace 1983 *The Complete Odes and Epodes* translated, with notes, by W. G. Shepherd with an introduction by Betty Radice (London, Penguin Books)

Hyde, Douglas 1969 *Love Songs of Connacht* Introduction by Mícheál Ó hAodha (Shannon, Irish University Press) (facsimile of 1893 first edition)

Jeffares, A. Norman 1996 *W. B. Yeats: Man and Poet* 3rd edition (Gill & Macmillan, Dublin)

Kinsella, Thomas 1970 *The Táin* (London, Oxford University Press)

Knott, Eleanor 1994 *An Introduction to Irish Syllabic Poetry of the Period 1200–1600* with selections, notes and glossary 2nd ed. (Dublin, Institute for Advanced Studies)

Lawson, Roderick *The Shorter Catechism with commentary and scripture proofs* new edition (Edinburgh, Knox Press s.d.)

MacBride White, Anna and Jeffares, A. Norman 1992 *The Gonne-Yeats Letters 1893–1938: Always Your Friend* (London, Hutchinson)

MacCaig, Norman sel. and ed. 1959 *Honour'd Shade: an Anthology of New Scottish Poetry to mark the Bicentenary of the Birth of Robert Burns* (Edinburgh and London, Chambers)

MacDiarmid, Hugh 1993 *Complete Poems* edited Michael Grieve and W. R. Aitken 2 vols. (Manchester, Carcanet)

Mackenzie, John 1904 *The Beauties of Gaelic Poetry* (Edinburgh, Norman Macleod) (originally 1841)

MacKillop, James 1998 *Dictionary of Celtic Mythology* (Oxford and New York, Oxford University Press)

MacLeod, Angus 1933 *Sàr Òrain: Three Gaelic Poems* (Glasgow, An Comunn Gaidhealach)

McLeod, Wilson 1998 'Packaging Gaelic Poetry' in *Chapman* 89–90: 149–51

Mac Mhaighstir Alasdair, Alasdair 1996 *Selected Poems* ed. Derick Thomson (Edinburgh, Scottish Academic Press for Scottish Gaelic Texts Society)

MacNeacail, Aonghas 1994 introduction to 'The Long Road to Now: a Snapshot Survey of Gaelic Poetry' *Verse* Vol. 11 No. 2: 29–36

MacNeill, Seumas and Richardson, Frank 1996 *Piobaireachd and its Interpretation: Classical Music of the Highland Bagpipe* (Edinburgh, John Donald)

March, Ausiàs 1992 *Ausiàs March: a Key Anthology* edited and translated by Robert Archer (s.l. Anglo-Catalan Society)

Marlowe, Christopher 1965 *Doctor Faustus* ed. John D. Jump (London and New York, Routledge)

Matheson, William 1970 *An Clàrsair Dall: Òrain Ruaidhri Mhic Mhuirich agus a Chuid Ciùil / The Blind Harper: the Songs of Roderick Morison and his Music* (Edinburgh, Scottish Gaelic Texts Society)

Meek, Donald Eachann 1998 *Màiri Mhòr nan Òran: Taghadh de a h-Òrain* (Edinburgh, Scottish Academic Press)

Ovid 1982 *The Erotic Poems* translated with an introduction and notes by Peter Green (London, Penguin)

Petrarch 1996 *The Canzoniere or Rerum vulgarium fragmenta* translated into verse with notes and commentary by Mark Musa (Bloomington and Indianapolis, Indiana University Press)

Pliny the Elder *Natural History* with an English translation by H. Rackham 10 vols (Cambridge, Massachusetts, Harvard University Press and London, William Heinemann) (Loeb Classics edition)

Pound, Ezra 1975 *Selected Poems 1908–1969* (London, Faber and Faber)

Propertius 1968 *The Poems of Propertius* translated with an introduction by A. E. Watts (London, Penguin)

Pyman, Avril 1979 *The Life of Aleksandr Blok* Vol. 1 The Distant Thunder 1880–1908 (Oxford, Oxford University Press)

Quinn, Kenneth 1980 *Horace: the Odes* edited with introduction, revised text and commentary (Basingstoke and London, Macmillan)

Ronsard, Pierre 1974 *Les Amours* Édition présentée par Françoise Joukovsky (Paris, Gallimard)

Shakespeare *The Sonnets* ed. with an introduction and commentary by Martin Seymour-Smith (London, Heinemann)

Sharpe, Richard 1982 *Raasay: a study in island history* (London, Grant & Cutler)

Sinclair, Archibald 1879 *An t-Òranaiche / The Gaelic Songster* (Glasgow, Archibald Sinclair and Robert McGregor)

Smith, Sydney Goodsir 1975 *Collected Poems 1941–1975* with an introduction by Hugh MacDiarmid (London, John Calder)

Spenser, Edmund 1912 *Poetical Works* edited with critical notes by J. C. Smith and E. De Selincourt (London, Oxford University Press)

Thomas, Hugh 1977 *The Spanish Civil War* 3rd edition (London, Hamish Hamilton)

Thomson, Derick 1989 *An Introduction to Gaelic Poetry* 2nd ed. (Edinburgh, Edinburgh University Press)

—— ed. 1990 *Gaelic and Scots in Harmony* (Glasgow, Glasgow University)

—— ed. 1994 *The Companion to Gaelic Scotland* (Glasgow, Gairm Publications)

Valéry, Paul 1971 *Le cimetière marin* edited and translated by Graham Dunstan (Edinburgh, Edinburgh University Press)

Watson, Roderick ed. and introd. 1995 *The Poetry of Scotland: Gaelic, Scots and English* (Edinburgh, Edinburgh University Press)

Yeats, William Butler 1972 *Memoirs* transcribed and edited by Denis Donoghue (London, Macmillan)

—— 1982 *Collected Plays* 2nd ed. (London, Macmillan)

—— 1983 *The Poems* ed. Richard J. Finneran (London, Macmillan)

—— 1991 *Selected Poetry* ed. with an introduction and notes by Timothy Webb (London, Penguin)

Young, Douglas 1943 *Auntran Blads* (Maclellan, Glasgow)
—— 1947 *A Braird of Thristles* (Maclellan, Glasgow)

THE ASSOCIATION FOR SCOTTISH LITERARY STUDIES

ANNUAL VOLUMES

Volumes marked * are, at the time of publication, still available from booksellers or from the address given opposite the title page of this book.

INDEX

Note: SM in the index stands for Sorley MacLean

Mackenzie, John
  The Beauties of Gaelic Poetry
    181
MacLean, Christina (mother of
    SM) 10, 30, 31–2, 205–6
MacLean, Flora (aunt of SM) 31
MacLean, Ishbel (daughter of SM)
    17n
Maclean, John (*1879–1923*) 139,
    142, 161, 198n, 245
MacLean, John (great-grandfather
    of SM) 30
MacLean, John (brother of SM)
    31, 34
  and SM's poetry 29, 35–6, 205
MacLean, Malcolm (father of SM)
    10, 30, 31, 32, 205
MacLean, Mary (sister of SM)
    33n
MacLean, Peigi (aunt of SM) 30–1
**MacLean, Sorley (Somhairle
    MacGill-Eain)**
  family and childhood 30–3,
    141–3
  religion 9, 32–3, 141–3, 145–6,
    202–5, 212
  at school 22, 31, 142, 146, 214,
    229
  juvenilia 143, 155
  at university 6–7, 143–4, 146–7,
    148, 157
  teacher training 6n, 77
  teaching 7–8, 9, 11, 241
  first publication 11
  military training 4, 5, 11, 139,
    264
  military service 11, 33, 255, 264
  wounded 33
  WRITING:
  ESSAYS:
  'My relationship with the Muse'
    10
  'Old Songs and New Poetry' 236
  'Some Gaelic and non-Gaelic
    Influences on Myself' 29
  LETTERS *see under names of
    correspondents*
  POETRY:
  'Aig Uaigh Yeats' 185
  'Aigeach, An t-' 147, 151

'Ann an talla' 138
'Ard-Mhusaeum na h-Eireann'
    210
'Ban-Ghàidheal' 35, 147
  date 138
  Scots version 38n
'Am Bàta Dubh' 139
'Calbharaigh' 35, 139
  date 139
  Scots version 38n
'Ceann Loch Aoineart' 139
'An Ceann Thall' 226
'Ceathrar ann' (Dàn XII) 2
  'A' Chorra-ghridheach' ('The
    Heron') 6, 139
'Clach air càrn' 173
'Clann Ghill-Eain' 139n
'Có seo' 139
'An Cogadh Ceart' ('The Proper
    War') 14, 245
'Coilltean Ratharsair' ('The
    Woods of Raasay') 139,
    147, 151, 241
'Coin is Madaidhean-allaidh'
    (Dàn XXIX) 138, 140, 147,
    151, 231–2
'Conchobar' 139, 226
'Cornford' 139
'An Crann Dubh' 139
'Craobh nan Teud' 139, 147,
    151, 183, 193, 224, 227,
    250, 265
'An Cuilithionn' ('The Cuillin')
    4, 7, 161, 162–3, 167, 169,
    172, 173n, 176, 209, 235,
    239, 241, 244, 269
  closing section 33, 166
  date 14, 138, 139
  dedicatees 196
  English 'projection' 36, 38
  excised lines 168
  form 147, 151, 152
  illustrations 36
  influences 145
  publication considered 35
'Dàin do Eimhir' ('Poems to
    Eimhir')
  chronology and dating 3–6,
    11, 138–40
  diction 153–4